for Nina S[...]

a friend in two centuries

With best wishes

Charles Hare
June 25, 2009

RISING CHINA AND ITS POSTMODERN FATE

RISING CHINA AND ITS POSTMODERN FATE

Memories of Empire in a
New Global Context

CHARLES HORNER

The University of Georgia Press | Athens and London

© 2009 by the University of Georgia Press
Athens, Georgia 30602
www.ugapress.org
All rights reserved
Set in 10.5/13.5 Adobe Caslon Pro by BookComp, Inc.
Printed and bound by Sheridan Books
The paper in this book meets the guidelines for
permanence and durability of the Committee on
Production Guidelines for Book Longevity of the
Council on Library Resources.

Printed in the United States of America

13 12 11 10 09 C 5 4 3 2 1

Library of Congress Cataloging-in-Publication Data

Horner, Charles, 1943–
Rising China and its postmodern fate : memories of empire
in a new global context / Charles Horner.
      p.   cm. — (Studies in security and international
affairs)
Includes bibliographical references and index.
ISBN-13: 978-0-8203-3334-2 (cloth : alk. paper)
ISBN-10: 0-8203-3334-4 (cloth : alk. paper)
1. China—Relations—Foreign countries. 2. China—
History—Yuan dynasty, 1260–1368—Historiography.
3. China—History—Ming dynasty, 1368–1644—
Historiography. 4. China—History—Qing dynasty, 1644–
1912—Historiography. 5. Historiography—China. I. Title.
DS779.27.H67 2009
951.0072—dc22   2008049646

British Library Cataloging-in-Publication Data available

for my granddaughter
Catherine Bayer Horner
and my grandsons
Charles Simons Horner and Thomas Morgan Horner
children of the twenty-first century

CONTENTS

ACKNOWLEDGMENTS

My main debt is to the scholars whose names appear throughout this book. Without their work in the demanding field of China studies a book like this could not have been written, for it relies on the primary work of others. Since 1995 I have been based at the Hudson Institute in Washington, D.C. Hudson's Chief Executive Officer Kenneth Weinstein has encouraged his colleagues to think about the future in a broad way that connects history, politics, economics, technology, and culture. This book began with a question he once asked me: what will China's leadership be thinking in twenty or thirty years? Research fellow Maria Farkas, a student of Japan, helped me bring greater clarity to my writing about my own recondite topic. Research fellow Eric Brown is half my age and at least twice as conversant with the new ways of thinking about China that inform parts of this book. Philip Ross of the Hudson staff is a third my age and at least three times as proficient in the use of information technology that produces books these days. My wife, Connie, read the manuscript and has helped add coherence to it. I am grateful to them all.

At the University of Georgia, Harold Wiarda, Dean Rusk Professor of International Relations and head of the Department of International Affairs, was this book's first sponsor, and he soon had the support of Gary Bertsch, University Professor of Public and International Affairs and director of the Center for International Trade and Security. In a relatively short time the two have built an important program for the study of world affairs. At the University of Georgia Press, editor in chief Nancy Grayson and her colleagues helped me find a balance that allows me to hope that this book will be of interest to specialists and generalists alike. Reviewers made many helpful suggestions for organizing and presenting the different components of the book, and they also prevented many errors. I very much appreciate their professionalism and attentiveness.

I have dedicated this book to my three grandchildren. More than that, I wrote this book for them as children of the twenty-first century. My own parents were born as the twentieth century was getting started. I was born in the middle of it and grew up with the words that bespoke its horrors—Hitler, Stalin, Auschwitz, Gulag. During the twentieth century in the China about which I write, tens upon tens of millions died before their time; many were just murdered outright; many more died in the backwash of war and revolution. The world came through the twentieth century, but it was a close thing. I was eleven years old when the first hydrogen bomb was exploded.

These children of the twenty-first century are fortunate in the time of their birth. Yes, it is a time of danger and uncertainty, and with no shortage of men intent on murder. But it is also the greatest age in the history of the world; there is more freedom, more hope, more opportunity—and, above all, more peace—for more people in more places than at any other time.

Just as it fell to my generation to seek to understand how it happened that the *Belle Epoch* when my parents were born became the nightmare of the year that I was born, these children will in their time try to understand how the world came from that to this. It is a stark, but an encouraging, contrast, and it should make for a more pleasant inquiry. But there is another thing: to paraphrase Benjamin Franklin's famous injunction at the birth of our own republic, this is a great age—if you can keep it.

These children will one day start to learn about the abrupt change between my Then and their Now. When they do, perhaps the brightness of that line will direct them early on to chapter 30, verse 19, in *Deuteronomy*. There, the Lord condenses his many commandments, directives, injunctions, and prohibitions into only one: "I have set before you life and death, blessing and curse. Therefore, choose life, so that you may live."

Charles Horner
Lexington, Virginia

A NOTE ON ROMANIZATION AND THE PRONUNCIATION OF CHINESE

There is no wholly satisfactory way of using Roman letters to represent the sounds of Chinese. During most of the nineteenth and twentieth centuries, English speakers used the so-called Wade-Giles system, devised by British sinologue Sir Thomas Wade in 1859 and then modified by another British sinologue, Herbert Giles, in 1912. It is in this system of romanization that we English speakers first met Mao Tse-tung, Teng Hsiao-p'ing, the rest of the dramatis personae of China's long history, and the gazetteer of China's towns and cities. Small things mattered. It was "Dung" not "Tung" because there was no apostrophe after the "T" to signify aspiration. But the apostrophe after the "p" told us that it was indeed "ping" as in "ping pong." Without that apostrophe, it would have been "bing" as in "bingo."

In the early 1980s things changed. "Mao Tse-tung" became "Mao Zedong," and "Teng Hsiao-p'ing" became "Deng Xiaoping." This new system was called *pinyin* (*hanyu pinyin*, to be precise), a system first put into use in 1958 in the People's Republic of China and officially adopted there in 1979. Since then, *hanyu pinyin* has been adopted by the Library of Congress, the American Library Association, and the International Organization for Standardization. Even so, the system is still not universal within the Chinese-speaking world. The Republic of China on Taiwan devised a close cousin of *hanyu pinyin* called *tongyong pinyin* and adopted it in 2002, but local jurisdictions still retain the right to adopt the romanization system of their choice, and some have exercised it.

None of this would matter to the ordinary English reader, except that the *hanyu pinyin* system often uses the letters of our alphabet in confusing ways, which in turn misleads the uninitiated about which sound is being represented. For example, different letters are used to represent the same sound. Thus, Chou En-lai, who signed the Geneva Accords of 1954 and who famously shook the hand of Richard Nixon in 1972, is now Zhou En-lai. His surname, which, yes, comes first, is pronounced "joe" either way, but "zh" is not the only way our "j" sound is represented. When the "j" sound is followed by a long "e" sound, then the syllable is written "ji" (as in "gee whiz"). And just when you think you have learned that an "i" represents our long "e" sound, you will come across the syllable "zhi"—which is to be pronounced as if it had an "r" tacked on, as in "Ger" in "Germany." The same rule applies to "shi" (as in "shirred") and to "chi" (as in "church"). But when the "ch" sound is followed by our long "e" sound, it is represented by a "q" so that "qi" is pronounced "chee," as in "cheesecake," and "qu" is the "choo" of "choo-choo train." This is how the Ch'ing (rhymes with "ring") dynasty, which ended in 1912, and which figures prominently in this book, became the Qing dynasty.

RISING CHINA AND ITS POSTMODERN FATE

PROLOGUE

In 1958, the brilliant sinologist and intellectual historian Joseph Levenson (1920–1969) published the first of the three volumes that would become his trilogy *Confucian China and Its Modern Fate*. The work was completed in 1965 and has since gone on to become what literary critics call a canonical text. *Rising China and Its Postmodern Fate* quite deliberately mimes Levenson's trilogy in its title, but it is not a literal resumption of the inquiry he began five decades ago. Rather, I think of his work as a marker, a major milestone on what must necessarily be a never-ending intellectual journey to make sense of "actually existing" China. So, in that sense, it is impossible to take up where he left off.

The Confucian China that collided with the modern world in the nineteenth century was the product of two millennia of intellectual and practical effort. It was a place of extraordinary achievement in every realm of human endeavor—philosophy, art, religion, engineering, architecture, science, governance, literature, theology, music, commerce. It had fascinated the world for centuries. It had become more than merely rich and powerful; its military forces were certainly intimidating, but its culture also dominated neighbors like Vietnam, Korea, and Japan. Over the centuries, the achievement that was Confucian China had come to possess a quality that the Chinese themselves called *wei* (a German might render the Chinese character as "awe-inspiringness"), for Confucian China was indeed awe inspiring, and daunting.

Over the centuries, Chinese came to attribute their success as a polity not so much to any complicated system of thought but rather to the way that their tradition transmitted virtues and values. These could be traced to Confucius himself (550 BC–479 BC), though other philosophers, thinkers, and commentators helped create the Confucian canon over the centuries. To be sure, this was a collection of Great Books, but it was also a code of conduct. Confucian China joined culture to politics, creating a beau ideal of the scholar-official—the mandarin—at ease both in the world of affairs and in the world of poetry, painting, and calligraphy. He prepared for entry into the governing elite after total immersion in a core curriculum that derived from the classics and the orthodox commentaries about them. It is fair to say that China became close to obsessive about this; *respectable* entry into the world of power and wealth (one could, for example, become a very rich, but *déclassé,* businessman) could be gained only through a centuries-old examination system, and success at these extremely competitive examinations could be had only through a thorough mastery of received tradition.

But the received tradition was more than a set of aphorisms about good government derived from the *Analects* of Confucius. There was, of course, wide-ranging literary and art criticism, as one might expect in a culture-first society. Even more, across the centuries, there had been sophisticated political and philosophical argument of all kinds, much of it with a ring recognizable to us today. As early as the first century BC, Han dynasty (206 BC–AD 220) thinkers had conducted a famous debate about the merits of a free market as against the maintenance of government monopolies. In the twelfth century AD, Song dynasty (960–1279) thinkers were deeply immersed in policy disputes about the proper responsibility of government in regulating prices or aiding the poor, as against relying on what we today would call civil society, in order to reduce dependency of citizens on the state. In the sixteenth century, Ming dynasty (1368–1644) theorists argued about monetary policy, the real causes of inflation, and the benefits and costs of the nation's increased involvement in international commerce. And, as we might expect of any great nation, there was a lively debate across the centuries about what we would call Grand Strategy and all its elements— military power, diplomacy, "soft power," psychological warfare, commercial relations.

Withal, Traditional China was a place of enormous human energy, physical and mental. Accordingly, in addition to the more familiar topics of politics and economics, this book also considers a wide range of Chinese creativity, including literature, city planning, and architecture. Each of these is a way of showing respect for the past and of displaying a vision of the future. In them, one can find grand designs that mime those of grand strategists.

In the wide range of its achievements, China had become far more than just a country; it was a world, a civilization, formidable in every respect. But in the middle of the nineteenth century, it began to come apart as a polity, an economy, and as a Great Power. And then the very way of thinking that had sustained all of the past's great achievements also began to come apart. This decomposition, of course, proceeded in parts, and thoughtful Chinese began to think about things differently. Doctrines of every description and place of origin were investigated. The venerable common curriculum was thought no longer to serve, and the emperor decreed its abolition in 1905. The imperial system itself was scrapped in 1912, and replaced by a republic.

There was civil war, and about a century after the great decomposition began, it seemed to end with the proclamation of the People's Republic of China on October 1, 1949.

Scholars of Levenson's generation had an unusually daunting task as they sought to explain how and why this had happened. They had seen the actually existing China of the 1940s, and their teachers knew China first-hand before that. But this new People's Republic of China was so radical a departure from everything that had come before, so different in its visual appearance and its manner of speaking, so startling in its recasting of the country's domestic practices and international relations, and so challenging to what most people thought of as the essential nature of China that even the most knowledgeable and sophisticated observers of the Chinese scene were made to wonder: What was this thing? Where did it come from? What does it portend for China and for the world? How should we cope with it?

As efforts at understanding began, Levenson and his colleagues were indeed present at the creation. One senses that this cohort of then-young scholars was stimulated by what had become the obvious challenge of China's great transformation, and they looked forward to tackling it. Their elders, after all, were pre–World War II men; they had by the mid-1950s become a bit stuffy, a little hidebound, too much the captives of old thinking about Old China; one could say that they were just too Confucian. Thus, there was a sense that the Modern Fate of Confucian China would also presage the fate of the world's older China-related scholarship. For all of its dangers and uncertainties, this new world of China itself, and the community of scholars bound to it, would not be a dull place. It would be no country for old men.

This thrill of encountering something new—really new—in the stodgy discipline of sinology would inevitably go the way of other thrills. As decades passed, the world got over the shock of New China and became accustomed to its odd ways of behaving and dressing and speaking. But, about thirty years ago, this comfortable habituation was upended once again. China made another radical change of direction, and the China that people of my age (b. 1943) had come to know became something altogether different. This time, however, the change seemed easier to fathom; China began to resemble other places; its citizens began to wear what other people wore; they began to drive cars, watch television, and send e-mail to each other. This China—yes, Westerners had seen things like it before in other places that they had visited—but the questions still had to be asked: What was this thing? Where did it come from? What did it portend for China itself and for the world? How should we cope with it? To these, a sinologue of my age might have added: How was it that my education in things Chinese had failed to warn me that a second iteration of New China would appear?

It is this last question that links Levenson's book to this one, but it is an unfair complaint. After all, when Levenson was a student in the 1940s, no one told him that Mao Zedong would proclaim the People's Republic of China at the end of the decade; no one told him to prepare for what seemed to be the outcome of China's two-hundred-year encounter with modernity: a parade in front of the walls of the Forbidden City, with ecstatic Chinese carrying aloft an enormous portrait of a German Jew. Levenson was twenty-nine years old at the time of this improbable spectacle. He was a student of ideas and their history, and so it was in that realm where he sought an answer to a master question: How did it happen that the Chinese, heirs to the longest continuous intellectual and cultural tradition in the world, decided to abandon it and to adopt communism in its place? Just this one question was more than enough. In posing answers to his question, Levenson had no particular obligation to offer predictions either reassuring or unsettling—so long as explication of thoughts Chinese did not somehow slip into exculpation of deeds Chinese.

Meanwhile, my own education about China started at about the same time that Levenson published his first volume. I was a teenager then, a 1950s high school student who had totally embraced modernity—the American version, of course—as embodied by Little Richard, Elvis Presley, and my older brother's 1957 Chrysler 300D coupe. True, my maternal grandfather had visited China in the 1920s and the 1930s, and we had the usual kind of lower-level *chinoiserie* around the house—books by Pearl Buck and Lin Yu-tang, a pair (peddled as real, but certainly fake) of Ming-era figurines given to my mother by one of my uncles, who had got them during his military service in Asia.

But actually existing China first appeared to me in an English class, where we read George Orwell's *1984*, the most penetrating and influential book ever written about totalitarian dystopias. Our teacher, as I remember it, showed us a long article that had appeared in *Newsweek* describing a vast, government-engineered upheaval in China called the Great Leap Forward. Chairman Mao's campaign was described (rightly, as subsequent eyewitness accounts and scholarly research later confirmed) as an ur-nightmare of totalitarianism, right down to his naming of it with a perfectly Orwellian phrase. Tens of millions would die. This was startling; I was learning that there were other teenagers halfway around the world who, so *they* were told, were privileged to live a *modern* life far in advance of my own. Fortunately for me, one of my classmates knew something about this; her family had found its way to our town after the Hungarian uprising of 1956. No, she said, one should never be surprised by what "they" did; if I wanted to know more about "them," I should talk to her parents.

In 1959 the Dalai Lama fled actually existing China for India, beginning an exile that still continues. The People's Liberation Army of the new People's Republic of China had entered Tibet, and a decade of guerrilla warfare had failed to oust it. The next year, I was an undergraduate at the University of Pennsylvania and the beneficiary of some erudite and provocative teaching. Derk Bodde (1909–2003) was the very essence of sinological erudition. He taught the history of Chinese thought, having translated from the original Chinese the definitive two-volume work on the subject by the eminent scholar Feng Youlan (1895–1990). Bodde himself had written on ancient China's thought and institutions and would later explore law and the history of science and technology, collaborating intermittently with the great historian of Chinese science, Joseph Needham. And Bodde had actually been there—as a student in the 1930s and as a representative of the Office of Strategic Services during World War II. He had published *Peking Diary: A Year of Revolution* (1950), his eyewitness account of the entry of Mao's army into Beijing in 1949.

To use a euphemism, Bodde was a well-wisher of the new regime, but he was subdued about it, at least in his young students' presence. The real *provocateur*, in my recollection, was John Melby (1913–1992). Melby, a PhD from the University of Chicago, had served in the U.S. Foreign Service and had been the principal author of the famous China White Paper, released by Dean Acheson's Department of State in August 1949. It was a preemptive strike in the "Who Lost China?" debate, and it would soon be joined by innumerable books, articles, and pamphlets.

In those days, studying China meant being taken through the intricacies of the history of China's Communist Party. Melby did this for us. After a while, it began to seem normal to discuss left-wing adventurism and right-wing opportunism and the Li Li-san line and various sorts of deviationism. But then the weekend would come, and the bonhomie of the fraternity house would provide the proper corrective. We did not think about how our Chinese counterparts spent their weekends.

Melby was also a raconteur with a large cache of anecdotes about his former bosses, colleagues, and enemies, whether American or Chinese. Beyond anything else one took away from him, his mere presence was a reminder that "China" as such had become a treacherous topic. More exciting still, it held potential for real scandal. Lillian Hellman, the famous playwright, and Melby were lovers. Their affair began in 1944 (it was to continue, intermittently, until her death in 1984), and Melby would claim that the State Department had fired him as a security risk because it believed that *she* was a Communist. For us, this raised the titillating possibility that Melby himself just once might have been—indeed, maybe still was—a Communist. We had all *heard* about Communists, of course, but to our knowledge none of us had ever been in the same room with one.

By 1965, the Great Leap Forward had run its course, and I arrived at the University of Chicago to begin graduate study in the history of China. The American China scholars there were an interesting mixture of the established Confucian and the restless modern. The Chinese China scholars, China-born, were just old enough to have received classical Chinese educations and just young enough to have gone through American doctoral programs. I felt that such men could never be replicated; they were an accident of history, and no one would ever again be able to have such powerful command of two vastly different academic traditions. Moreover, they had lived through China's wars and revolutions and, for one reason or another, had become part of the Chinese diaspora, that centuries-old emigration that had also created the world's Chinatowns.

Two of my teachers from that time, neither one an American, figure in important leitmotifs in this book. Both were born in 1917 and, as of this writing, both are still at work. William H. McNeill, son of a Canadian clergyman and church historian, published what is still the best one-volume history of the world, *The Rise of the West* (1963). His influence on the study of world history and global history has been growing ever since. In several places in this book, I repair to his beguilingly simple insight that China, though often thought of as a world unto itself, was nonetheless a part of the whole world; China's own history could not be adequately understood unless one kept that in mind when contemplating the Middle Kingdom.

He Bingdi (Ping-ti Ho, as he was known in the romanization system then in general use) was *the* great scholar of China's so-called early modern period. He was not one for narrative political history of the ordinary sort. Instead, he had an enormous range of interests and wrote about things as diverse as developments in agricultural practices across the centuries, the evolution of financial institutions, the spread of native-place organizations, and the origins of Chinese civilization itself. His book, *Studies on the*

Population of China, first published in 1954, remains definitive and is still in print.

But in this book I make much of what He Bingdi may well have regarded as but an afterthought, though it led to a journal article in 1967 that still resonates. He set out to rehabilitate the Qing dynasty (1644–1912) and to rescue it from the bad reputation it had acquired over the decades for being in charge at a time of Chinese decline. He had his own particular explanations for the achievements of the dynasty, and these would be challenged a generation later. But the poles of this spirited debate—and the span of a generation that separates them—are now the starting points for arguments about the most basic terms in sinology, not least the meaning of the very word "China" itself.

In 1967, actually existing China was once again in a man-made convulsion, this one called the Great Proletarian Cultural Revolution. Though not so destructive as the Great Leap Forward of the previous decade, it was comparable in the human and material costs it imposed on a people not yet recovered from that earlier catastrophe. Chinese today call 1966–1976 the Lost Decade. If it is remembered at all in the West, it is because of its antic linguistic detritus. The Great Proletarian Cultural Revolution was spearheaded by Red Guards who chanted quotations from Chairman Mao that were printed in the Little Red Book. The enterprise was managed on Mao's behalf by his wife and three others who, when brought to book after Mao's death in 1976, would become world renowned as the Gang of Four.

In the middle of this upheaval on the Chinese mainland, I arrived on the island of Taiwan to continue my graduate studies. At that time, Americans interested in the academic study of China did not go, because they could not go, to China. They went to Taiwan or Hong Kong or Singapore. (Japan was also a center of China studies, and I spent a year there after Taiwan.) At that time, the island was under martial law, Chiang Kai-shek was still alive, and there were billboards all around exhorting the populace to prepare for a return to the mainland. As an American, protected from the police state in power, I could appreciate the surreality of my immediate surroundings; I could also, via shortwave radio, tune in on the Cultural Revolution being waged on the mainland, just ninety miles to the west. The narrator seemed always to be the same shrieking woman.

In fact, the entire region was a place of mind-numbing violence. Abutting the upheaval in China proper was the warfare throughout the Indochina Peninsula. The Vietnam War, which is what Americans call the period of United States involvement there, had already been preceded by military and political violence in Laos, Thailand, Malaya, Burma, and Vietnam—into which America's military forces were but inserted—and then followed by truly horrific mass murder after they were withdrawn. In 1967, of course, Cambodia's notorious Killing Fields had not yet been harvested, but on Taiwan there were personal accounts aplenty about 1965, Indonesia's famous "year of living dangerously." Hundreds of thousands of Chinese in Indonesia were massacred in the wake of an abortive, China-backed effort by Indonesia's Communist Party to overthrow the government in Jakarta. Many survivors of this great pogrom found their way to Taiwan; after a while, high-quality Indonesian batik began to appear in the local shops. Rising China—Confucian China's Modern Fate of the moment—is bound to the violence of its history. How does that legacy shape China's present? How would it shape China's visions of its future?

In 1970, I brought these and many other questions back to the United States, but they would have to keep. Only after two decades of other work did I get back to the study of China in the early 1990s. I knew about and had seen firsthand the vast changes in China that began after Mao Zedong's death in 1976. It was easy to observe how this great transformation of China's economy and society had affected the country's modes of living and its international trade rankings. But as I began to learn about what had happened to China studies during my almost quarter-century leave of absence, it was not only China's economy that had opened up. There had also appeared an entirely new discussion of the meaning of China's experience in the modern world. It was a discussion carried on in an environment of easier communication and freer artistic expression. For the first time in a very long time, it provided Chinese *themselves* an opportunity to assess openly their post-Confucian Modern Fate.

This had not been the case for decades. The chaos, confusion, and repression that was Modern China was hardly conducive to the study of history and of the humanities. Now, just as an earlier generation of China scholars had pondered what a thoughtful Chinese man of 1895 would make of his situation, I began to ponder what a thoughtful Chinese person of 1995 or 2005 would make of a Chinese world that had been turned upside down yet again.

I am fortunate to have advantages in looking for answers to my questions that my teachers did not have when they sought theirs. There is, first of all, the mere passage of time, which provides the benefit of perspective. But I also have the advantage of greater efficiency, for there are now many more people to help me. Certainly, the most important among these are China's scholars. They could not do this in Mao's time, when they were effectively forbidden to study their own country or to learn of any foreign study of it. China's system of education was consciously designed to separate them from their real past, and to substitute for it a kind of doggerel. But these past thirty years, Chinese scholars have been making up for lost time, and in crucial respects, China's intellectual scene is now among the most vibrant in the world, bringing together as it does competing ideas both foreign and domestic.

I have yet another advantage—the resurrection of non-Chinese sinology as a wide-ranging scholarly discipline. For centuries, sinology had been a worldwide undertaking—especially well established in Britain, France, Germany, the Netherlands, the United States, and Japan—but just as the Chinese were cut off from their own inherited learning, sinologists around the world were cut off from China altogether. They had to rely on materials housed outside the country. Among non-Chinese sinologues of an earlier generation, there grew up a division of labor. Some were trying to fathom the critique of Confucianism that had led to its seeming demise, and among these, there were many who did not regret its Modern Fate. But there were others who also became Confucian China's conservators; regardless of their own personal political opinions, they saw China's tradition as they had always seen it—a treasure that belonged to the whole world. Indeed, it is no overstatement that China's Great Books and all they represented, while in peril at home, were kept alive and sustained outside the country.

The relationship between foreign students of China and their country of interest has now been rebuilt, with connections today far more powerful than those that existed before the advent of the Maoist state. Scholars from around the world now have access to archives and opportunities for field research that would have been unimaginable a generation ago. These have been compounded by an information and communications revolution, with its e-mail, affinity message boards, and instantaneous transmission of documents of all kinds. Sinologues around the world can read Chinese newspapers and academic journals online. Great libraries can now be linked to one another. In short, there has been a major revolution in China studies. Fifty years ago, when Joseph Levenson reflected on China's state of mind, he was certainly not unaccompanied, but his intellectual travels were far lonelier than mine.

My journey also begins at a very different place. The Chinese thinker of 1905 lived amid chaos and failure. His prospects and the prospects for his country were uncertain; indeed, there were many reasons to believe that they would be tragic. But the Chinese thinker of 2005 lived without such dire foreboding. Today, he can contemplate China's current and anticipated weight in the world; his country has a reasonable expectation of national success rather than one of national disaster. This simple distinction is the starting point of this book.

Ever since the Chinese imperial system began its fatal decline in the nineteenth century, Chinese thinkers of every outlook shared in a search for an explanation for this nation-transforming catastrophe and its profound effects on the world beyond. It was not that cataclysm and breakdown were unknown to the Chinese. Their history was filled with such episodes, and these had become part of the country's cultural tradition and central to its deepest sensibility about the nature of the world. At the same time, China's history was filled with uplifting accounts of restoration of prior grandeur, and these also had well-established explanations. In the modern period, however, the search for explanations of rise and fall incorporated entirely new ways of investigating and comprehending the nation's past and reflecting on its present situation.

Over the centuries, traditional Chinese historiography had perfected its methodologies and refined its moral lessons, and had always found a way to provide for the validation of those techniques and teachings. But in the modern era Chinese historians sought to do neither; they were on an unprecedented search for a fatal flaw in the system, a historian's philosopher's stone that would explain modern China's miseries. When the great crisis began, there was but one way that Confucian China had of understanding itself—its own tradition. But Confucian China's encounter with the modern world introduced entirely new ways to Confucian China, including new ways of understanding itself.

These were as different as Christian historiography, or Marxist historiography, or the Whig interpretation of history. In the past thirty years, the intellectual imports from the modern world have become a torrent of ideas. This has made the interaction between the traditional and the modern more complicated than it has ever been, just as the advent of Rising China has made the resolution of the issues seem more urgent. China is seeking to assemble a set of lessons from the country's past that can serve as a guide, and even an inspiration, for China's return to prominence and power in the world. For this task, China now has before it not only its own experience, but also the experience of the whole world. Stories from the past meet the flood of information and ideas that are now pouring into the country every day.

This book begins by looking at past events in the light of how they have come to be interpreted in the present. My purpose is to discuss how contemporary China's view of great periods in the nation's history is influencing the development of China's view of itself and of the world. Chapters in China's great history will underscore the point that the twenty-first century is hardly the first time that China has had to define and then redefine itself as its own circumstances and world circumstances require.

China's past experiences have been rich and varied in this regard. Though "China" is often thought of as something fixed and immutable, it has shown instead that it can change its shape, organize itself in different ways, relate to the world in different ways, and alter the ways it thinks about the world. Chinese political philosophy may rest on a long tradition, but this apparent consensus has never precluded sharp and spirited debate about proper policy. Chinese do not all think alike. They have had intense arguments about politics; some were so bitter that they could be resolved only by violence and civil war.

Good historians are not supposed to look at the past principally in the context of present-day arguments or in the way interpretations of the past quite deliberately inform present-day political debates. But this book does both. It also does what good political scientists are not supposed to do either: it not only engages in "mirror imaging" but, even worse, it engages in "rearview mirror imaging;" it suggests that the past will be more usefully understood if we impose on it concepts and vocabulary from our own time.

Three great dynasties serve as examples. What they stand for now is very different from what they were once were thought to be. A generation ago, the Yuan dynasty (1271–1368), because it was the creation of close descendents of Genghis Khan, was tainted by its Mongol origins. Today, the Yuan dynasty is appreciated for its integration of China into a genuine world system, a system consisting of several great cultures and traditions, each one useful in developing China's polity, society, economy, and culture. This particular Rising China was a place of great strategic ambition that sought to expand its influence into Central Asia and Southeast Asia, and that, in support of these objectives, mobilized large armies and great armadas.

A generation ago, the Ming dynasty (1368–1644) was thought of as isolationist. Today, it is now compared to the Yuan, for Ming China became part of an even larger worldwide system that now included the New World, a system that quickly developed complex political, economic, and strategic links among Europe, South America, the Near East, South Asia, and East Asia. These were truly enormous changes, creating a world far more complicated and integrated than the already-complex world of Yuan times. China's intellectual horizons also expanded, for the expansion of Ming China's sense of the known world led also to an expansion of Chinese thinking about that world. Ming-era Rising China sought, first, to understand what was happening around it and, second, to adapt China to it. The appearance of this new international economic and political system presented novel problems. China's own society could now be profoundly shaken by events on the other side of the world, events altogether different from those of Mongol/Yuan times. Ming-era China, through the use of its maritime power, tried to enhance its position in this new configuration. Not surprisingly, the history of that effort has now been enlisted by strategists in today's Rising China who would like to do the same thing.

A generation ago, the Qing dynasty (1644–1912), founded by invading Manchus in 1644, was best known for having presided over China's greatest humiliations and for leading the country down a series of blind alleys. But not least because it is the dynasty closest to us in time, the Qing has begun to provide us with powerful insights into the Rising China of the twenty-first century. The Qing emperors created a vast, Asia-based continental system, akin to what the Yuan dynasty had done, yet more sophisticated and enduring. Qing strategists, faced with a transformation in the world system far greater and far more threatening than even the astonishing worldwide transformation of the Ming era, tried to steer their empire—keeping in mind that China proper was only one part of that empire—through dangerous times. Historians now stress the continuity between that time and our own, and there is much to learn about today's Rising China by looking more closely at the Late Qing era.

Like the China of the Late Qing, a China thought to be in decline, today's Rising China is a multiethnic polity; today's People's Republic recognizes fifty-six minorities, many inside of China today because of earlier Manchu conquests. Today's Rising China is also thoroughly enmeshed in an integrated international system, akin to the era of globalization during the Late Qing, that is, between 1870 and 1912. Just as the globalization of the late nineteenth and early twentieth centuries was a time of astonishing technological advance that, in one generation, introduced the world to electricity, automobiles, motion pictures, wireless, and airplanes, so too are today's new technologies—in telecommunications, in biology and medicine, in computer science, in nanotechnology—a defining feature of twenty-first-century globalization.

There are other connections. In the Late Qing period, China's popular opinion of the traditional kind—an opinion expressed in peasant violence and rebellion in the name of folk religion or Han Chinese racial solidarity—began slowly to give way to popular opinion of the modern kind, supportive of new Western-derived concepts of politics that included words like constitutionalism, representative government, democracy, socialism, and communism.

For twenty-first-century China, where massive changes wrought by globalization have begun, twentieth-century Europe offers a cautionary tale. The changes may start slowly, but then at an ever-increasing tempo society is transformed from rural to urban, from agrarian to industrial, from industrial to technological. A merely populous society becomes a mass society, where ways of life, modes of thought, and tastes in art and culture unimaginable a generation before spread throughout the country. First, there is "the rise of the masses," followed by what Spanish philosopher Jose Ortega y Gasset (1883–1955) called "the revolt of the masses," followed by the erosion of deference to old authorities, followed by cultural incoherence, political confusion, and, finally, breakdown.

The Chinese call this condition *luan* ("chaos"), and in one form or another it has been the specter haunting every Chinese governing group since the time of Confucius. The cataclysms in Europe in the twentieth century and the appearance there of crazed social theories and murderous political ideologies testify to the dangers of rapid modernization. In this respect, the same modernization that must occur before any grand vision in China has real power behind it is also a great threat to that design's realization. Understanding how today's Chinese construe this dilemma is an essential part of speculating about the country's future.

China reached a low point in 1900, when the armies of eight foreign countries occupied Beijing after suppressing an outbreak of violent xenophobia known as the Boxer Rebellion. In 1949, after decades of war and violence, the People's Republic of China was established, and it set out to restore China's position among the leading nations of the world. For all its revolutionary fervor, historians now call attention to how New China also drew on much that was well established in Chinese tradition. Historians connect Maoism to Chinese heterodoxy, the polar opposite of Chinese orthodoxy; thus, one can look at the story of Modern China as the struggle between the radical utopianism embodied by Mao Zedong, the Great Helmsman of the Chinese Communist Party, on the one hand, and practitioners of time-honored statecraft and state-building, like the "self-strengtheners" of the Late Qing era or the "pragmatic" followers of Deng Xiaoping on the other.

The world was both fascinated and frightened by the Rising China of Mao Zedong. In the 1960s especially, China seemed to be at one with powerful forces sweeping the world that bid fair to overturn the entire international order. In an effort to understand how this had happened in China, historians now follow many paths of interpretation and argument in trying to identify elements in Mao's China that were "Chinese," that were "Communist," and that represented features common to all political and social systems. Maoism, as practiced in the first twenty-six years of the People's Republic, turned out to be short lived; in the end it remains a mystery. There is no broad understanding of why or how it came to grief, whether its failures were peculiar to China's circumstances, history, and culture, or whether its failure—to paraphrase some old Marxist lingo—was principally a manifestation of the General Crisis of Communism in the Current Historical Epoch. This was the fate of communism as established in China; fifty years ago, it was thought it would be there for the duration. Today's China also seeks to understand the fate of other grand national designs by studying the collapse of the Soviet Union and, by extension, the success of the United States. In the nineteenth century, Marx and Engels famously announced that the specter of communism had begun to haunt Europe. Now, in the twenty-first century, it is the specter of the collapse of communism that haunts the leaders of the People's Republic of China.

In this they are probably both burdened and edified by the legacy of that most obscure of the ancient Chinese classics, the *Book of Changes*. For centuries, commentators have sought to explicate this opaque text, and yet it can be reduced to one profound observation: Things change. Confucian China became Modern China, which became Rising China, and which is now on its way to becoming something else.

CHAPTER 1

A MEMORY OF EMPIRE:
THE NEW PAST OF OLD CHINA

On November 19, 2004, Xu Jialu, vice chairman of the Standing Committee of the National People's Congress, announced the completion of a vast literary enterprise he had been supervising. For more than thirteen years Xu had been editor in chief of a translation of China's twenty-four official dynastic histories from the classical literary Chinese in which they had been composed into modern vernacular Chinese, the language as it is spoken and written today. The project had employed more than two hundred professors from seven academic institutes and universities. These twenty-four histories represent the accumulated effort of centuries and cover all the officially recognized dynasties save the last one, the Qing (1644–1912). Taken together, the histories contain about 470 million Chinese characters in their original classical language and more than 600 million characters when rendered into the modern tongue. These writings are what the Chinese call *zhengshi*, "official" or "standard" history. They begin with the renowned *Records of the Grand Historian*, completed in 93 BC during the reign of the Han dynasty. *Records* established the model that would be used until 1739, when the standard history of the Ming dynasty (1368–1644) was finally completed.

The twenty-four histories are more than chronology. They include bi-ographies of the emperors, as well as of selected "eminent persons," and treatises on subjects as varied as law, geography, astronomy, trade, military affairs, bureaucracy, and civil engineering. Over the centuries, the writing of standard history took on a life of its own. Each new dynasty wrote the his-tory of the failed dynasty that preceded it. The preparation of such histories became a large-scale bureaucratic activity involving sometimes hundreds of compilers and writers. Therefore, the obligatory political and moral judg-ments could not be attributed to a single person; the profession of historian as it has come to be understood in our day—that is, one individual working alone—did not exist. The writers of standard history were drawn from the same group of Confucian-educated literati who formed the mandarinate—imperial officials chosen by China's renowned civil service examinations—and they were thought to be performing the same high duty to the emperor as their colleagues in any other government ministry. Standard history was thus always broadly political in its intention, but for all the repetitiveness of its core moral judgments over the centuries, new—and dangerous—issues sometimes needed to be addressed.

Of particular relevance to any discussion involving the Yuan and Qing dynasties was the plain and embarrassing fact that, sometimes, the ruling houses of China were not Chinese at all. Their gaining of the Mandate of Heaven would thus compel Chinese officialdom to confront a basic dis-tinction between Han Chinese people and those of different races, between what the Chinese had long called the "inside" peoples and the "outside" ones and, most important of all, between what was traditionally regarded as "civilized" and what was regarded as "uncivilized." The ascendancy of Inner Asian peoples like the Mongols or the Manchus (and some others also) raised very large and treacherous problems of interpretation for literati reared in the conceits of a Middle Kingdom. In these ways the combined effort of centuries served to produce an accessible and useable past.

But useable by whom, and for what? As the nineteenth century unfolded and as the Chinese imperial and social system began to unravel—and, in particular, as Europeans from distant places, barely known foreigners who were neither Mongols nor Manchus, gained ever more influence in, over, and around China—the past became part of the crisis of the present. In the last half of the nineteenth century and in the first half of the twentieth, there were movements for reform, then renovation, and, finally, revolution. The past got caught up in this, for it had to be changed. By the 1920s a va-riety of intellectual efforts had coalesced into something that sounds droll to our ears today, the "Movement for the Reorganization of the National Past." Many varieties of older Chinese thought and newer Western thought flowed into it. This movement embodied recognizable features of modern historiography especially in its critical attitude toward traditional historiography and biography. One of its principles—"boldness in hypothesis, but caution in proof"—suggested that the study of history could become more scientific and less impressionistic. Historians could then stand apart from political affiliations and partisan causes.

In the meantime, energetic scholars reclassified historical materials and collated new editions of ancient works with new commentaries and prefaces, making ancient texts more accessible to the general public. World War I and the Bolshevik Revolution in Russia introduced new concepts into the mix, most notably Marxist materialism. Japan's relentless efforts after 1895 to overturn the traditional intra-Asian balance of power and gain ascendancy over China, an effort that culminated in the Second Sino-Japanese War, between 1937 and 1945, introduced what today's academics call "nationalist narrative" into Chinese historical writing. The People's Republic of China that emerged after the chaos of that conflict embodied the ultimate in creating a "purposeful past." As Jin Qiu, an analyst of Chinese historiography, has summarized it, Mao and the Communist Party well understood the power of history, which could be used to legitimize or sabotage his political rule. Mao's personal involvement in academic discussions and his extensive purges of intellectuals had tremendous impact. He pushed the practice of using the past to serve current political purpose to the extreme. The government thus created an atmosphere that became increasingly brutal toward historians who wanted to conduct independent academic research. Anything without official endorsement was viewed with increasing suspicion, for it could serve antiparty purposes.

The death of Mao Zedong in 1976 and the end of the Great Proletarian Cultural Revolution, marked by the return to power of Deng Xiaoping shortly thereafter, set off an intellectual explosion comparable in every way to the explosion triggered by Deng's economic reforms. An older cultural revolution in the study of history and historiography could now resume, and it featured a wholesale resumption of Chinese historians' interest in, and inspiration by, the outer world. Q. Edward Wang, a scholar of both early modern and contemporary Chinese historiography, has documented this enthusiasm and its enormous productivity both in the rediscovery of what had once been well known in China and in the discovery of new things that had gone unknown during China's period of Maoist isolation and repression. The revolution also had a personal dimension as prominent historians from all over the world traveled to China to bring their Chinese colleagues up to date on the latest developments—fads, some might say—in the study and writing of history. Wang pays attention especially to the Culture Fever movement of the 1980s and the interest of a rising generation of Chinese intellectuals in what was modern and Western—"a project underscored by a century-old anxiety for their country's weakness in confronting and competing with the West."[1] Culture Fever, in turn, set off Book Series Fever.

During the 1980s, as Wang further records, there was a torrent of translation that included works by modern theorists as disparate as Benedetto Croce, R. G. Collingwood, G. P. Gooch, and Arnold Toynbee, and venerable practitioners such as Herodotus, Thucydides, Livy, Tacitus, Machiavelli, and Gibbon. The craze even produced some highly improbable best sellers—Ernst Cassirer's *An Essay of Man*, which sold more than two hundred thousand copies, and Geoffrey Barraclough's *Main Trends in History*, which sold more than one hundred thousand. The massacre in Tiananmen Square on June 4, 1989, brought these expansive speculations to an abrupt halt. Suddenly it was far from clear what even the reformist Deng Xiaoping regime was willing to tolerate in its new environment of openness. Though we know little of how these issues were actually thrashed out at the upper reaches of the Chinese Communist Party, we do know that about three years after the 1989 massacre Deng personally renewed his call, not only for reform, but for "more reform." Among historians this was taken as permission to resume their discussions and debates about the writing of history as a profession and the meaning of history as a profound question for civilization.

The scholar Edward Krebs has also noted how the commercialization of Chinese society worked to reinforce these proclivities among the country's intellectuals. At first, he observes, China's intellectuals felt threatened by the growth and influence of the business class, but

> by the middle 1990s, the growth of the market economy also brought positive changes for scholars, writers, and intellectuals in most fields. China's publishing market began to incorporate the positive effects of commercialization; one effect has been the continuing introduction of historians and historical thinking from abroad. Historians, and scholars in other fields, generally enjoy more opportunities to publish and to gain a readership for their work. The publishing market today is a big factor in the development

of a marketplace of ideas, probably more open than at any time since the
1910s and the 1920s. . . . The past two decades have brought historians from
being the modern equivalents of the scholars who served in the history
bureaus of a dynastic government to the status of somewhat more outspoken
and independent scholars with opportunities to influence a growing urban
reading public.[2]

One can rightfully wonder how this ongoing assimilation of Western
practices of academic, narrative, and highly specialized historical study into
China shapes the insights and methods that we associate with the traditional concerns and topics of the Chinese historian. China's scholarly
practices of the past without doubt remain a powerful presence, but as we
shall see, Western and Chinese approaches to the interpretation of China's
history are coming increasingly to resemble each other, so that contemporary scholarship in one part of the world is increasingly indistinguishable
from that in another.

Today this has revealed an intellectual convergence. For the past four
centuries the study of China has been an international undertaking with
non-Chinese having the dominant though not the exclusive influence over
the world's perceptions of the country and its history. This had been especially true since the mid-nineteenth century, because of the enormous
difficulties that the collapse of civil order and subsequent Maoist brutalities
presented to Chinese people who might be interested in learning about
their own tradition. Sinologues outside the country had to develop a kind of
self-reliance, relying more on themselves than they might have if the times
had been normal. In the United States in particular the professional study
of China and the university teaching that derived from it were initially
and importantly the work of American missionaries resident in China and,
later, their China-born sons. C. Martin Wilbur (1909–1997) and A. Doak
Barnett (1922–1999) are representative examples, though in citing them one
should not gloss over the enormous influence of Chinese scholars based
at universities in the United States from, say, 1930 on. After all, these men
were old enough to be among the last to receive classical Chinese educations, yet still young enough to be Chinese pioneers in earning doctorates
from American universities.

Beyond their role as China scholars, Americans of backgrounds similar
to those of Wilbur and Barnett also filled important positions in the U.S.
Foreign Service. Most of the so-called Old China Hands were China-born,
and their influence was felt even after the reopening of the U.S. embassy in

Beijing in 1979. It was as if a government-in-exile had returned. The man who had closed the Beijing embassy in 1949 was John Leighton Stuart, a prominent China-based Presbyterian educator who was president of Yenching University when General George Marshall sponsored his appointment as ambassador. Since the embassy was reopened after the resumption of United States–China formal diplomatic relations in 1979, three of the ambassadors who served there were China-born—Arthur Hummel Jr., J. Stapleton Roy, and James Lilley.

The establishment of the People's Republic of China, and especially its deep isolation from the Western world in general and the United States in particular, destroyed the human linkages among the sinologists of the world that had existed for centuries. Meanwhile, the sociology of American sinology was also changing, tracking larger changes in American higher education and its new post–World War II meritocracy. Just as the student bodies in the Ivy League became less predominantly traditional Protestant, so too did the field of China studies, sometimes establishing new ties between ancient intellectual traditions. Back in 1992, for example, the late Benjamin Schwartz, then Professor Emeritus at Harvard and one of America's greatest sinologists, noted that "some of the most meaningful encounters between the Jews and China have occurred only in recent years, as the number of scholars of Jewish origin who are interested in both traditional and modern China has grown significantly."[3] Predictably, the transformation of China from a crumbling place in need of patient American tending into a leading-edge revolutionary state bent on supplanting American influence everywhere transformed the nature of America's interest in the place. Students at Harvard and Yale, once drawn to China as a country ripe for religious and political conversion by America, became interested during the 1970s in the connection between the advent of the People's Republic and other great upheavals in world politics. But far more important than anything sociological or political was the fact that these younger students of the older China scholars had a profoundly, indeed decisively, different educational experience. They were trying to learn about China at a time when Americans did not go there. Instead, they had to go to the British enclave of Hong Kong and peer into the mists on the other side of the border, or they would go to Taiwan, not yet the economic success it would later become and, for all its claims, still something of a backwater.

Today, graduate students and professors travel throughout China in search of research material, and the China they see is different from anything their teachers could have imagined. They are now part of the historic process of re-establishing the personal connections that had been important for a century and a half. Our own university system, to take an example important to students of China, has educated hundreds of thousands of Chinese students from every part of the Chinese world, even as China itself has become the place where American students and scholars go to learn about China. Initially, these Chinese students directed themselves mostly to the sciences, later to business and management, but increasingly during the past decade to the study of China itself. A new consensus about China's modern historical experience is thus being fashioned by young Chinese from the mainland, by many tens of thousands from Taiwan, and by thousands more from other places in the Chinese diaspora who have also studied in the United States.

One immediate consequence of this is that China has come to seem less exotic and more ordinary, a place like other places, still inscrutable perhaps, but no longer inaccessible. Some traditionalists may ruefully regret the loss of individuality and idiosyncrasy in the study of this great country's history, but it is nonetheless easier to focus on today's debates about the past that influence the present and foreshadow the future, without dwelling overly much on their place of origin.

Mao's instruction to "use the past to serve the present" was a watchword of his tyranny, and almost all of China's historians today are deeply ashamed of it. Yet the habit dies hard. Today there is a movement underway to create a new past that can inform a new generation's grand designs, and many Chinese hope that it augurs a great leap forward for their country.

CHAPTER 2

THE YUAN DYNASTY AND THE *PAX MONGOLICA*

"Today, thanks to God and in consequence of Him," noted the great Persian historian Rashid al-Din (1247–1317) in the introduction to his magnum opus of 1308,

> the extremities of the inhabited earth are under the dominion of the house of Genghis Khan, and philosophers, astronomers, scholars, and historians from North and South China, India, Kashmir, Tibet, the land of the Uighurs and the other Turkic tribes, the Arabs and the Franks, all belonging to different religions and sects, are united in large numbers in the service of majestic Heaven.
>
> And each one had manuscripts on the chronology, history and articles of faith of his people, and each has knowledge of some aspect of this. Wisdom, which decorates the world, demands that there should be prepared from these chronicles and narratives an abridgement, but still an essentially complete work. . . . This book in its totality will be unprecedented—an assemblage of all the branches of history.

Al-Din's book, *Collected Chronicles*, was for that time—indeed, for any time—an enormous undertaking, assembled by writers and researchers who, among them, commanded a wide array of languages—Chinese, Persian, Kashmiri, Uighur, Mongolian, Hebrew, Arabic, Tibetan, and Frankish—and an even wider range of special interests—agronomy, geography, science, medicine, mathematics, religion, philosophy, government, and genealogy. The work also relies on traditional oral history for accounts of steppe nomads. Rashid al-Din himself was a court physician until given this task by the then–Mongol ruler of Iran and, in completing his assignment, created "an unparalleled source of information, a veritable gold mine that is still largely untapped."[1]

The work, as Rashid al-Din properly implies, is an astonishing catalogue of the diversity of the Mongols' imperial portfolio and their respect for, and interest in, the many peoples they had brought under their rule. And yet, such a literary undertaking is hardly the kind of project one associates, even in our own time, with the word *Mongol*. In its multilingual origins, one can safely assume that one purpose of the work's patrons was an educative one—a way for at least some of the constituent parts of an empire that stretched from Beijing in the East to Baghdad in the West, from Vienna in Central Europe to the heart of Muscovy in Russia, to learn something about each other.

The twenty-first century is interested in thirteenth-century Mongol cosmopolitanism because of its connection to China, how the Mongols made China part of what we today would call a world system. How did that experience affect the outlook of future empire builders in China, whether the native Chinese Ming founders or the Inner Asia cousins of the Mongols, the Manchus, who created the Qing? The *Pax Mongolica* was in and of itself a further elaboration on what was already a centuries-old argument about what "China" was, an argument that remains unsettled in the twenty-first century. What, in fact, is China? How did it become what it is? How is this thing called China going to live in something called the modern world?

Just as we do not usually link the words *Mongol* and *cosmopolitanism*, we do not usually think that unfamiliar subjects like thirteenth-century China are implicated in nation-defining thoughts and actions of today. But if we properly ascribe to ancient China—especially ancient Chinese thinking about history, governance, and Grand Strategy—a place of influence in the thinking of China's present-day historians, mandarins, and strategists, we dare not overlook ideas that have entered the Chinese mind since then.

And, at every stage over the centuries, precisely because the examination of these issues and the writing of their history have been intensely political, consideration of the Mongol ascendancy in China is more than an antiquarian pursuit. Through no fault of its own, *Pax Mongolica* has entered contemporary discussion, and new interpretations of that era now feed into, even as they derive from, perennial arguments about China—what it is, where it belongs in the world, and what will become of it.

"Historians of China," as Richard von Glahn points out, "have often deemed periods of foreign rule as aberrations or deviations from a Chinese pattern of historical evolution. The notion that the Mongol Yuan dynasty caused a rupture in the normal trajectory of Chinese history with uniformly negative consequences has been challenged [and] we should move beyond the obsolete notion that Yuan history was a tale of failed sinification. . . . The epoch of Mongol rule has come to occupy a crucial place in narratives of the 'Rise of the West' in recent world-historical scholarship. . . . Mongol rule in Yuan China created an unprecedented geopolitical context that affected social and political life in profound ways."[2] Our new appreciation of the influence of Mongol rule rests on the simple fact that, for the first time in its history, China was governed as part of a world system larger than itself, as part of *someone else's* empire.

It would have that experience again between 1644 and 1912 when, for almost three centuries, its government was not the government of China *qua* China but, instead, China was part of someone else's empire—in this case the vast empire of the Manchus, another traditionally disdained people from Inner Asia. An experience like this can lead a country in different directions. It can make it more worldly and sophisticated, more flexible and venturesome, more energetic and more interested in the future. The effects can also be quite the opposite, even as both sets of effects work at the same time. In the end it will depend on what use a country will make of its new-found connections to the larger world.

The great enterprise that was the Mongol Empire began with Genghis Khan (1167–1227.) After he died, the vast holdings he had assembled passed to one of his grandsons, Mongke Khan (1208–1259), who enlarged them even more. Mongke was especially interested in expanding into China and spent many years doing precisely that; indeed, he died there in a battle in Sichuan in the western part of the country. (A Mongol army returned to

Sichuan in 1279 and avenged his death, carrying out the infamous sack of Chengdu, the provincial capital. Though the story has probably been improved in the telling, the consensus estimate is that at least one million people in the city were killed. This exceeded even the eight hundred thousand thought to have been killed when a Mongol army in Southwest Asia commanded by Hulegu Khan, one of Mongke's brothers, occupied Baghdad in 1258.) Khubilai Khan (1215–1294), another of Mongke's brothers, was also involved in the China campaign; during the 1250s he was sent to gain control of what is now Yunnan province in the southwestern part of the country. Khubilai's success there established an important Mongol base for subsequent expansion into southern China and later into Southeast Asia.

The intricacies of the subsequent re-organization of the Mongol Empire after Mongke Khan's death are not a concern here. Suffice to say, the once centrally governed empire was divided into four parts, and Khubilai inherited the part that included Mongolia and China. The Yuan dynasty in China was proclaimed in 1260, but Khubilai still needed to expand and consolidate the khanate, or realm, he had inherited from his older brother. While his title to his fourth of the Mongol Empire was secure, his title to the throne of China was widely disputed and violently resisted. There were other claimants, and it took many years to deal with them. Thus, Khubilai did not sit on the throne of One China until 1280, the year that customarily marks the beginning of the Yuan dynasty.

We can assume that Khubilai's approach to transforming his Mongol khanate inheritance into a proper Chinese dynasty began with the fact that, by 1260, China was already an important power base for the larger Mongol Empire. The Mongols were always a tiny minority wherever they ruled, and bringing more of China into the fold made them a tinier minority still. Khubilai needed to develop as much local support as he could, and he needed also to draw on support from the other parts of the Mongol Empire. After all, it was still a family business.

Khubilai's strategy for securing China for the Mongols illustrates both components of the Mongol Empire's Grand Strategy—co-optation of those on the scene and cooperation with other parts of the empire. Building local support came first. As the historian Frederick W. Mote has pointed out, "we perceive that the Mongols in China, as in the steppe, as in Central Asia and Persia, and in Russia, adapted fully to various civilizations in all the realms they conquered. What the Chinese have observed as obeisance to their universal culture was in fact a pragmatic decision about how best to serve Mongolian interests in all places and times."[3] As a partner in his brother's military campaign in China, Khubilai had already begun to build the core of a future government for all of China. He had many Chinese advisers, he took an interest in agriculture, taxation, and commerce, and the area under his control acquired a reputation for stability and prosperity. He agreed to the opening of Chinese schools and to the use of some Chinese rituals at his court. He listened to the arguments between Daoists and Buddhists and came down on neither side. Even before his brother's death and his formal acquisition of the China khanate, Khubilai built a capital city near Dolon-nor in what is now Inner Mongolia, about a two-week excursion from Beijing in those days.

The site was not altogether a part of the settled agrarian Chinese world, but it was not wholly part of the Mongolian steppe nomad world either. At the same time, Khubilai's military operations were run by Mongol generals, and he turned to others from the empire, Uighurs and Turks especially, to serve as interpreters, local governors, and court officials. As Morris Rosabi, the authoritative biographer of Khubilai Khan of our own time, summarizes it, "by the time of Mongke's death in 1259, Khubilai had recruited advisers and administrators representing a variety of different religions, ethnic groups, and occupations. Although he was not the first Mongol to seek advice and assistance from the peoples they had subjugated, he was unique in having such a large coterie of advisers."[4] As we can imagine, it took a while for the family to settle the disposition of Mongke Khan's estate, in that it consisted of the largest contiguous piece of real estate in the history of the world.

As for Khubilai Khan's portion of it, he was paramount only in north China; the Song dynasty—this portion of Song history known to us now as the Southern Song (1127–1280)—was a formidable rival, reeling, to be sure, from its loss of control of the northern part of the country but still rich and powerful. It ruled a region of great cities and productive farms and was a center of wide-ranging domestic and international commerce. It also had something wholly foreign to the Mongols and their characteristic mode of warfare—a powerful navy, whose warships were armed with rockets, flamethrowers, and fragmentation bombs.

"The war began in earnest in 1268 and lasted until 1279," writes Rosabi. The Chinese had constructed almost impregnable fortifications at Hsiangyang, the last stronghold on the route to the central basin of the Yangtze. To overcome the defenders' resistance, the Mongolian troops needed naval supremacy and also required proficiency in siege warfare and artillery.

To provide this expertise, Khubilai selected an international group of commanders, eventually recruiting Mongols, Chinese, Uighurs, and Persians for his army and Koreans and Jurchens for his navy."[5] This multinational force besieged the city, then overran it, and went on to capture the great Song capital city of Hangzhou (the same city that would later be made famous by Marco Polo). Separate armies pushed into Guangxi and Fujian. The Song court itself was trapped in what is now Guangzhou, and its end had a poignancy that would inspire playwrights and poets for many centuries thereafter. The last Song emperor was a seven-year-old boy, and as the Mongol forces closed in, one of his loyal commanders grabbed him and tried to escape with him by ship. Both of them drowned. Thus did Khubilai Khan come to institute Mongol rule over the most populous country in the world.[6]

The new dynasty now faced the perennial problem of insinuating itself into the orthodox line of succession even though, of course, it was not Chinese. Khubilai had begun to address this problem almost immediately upon his proclamation of the Yuan dynasty in 1260, well before the triumphs of 1279. Hok-Lam Chan, who has studied the ensuing work of the reconstituted National History Office, describes it as "one of the most ambitious projects undertaken in the history of official Chinese historiography."[7] But it was not Khubilai's task to complete. It was to take about eighty years to agree on what to publish, but within a three-year period, 1343–1345, the Yuan dynasty history office issued about 700 volumes in toto, about 450 of them devoted to its immediate Chinese predecessor, the Song (960–1279), and the other volumes to two kindred alien dynasties, the Liao (906–1025) and the Jin (1125–1234). As the overlapping dates suggest, the four had contested among themselves for control of the country, but only the Song and the Yuan were able, at one time or another, to rule the entire country.

Aside from practical problems, not least the organization and exploitation of astonishingly large quantities of captured archival materials, the work presented many knotty doctrinal and political questions. The struggle to control the interpretation of the history of the Song dynasty and the history of relations between the Song and Yuan dynasties was to continue for centuries, as would the argument over the legitimacy of the Yuan dynasty. The historians who carried on this work for the Yuan dynasty knew they were to place Mongol rule in the orthodox line of succession. They did this by issuing official histories of all of the dynasties that the Mongols had defeated on their way to control of China, that is, not only the "Chinese" Song dynasty, but also the "alien" Liao and Jin.

All three dynasties, especially the alien ones, now had an independent history of their own and were therefore legitimate. How could it be otherwise? Within the tradition of standard history, already more than a thousand years old when the Mongols came to power, the publishing of proper dynastic histories about them under the emperor's aegis made it so.

A helpful perspective on what this set in motion is also provided by Hok-Lam Chan, as he describes the centuries-long ideological struggle that would develop about these interpretations. The new Ming ruling house that appeared in 1368 after the collapse of the Mongols attempted to connect itself to "Song loyalism," that is, to the anti-Mongol resistance of the thirteenth century. Later on during its tenure, the Ming dynasty decided upon a wholesale revision of the still-official Yuan reading of Song dynasty history. It began after the greatest military defeat suffered in the early Ming period. In 1449 the reigning emperor personally led Ming armies into battle against a Mongol force at a place called Tu Mu, northwest of Beijing, beyond the Great Wall. It was a huge defeat for the Ming; about 250,000 Chinese soldiers were killed, and the emperor was captured. According to Chan, "This humiliating setback caused a wave of sentiment against not only the Mongols but all the alien conquerors in Chinese history." He calls this "proto-nationalism," as he recounts how the resulting product, the new Ming history of the Song era, came to be filled with "anti-foreign propaganda" and "fabricated chronology."[8] From today's perspective, there is great irony in using the open-minded and sophisticated Song dynasty, now renowned as one of the truly great ages in the history of Chinese culture, as an occasion for xenophobia.

The Rising China of the Great Khan was a complex creation. It involved a mix of military and political tactics and a balance between China's own internal situation and its newfound place in a world system created by non-Chinese people. Though Khubilai had crushed the Song dynasty, he seems to have understood the sources of its wealth and prestige. He acted to rebuild the seaborne trade networks that were a component of Song power. Indeed, as we will see later, he went on to organize large naval expeditions in the region, on a scale without precedent among Chinese and Mongols alike. He also carried forward much of the Song fiscal system that had shown its value in promoting agriculture, commerce, and manufacturing. He called on the great Chinese tradition of civil engineering in carrying out large public works and transportation projects.

But in his governing scheme, there was also a large role for what political scientists today call soft power. One of the things that had been least expected of a "barbarian" ruler of that age was that he would become an active promoter of Chinese philosophy, literature, art, and architecture. Accordingly, Khubilai arranged for the translation of Chinese classics into Mongolian, for which he had instituted a new script. He encouraged scholars to keep up the Song era's interest in science, technology, and engineering; as the history of Chinese science has developed as an independent academic discipline in our own time, important Yuan-era work in many areas of science, both theoretical and applied, has become well known to us. Khubilai endorsed the teaching of the orthodox interpretations of Confucianism that had been developed in late Song times, and he was a patron of various projects in the arts. Contemporary Chinese look back on Yuan times as an age of outstanding achievements in drama and painting.

The Yuan period is now also praised routinely for the dynasty's openness to international cultural relationships of all kinds. China proper benefited from the *Pax Mongolica*, which facilitated travel, trade, and communication along the ancient Central Asian Silk Road. Islam also gained direct access to Chinese living in the northwest, and Han Chinese converts (known today as the Hui Muslims) joined the Turkic Muslims in that area. The first Roman Catholic archbishop in China was seated in Beijing in 1307, beginning the long history of Catholic activity in the country. And, of course, there is Marco Polo, whose account of his sixteen-year stay in China (1275–1291), when published in Europe, set off a centuries-long Western fascination with Cathay.

But for all of this, it is highly probable that, beneath the dynasty's embrace of cultural politics as such, there was an understanding of the deeper strategic value of these actions and gestures, for they can be readily interpreted as bolstering legitimacy for further Yuan expansion. In Central Asia, though ultimately thwarted in his ambitions, Khubilai likely assumed that his patronage of Muslims in his country and their important presence at his court in Beijing would add yet another useful visage to the several he already displayed. In East Asia and Southeast Asia, China's centuries-long sway rested in part on a cultural consensus. It was visually manifested by the use of Chinese characters in writing Japanese, Korean, and Vietnamese and by the use of Chinese itself by educated people in these countries; it was intellectually cemented by the widespread acceptance of Confucian teachings. Thus, there was a pre-existing cultural ethos in these countries that rested on culture and on the language in which it was expressed—the *lingua sinica* as *lingua franca*.

Khubilai did far more than present himself as a grand unifier of Asia merely in appearance. He devoted substantial energy and resources to it. How much of his pan-Asianism derived from his understanding of the theory and practice of China's tributary system is hard to know. It is known that even in the midst of his contest with the Southern Song, and fully a dozen years before he became emperor of all of China, Khubilai Khan was interested in turning Japan into some kind of vassal state. During the 1250s, his older brother, Mongke, had established Mongol control over Korea, that proverbial dagger pointed at the heart of Japan, and Korea became the launching pad for Khubilai's first major military move against Japan.

Naval warfare was a novel experience for the Mongols, and their first adaptation to it had been to develop a capability for coastal warfare as part of the war against the Southern Song. A major invasion across open sea, even so narrow a stretch as that which separated Korea from Japan, was to prove to be a challenge of another magnitude. In 1274 the Mongols sent a fleet of several hundred ships carrying a mixed force of Mongols, Chinese, and Korean soldiers. The attackers established a beachhead at what is now Fukuoka on the main island of Kyushu, but in the ensuing battle the invaders were forced to return to their ships, many of which were sunk in a storm.

Several years later, with the Southern Song now defeated and the Mongol hold on the Chinese throne unassailable, Khubilai's effort to overcome Japan resumed. This time there were to be two invading fleets, one sailing up from South China and consisting of captured Song naval vessels, and the other leaving from Korea. The accounts of what happened thereafter are inconsistent: some assert that the fleet from South China never did show up; others maintain that it did, but too late. In any case, we are led to believe that the Mongols' armada consisted of perhaps two thousand vessels of all sorts and an army of about a hundred thousand men. In any event the invasion of 1281 turned into a disaster of epic proportions. The Japanese employed a kind of guerrilla warfare at sea, making it hard for the invaders to disembark. Confined to their relatively small vessels—and with their horses, too—the invaders soon fell victim to an epidemic. In their subsequent mythmaking about the battle, the Japanese came to credit their escape to a providential typhoon, later to become famous as the *kamikaze* ("divine wind"). Even though the myth has exhausted its political utility inside Japan, it still lives on. However, through painstaking translation and annotation of contemporaneous thirteenth-century Japanese materials, the historian Thomas Conlan has demonstrated that the Japanese have been selling themselves short for centuries. They mounted a stalwart, skillful, and successful defense of their islands without the need for divine intervention.

The Mongols also attempted to expand their authority into Southeast Asia. Apparently this project also began before the Mongols achieved their final victory over the Southern Song. As we have noted, Khubilai Khan's own introduction to China was as commander of one of his brother's armies in the 1250s. Khubilai had been sent to establish Mongol control over what is now Yunnan province in the southwestern part of the country. Then, using Yunnan as their base, Mongol forces pushed far into what is now northern Vietnam, but they could not consolidate their control and had to withdraw under duress. There followed a period of strained relations between the Vietnamese monarchy and the Yuan court and prolonged bargaining about the extent of actual Mongol political and economic influence in the area.

War resumed in earnest about 1280, once Khubilai had established his authority over all of China. This time, it was Khubilai's son who was given command of the Mongol forces. Their ostensible purpose was to pass innocently through northern Vietnam en route to invading the kingdom of Champa, in what is now southern Vietnam. But the Vietnamese were not interested in providing safe passage, seeing the action as a ploy to permit the permanent stationing of a large Mongol army in their country. Initially, the armed resistance offered by the Vietnamese was ineffective, but it gradually wore down the invaders, to the point that Khubilai's son left his army to fend for itself and returned home. The men he left behind did not fare well, gradually succumbing to the three-part bane of all warriors in tropical jungles—heat, disease, and malnutrition.

Still, the Mongols were indefatigable. In 1287 there was another outbreak of fighting, this time leading to a short-term Mongol occupation of what is now Hanoi. This venture, too, was also abandoned. For good measure, and in the interim, Khubilai sent a large army into Burma, but this also turned out to be another short-lived expedition. Finally, Yuan archives record that a large Mongol naval force attempted a landing on the coast of Java but soon gave up that effort also.

These episodes seem quixotic to us, and even now Mongol intentions are debated by historians. But even with due allowance for the failures of the naval expeditions to Japan, mainland Southeast Asia, and the Indonesian archipelago, one cannot but be impressed by the scope of the ambition and the scale of the undertakings. Thus, the Yuan demonstrated in the thirteenth century a capacity to marshal and deploy armed forces in Central Asia, in China, and in East Asia on a scale well in advance of anything the world would see for centuries. Even if the surviving records exaggerate the size of the armies and the fleets involved, the probable logistical requirements for these expeditions on both land and sea had to be enormous. In these respects the Rising China of the Great Khan provides us with an intriguing example of the potential for imperial aggrandizement of a China-based regime sufficiently productive and well-enough organized to mobilize the resources of that vast country and its dependencies.

The West is most familiar with two great architectural monuments of imperial China, the Great Wall and the Forbidden City. But there are many others. For almost all of the past eight hundred years or so, China's capital has been in or near Beijing. It goes back to 1267 when Khubilai began a twenty-five-year construction project to create a capital for the Yuan dynasty at a place then called Dadu, where today's Forbidden City in Beijing would later be located. This was the first time that this now-famous site housed the nerve center of a dynasty ruling all of China. When the Ming dynasty took power, it extended the original settlement southward, a stage in the long process that created modern-day Beijing. The famous Forbidden City, begun in Ming times, was later used by the Manchus as the nerve center of their empire. What is now Tiananmen Square was once within the borders of Dadu, and over time the main north-south axis of Dadu was extended southward to become the main north-south axis of Beijing. Some ruins of the original Dadu can be seen today in a park in northern Beijing.

The construction of Dadu was an enormous project and drew on the resources not only of China but also of the three other khanates of the Mongol Empire. The eclectic origins of the city's design and construction were revealed in the imperial palaces, temples, and government office buildings, all on a grand scale. As in any great imperial capital, visitors came from all over the world, with Dadu becoming famous in Europe as a result of the account of Marco Polo. In the famous account of his travels that appeared at the end of the fifteenth century, he offered extravagant praise for Khanbalig palace in particular:

> You must know that it is the greatest palace that ever was. The roof is very
> lofty, and the walls of the palace are covered with gold and silver. They are
> adorned with dragons, beasts, birds, knights, and idols. The main hall of
> the palace is so large that 6,000 people could easily dine there, and it is a
> marvel to see how many rooms there are besides. The building is altogether
> so vast, so rich, and so beautiful, that no man on earth could design anything
> superior to it. The outside of the roof is colored with vermillion, yellow,
> green, blue, and other hues, which are fixed with a varnish so fine that they
> shine like crystal and lend a resplendent luster to the palace as seen from
> far away.[9]

The regime now in power in Beijing could have decided to turn the legacy of Dadu into an example of extravagance and self-indulgence, not at all in keeping with the Communist Party's devotion to "hard struggle and plain living." Today visitors can walk on the surviving walls of Dadu in Beijing and see how they lead into a public park, almost directly below a new expressway that runs overhead. At the entrance to the park visitors will find the *Sculpture of Eight Steeds in Pasture*. On a nearby waterway they will see a permanently moored barge, *Ancient Boat with Tea Fragrance*. There is also a large granite sculpture, *Grand Foundation Ceremony of Dadu, Capital of the Yuan Dynasty*, that shows Khubilai Khan looking down on the scene, flanked by a double column of elephants. They will then come upon a statue of the great civil engineer Liu Bingzhong, next to a large terracotta mosaic that illustrates the complex system he designed and had built to connect Dadu to Hangzhou, and thereby to the sea.

The park and the statuary are there for the same reason that Khubilai began the project in the first place, not only as a tribute to his own success and power but also as a way of representing himself and his imperium to the world. He wanted the world to think of his accomplishments in a certain way, as if the successful execution of strategy, warfare, and diplomacy were necessary requirements for greatness, but not sufficient in and of themselves. In this respect he was affording culture pride of place ahead of politics, which was already the traditional Chinese way. In the end the power of this suggestion not only brought the Rising China of the Mongol Khans to heel, but centuries later it would force upon Mao's Communists a great retreat.

CHAPTER 3
THE MING DYNASTY AND THE
PAX SINICA

In March 1997, Joanna Handlin-Smith, a specialist in the Ming era, convened a panel of China scholars at the annual meeting of the Association for Asian Studies in Chicago. Its purpose was to assess the state of studies of the Ming dynasty (1368–1644). It had been twenty years since a comparable panel had addressed the condition of Ming-era scholarship, the occasion then being the publication in 1976 of *The Dictionary of Ming Biography*, a large-scale scholarly collaboration, seen as a companion to the famous biographical dictionaries that had been compiled for both the Qing era (1644–1912) and the Republic of China (1912–1949). Before the appearance of this compendium, China scholars, in Handlin-Smith's description, had dismissed the Ming dynasty as a mere adumbration of the Qing and, therefore, unworthy of close scrutiny. But since then Ming studies have dramatically advanced, and we have enlarged our thinking to accommodate information that once seemed anomalous.

She might also have added that the Ming dynasty had not endeared itself to post-1950 Chinese. Its founder, Zhu Yuanzhang (1336–1405), was a no-nonsense peasant, a self-made emperor, brutal in his methods and notorious for his anti-intellectualism. Ming autocracy was the term commonly used to describe his Ming polity and that of his heirs. Accordingly, he had become a personal favorite of Mao Zedong, who took pains to identify with the Ming founder, just as dissenters of various degrees of subtlety also took pains to identify themselves with courageous officials and writers of Ming times who told truth to power.

The Ming dynasty, so far as Chinese were concerned, was treacherous historical terrain indeed. It had figured prominently in the launching of the Great Proletarian Cultural Revolution of the late 1960s. One of its first victims was the eminent Chinese historian Wu Han (1900–1969) who, in 1944, had written a biography of the Ming founder that portrayed him as the instigator of a reign of terror, a torturer, and a murderer of principled officials. In that Wu was known as a progressive, it was assumed he had Chiang Kai-shek in mind as the contemporary analogue. Thus, Wu became a favorite of New China and was appointed deputy mayor of Beijing.

He also continued his study of the Ming era, focusing on Hai Rui, an official of the time who had had a celebrated confrontation with one of the Ming emperors that had cost him his job, and almost his life. The historian, now turned playwright, also wrote a drama about Hai Rui's dismissal from office. Unfortunately for the venerable scholar, Mao Zedong construed the play, almost certainly correctly, as an attack on him and his policies; Wu was soon the target of concerted denunciations in the press. He became a national hate object, a stand-in for all the bourgeois intellectuals who needed to be extirpated from New China. His wife was sent to a labor camp, where she died in 1969. Wu himself died in prison, also in 1969. Their daughter was arrested in 1975 and committed suicide the following year.

Today, the study of the Ming era is not so dangerous an undertaking, not least because the regime now in power welcomes it, but for very different reasons. In fact, the new scholarship has fashioned a portrait of the Ming era that makes it appear not merely grand and innovative, but grand and innovative in ways that seem wholly connected to China's contemporary circumstances.

There is, first of all, a new and deep appreciation for what is now known as the Ming commercial revolution, a revolution that entailed sustained development of internal trade and technology, extensive seaborne commerce, and the integration of China into a new global economy created by the absorption of the New World into the Old World's political and economic system. Thus, silver from Spanish America financed an expansion of intra-Asian and intercontinental trade, producing often bewildering and hard-to-explain effects. The perplexities and mysteries of this first great era of globalization set off wide-ranging debates within China about the connections among trade, wealth, national power, and popular contentment.

One byproduct of the discussion was a remarkably sophisticated analysis of monetary and fiscal policy, theoretical and applied. This, in turn, has led to a deeper inquiry into the nature of capitalism as both an international and a Chinese phenomenon. These questions are also now joined to a reexamination of China's maritime and naval traditions, especially of what they mean to a China that is once again in the midst of a huge economic, commercial, and social upheaval intricately connected to the world at large.

The Ming era is now also appreciated for the sophistication and variety of its urban civilization, though much of it was not appreciated by many at the time. It was, in its way, a time of vulgar mass consumption and unrestrained materialism—an era of self-indulgence that the stern moralist then and now cannot help but find offensive aesthetically and also threatening to the stability of the society. In this respect Ming China's rise and fall, like all such great eras, bequeaths a cautionary tale that haunts its compelling allure. Yet the efflorescence of mass culture in Ming times gave to the then-Chinese empire a growing store of soft power—opportunities to expand China's influence in the realm of art, ideas, and literature that, in turn, helped enhance and consolidate China's hold on the economics and politics of East Asia.

The idea of a Ming commercial revolution derives from what had become a tedious debate about the nature of Chinese society prior to the founding of the People's Republic in 1949. Orthodox Marxist historiography required an officially sanctioned reading of China's history, especially its economic history. Capitalism, so it decreed, did not exist in China but, rather, was brought to China, and later imposed on China, by imperialism. Western students of China's economic history had been looking for capitalism in China prior to the West's arrival there and argued among themselves about what they had found. Chairman Mao himself had opened the investigatory door a crack by once conceding, in what seemed an afterthought, that though China had not had capitalism, it could be said to have had some sprouts of capitalism. Now, a generation of Chinese economic historians, sheltered by one of the chairman's musings that had instantly become a profound insight, could set out in search of such sprouts, to find where they might have been planted, to learn more about how they were cultivated, and by whom.

But it was not until after the death of Mao in 1976, when China had officially set out on the road to a "socialist market economy," defined by Deng Xiaoping as "socialism with Chinese characteristics," that bolder hypotheses about the country's economic history could be brought forward. Indeed, within the intellectual ferment of "Reform and Opening Up to the World," what could be more opportune? What if Deng's program could properly be placed not only in the context of China's history, but also in the history of the world? Was there a better place to begin than in the Ming era? The new understanding of this, both in China and the West, owes much to the publication in 1985 of a monumental three-volume history, *Zhongguo zibenzhuyi fazhan shi* (A History of the Development of Chinese Capitalism).[1] This study was the cumulative result of more than twenty years of work by economic historians Xu Dixin and Wu Chengming. They had combed through a mountain of documentation from the late Ming dynasty until the Opium War and had collected data about the quantities of commodities and manufactured products that moved around the country, examining the growth of commerce over time and through space. They tried to figure out, more precisely than anyone had attempted before, how things were made, that is, the effects of technological innovation, and how things in society were organized either to facilitate or impede the making and movement of goods.

Xu and Wu were Marxists and were therefore interested in the role of the state and how it both reflected and directed what Marxists call the relations of production. Though their book appeared in 1985, much of the research had, perforce, been conducted in an environment far more restrictive than today's. Thus, it was inevitable that more data would be unearthed, but more significantly, albeit indirectly, China, in revealing to the world its long-repressed talents at capitalism, was now run by a government that wanted to make the post-Mao radical redirection seem like a resumption of China's normal way of life.

Close examination of Ming-era commercial history has become important from other perspectives that also have to do with China's self-definition. Just as today's rise of China is supposed to tell us something about the future, the Chinese see in Ming history an opportunity to unravel an old story and begin a new story that places China where they think it more properly belongs. The past several centuries of world history have been understood as an account of the Rise of the West and its companion piece, the Fall of the East. In this story, as Yang Zhaoyun of Australia National University has pointed out, "it was the Ming dynasty and, for many, it is still the Ming dynasty, which is stereotypically regarded as the beginning of China's descent into conservative isolationism and stagnation relative to a dynamic Europe." This stagnation, which Yang regards as an illusion, has been seen not only as an outgrowth of ingrained Chinese principles of governance and philosophy, but also as the product of large meta-historical events like, for example, a "Little Ice Age" of cold climate during a time of reduced solar activity between 1450 and 1540, or bubonic plague, or Mongol invasions, or a precipitous decline in population, and so on.

Other, more down-to-earth assertions have presented what Yang Zhaoyun calls "the illusion of agrarianism," that is, the notion of the Ming era as a time when technological innovation and commerce were stifled by a conservative, agrarian-minded state ideology. Yang even cites Joseph Needham (1900–1995), the great historian of Chinese achievements in science, technology, and mathematics, who, nonetheless, helped contribute to the portrait of Ming backwardness. Needham had seen a lack of substantial progress in China after 1450, which, he wrote, "was a result of a fundamental institutional incompatibility between the bureaucratic administration of an agrarian society and the development of a money economy." Needham made a highly critical assessment of the increasing use of silver as a medium of exchange, a practice that had begun toward the end of the fifteenth century, calling it "a step backward that subjected the population to the tyranny of the harshest currency of all, similar to the situation that would pertain nowadays if consumers were required to buy their petrol and pay their grocery bills with chunks and bits of gold."[2]

The final illusion, and the one that will figure more prominently in the discussion later on, is what Yang calls the "illusion of isolation," which derives from a too-literal reading, and a frequent misreading, of what appeared to be the content and conduct of China's international relations—once understood primarily as the workings of a tributary system that was, in turn, a by-product of self-defeating imperial conceits.

Ming isolationism, as a shorthand formulation of the dynasty's foreign policies, is a subject all its own, but before addressing it as a historical issue and what the study of it implies for China's understanding of its place in the world today, it is useful to establish a context by summarizing the accumulated weight of two decades of scholarly work by Chinese and non-Chinese historians alike.

For one example, new food crops were introduced, many imported from nearby Southeast Asia early in the Ming reign, and also from the New World during the sixteenth century. Agricultural techniques were refined to include new methods of irrigation and crop rotation. Cash crops became important in the economy, and there were periodic and widespread government efforts at re-forestation. All this led to a rapid increase in population.

The population of cities grew rapidly, spurred by the growth in agricultural production. As cities grew, many attained the critical mass needed for sustained growth in manufacturing and commerce. Indeed, some of the better-known cities acquired an international reputation in Ming times. According to Michael Marme, "Suzhou [west of Shanghai] was one of the pre-industrial world's great cities. . . . It dazzled Europeans familiar with the most sophisticated forms of urban life in the West. . . . Suzhou [was the] 'leader' in the creation of a Ming Chinese world system, . . . not merely a regional metropolis. . . . [It] can be equated with one of Braudel's 'world cities' . . . [a] hierarchically structured [system] of exchange centered on the world city at its core. . . . It also tended to import raw materials and semi-finished goods while exporting finished ones."[3] Like Shanghai today, Suzhou was also a center of artistic creativity of all kinds, a place of nation-wide influence far beyond its economic and commercial boundaries.

Advances in technology led to rapid growth in the manufacture of goods for mass consumption. Cotton growing and weaving became widespread, and a large market in textiles, including a large market for exports, was created by improvements in cloth printing technology. A nationwide publishing industry was built on cheap books made possible by improvements in printing. Porcelain and ceramics, once again made for mass consumption, flooded the domestic and world markets.

China became embedded in a genuinely global financial system. The system came into being as New World precious metals entered into world trade and silver became the currency of account that financed an exponential expansion of international trade and an especially enormous growth in Asia's intra-regional trade. At the same time, the presence of large quantities of silver inside China made possible a reform of the Ming fiscal system, as taxes came to be paid in hard cash, rather than in kind or in corvée labor service.

These developments worked together to create a legacy of commerce that continues to fascinate. Gang Deng, an economic historian, has analyzed a trove of data that demonstrates the use of cargo ships that, for one example, could carry a load of as many as ten thousand woks bound for the kitchens of Asia. Hundreds of thousands of ceramic pieces were routinely manufactured for foreign export. Hundreds of thousands of rolls of silk cloth, reckoned in the millions of square meters, were joined by tens of millions of rolls of cotton cloth over these centuries. Gang also cites the work of Lin Ranchuan, another Chinese economic historian who has carried out extensive studies of China's market economy in late Ming times and who, for only one of many examples, looked into the paper-making industry in Guangxi province alone and found that it employed sixty thousand workers in six hundred water-powered mills, which cranked out a hundred thousand reams of paper each year. There were large sugar refineries in Guangdong, each of which could turn out hundreds of tons per year. Another student of this era has made intricate calculations of the number of trees that needed to be harvested annually to sustain the shipbuilding industry or the manufacture of wooden chests for the packing of the exports it made possible.[4] These seemingly idiosyncratic data are in fact important for what they also reveal about the institutional, organizational, and attitudinal consequences of this human energy. The building of factories and ships required capital accumulation and credit facilities, akin to latter-day banking. Dense transport networks were established to connect inland China to seaports. Chinese merchants set up what we would call offshore operations establishing commercial and paramilitary bases in Southeast and South Asia.

Great fortunes were made, and multigenerational business dynasties were created. Gang describes the extraordinary reach of some of these families: Returns from trading operations enabled the Zheng family, supporters of the Ming dynasty against the rise of Manchu power in the late 1500s and early 1600s, to operate an independent political entity with 170,000 troops and a fleet of 8,000 ships for some forty years against the Qing. In the early 1600s the Zheng fleet invaded the Shandong peninsula, later laid siege to Nanjing, and also launched a major attack against Taiwan. Earlier on, Wang Hi, another of these merchant dynasts, launched attacks against several cities on the Chinese coast.[5]

Obviously it is hard to draw a bright line between the seaborne activities of maritime merchant princes on the one hand and criminal organizations of smugglers and pirates on the other. Oftentimes the latter found a way to turn themselves into the former, because respectability was always for sale. Many of these men came to be offered official government positions and, as a result, paid a share of their revenues to the state in taxes, replacing the bribes they had earlier paid as part of the cost of doing business. But what-ever name one gives these actions, it is the scale that impresses. By many estimates, any one of the larger private Chinese trade networks greatly sur-passed in total intra-Asian turnover the combined operations of foreign in-terlopers like the Dutch and the Portuguese.[6] Similarly, though only about 2 percent of the population was involved directly in maritime activity as such, the trickle-down effect was substantial, stimulating shipbuilding, log-ging, metalworking, transport infrastructure construction, quarrying, and service industries like banking. There also arose a small but well-placed cadre of Chinese with multiple linguistic and managerial skills who pos-sessed the requisite cultural sensitivity. Gang writes of one such man in the Ming era who began his career in Macao as a Roman Catholic convert, married a Japanese woman, and, with his Japanese father-in-law, built up a large commercial empire, while siring a large family of Ming loyalists.

The Ming Commercial Revolution also became part of a centuries-long process of China's larger intellectual revolution. In 1970, decades before this era was understood in a detail comparable to that of today, William Theodore de Bary, our country's greatest scholar of the history of traditional Chinese thought and civilization, was already investigating a type of indi-vidualistic thought emerging around this time.[7] One man of great interest to him was Li Zhi (1527–1602), "one of the most brilliant and complex fig-ures in Chinese thought and literature . . . the greatest heretic and icono-clast in China's history."[8] Li Zhi anticipated what de Bary calls "the modern dilemma of Confucianism: how can a moral philosophy based essentially on human relations survive in a world of rapid change and mobility? . . . One can say without exaggeration that Li anticipates in the sixteenth cen-tury the criticisms of the classical Confucian tradition which erupted in the twentieth century during the so-called New Culture movement."[9] Li was among other things a defender of commerce and merchants in a soci-ety still dominated by an anticommercial ethos—but not by a disdain for money and luxuries. Born into a family of prosperous maritime traders, Li had developed an Adam Smith–like view of things, maintaining that all individuals, even worthy Confucian sages, were selfish, and that the pursuit of wealth as such was a normal and moral endeavor from which others also benefited.[10]

At a time when China today follows Deng Xiaoping's dictum that "some get rich first so that others can get rich later," one notices that the boom time half a millennium ago gave rise to speculations, or maybe just sooth-ing post-hoc rationalizations, about the value of enlightened selfishness.

Writing in 1970 and acknowledging that he was involved in "large speculations about a future which defies definition in traditional terms," de Bary nonetheless made a case for a kind of intellectual investigation considered anachronistic at the time. "Insofar as China might derive some value from its own past—and nationalism cannot be discounted as a powerful force in that direction—the Ming experience with its variety of individualistic thought may yet prove to have some relevance."[11]

The discussion thus far of Ming-era commerce and industry has been consciously informed by something historians warn against, "present-mindedness," that is, reading the present back into the past. Such reimagining of Ming times as an outward-looking age when China embraced innovation and novelty comports well with how the post-Mao leadership has wanted Chinese to view their country. Whether consciously directed by the regime or not, historical re-examination of this kind is in keeping with the regime's larger agenda and is therefore a welcome trend, a contribution to China's ongoing effort to develop what can be called its socioeconomic culture.

This term quite consciously mimes the more familiar term, strategic culture, introduced into the analysis of China's international behavior by Alistair Iain Johnston in his groundbreaking book, *Cultural Realism: Strategic Culture and Grand Strategy in Chinese History*. To oversimplify, Johnston compared what was often *said* about the Chinese view of conflict—especially its stated preference for stratagem, guile, and nonviolence—and what the Chinese actually *did*, which was to see the world as an unceasingly dangerous place where violence, not friendly persuasion, was determining. To the notion of strategic culture, Stephen Peter Rosen has appended the concept of strategic tradition, which, once again to oversimplify, is the accumulated wisdom that directs a country's strategic and military behavior, because it embodies what a country reflexively thinks it *is* and, accordingly, what it reflexively *does*.[12] Obviously, it takes time for such cultures and traditions to develop.

It is helpful to keep both of these notions in mind as we now focus on one aspect of Ming history that the Beijing regime seeks consciously to integrate into the country's strategic tradition—China's sea power. Unlike much of the older received strategic tradition, which liked to portray China in a near-perpetual strategic crouch, fending off the Mongols and other threatening nomads from Inner Asia, Ming sea power in the fifteenth century is the expression of a self-assertive and self-confident Rising China. This has become highly relevant to China's approach to high politics as the twenty-first century begins.

In September 2003 China announced that it would launch a series of activities to mark the six hundredth anniversary of the first voyage of the Chinese mariner Zheng He (1371–1425). According to Xinhua, China's official news agency, "From 1405 to 1422, Zheng's fleet made seven trips to some thirty countries in Southeast Asia, the Indian Ocean, and Africa. . . . Marine specialists believe that Zheng's fleet surpassed all other marine navigators of its time in scale, sophistication, and organizational skill." The commemorative activities would consist of summer camps, seminars, meetings, exhibits, and international marine fairs. In the best manner of China's political campaigns of old, Yao Mingde, the official-in-charge, announced the theme: "Love the Motherland. Foster good-neighborly relations. Advance navigation technology."[13]

Two years later, on National Maritime Day, which had been proclaimed in Zheng's honor, the Ministry of Communication, the State Commission on Science and Technology for National Defense, and the Shanghai municipal government combined forces to stage a large-scale exhibition in Shanghai. Later in the year, the National Museum on Tiananmen Square in Beijing presented an exhibition of artworks and artifacts from the imperial collections—"gigantic," one attendee described it—that bore on Zheng's voyages.

Both Hong Kong and Macau issued commemorative postage stamps, with officials journeying to the main post office in Kunming, capital of China's southwestern province of Yunnan and Zheng's birthplace. They found that Yunnan Provincial Television was at work on a documentary about Zheng.[14] Allan Chiang, postmaster general of Hong Kong, enthused: "The production of this set of stamps has enriched my understanding of the greatest adventurer and navigator of our nation. . . . His expeditions fostered trade and goodwill. Today, these stamps serve as an ambassador spreading our culture to people all over the world. . . . They carry letters of love, or care, or business opportunities."[15]

Meanwhile, also in July 2005, and as part of the celebrations in China, a group from Taiwan set out on a three-year voyage to re-enact Zheng He's voyages and planned to visit thirty ports in a replica of a Ming-era ocean-going junk, the $5 million cost of the expedition to be defrayed by a local businessman. Other overseas Chinese compatriots in Singapore staged a massive exhibition, and a theater group presented a modern-day musical about Zheng. Semarang staged a re-enactment of Zheng's arrival there. The prime minister of Malaysia officiated at the opening of a commemorative exhibit in Kuala Lumpur as a thousand attendees looked on, and his Chinese cohost, attentive to Malaysia's Muslim majority, made much of the fact that Zheng He had been a devout Muslim, born in Central Asia. As such, he is an improbable candidate for lionization by today's Han Chinese nationalists, and yet his heroics fit well with the adventurous spirit of today's China.

But Zheng He and his expeditions were hardly a latter-day rediscovery. The story of "China's Columbus" and "China's Sinbad" had been told many times before. It has recently found its way into a bilingual picture book for children.[16] Still, the best general account of the voyages, *When China Ruled the Seas*, was written by Louise Levathes and published in 1994. It is instructive to look at it a decade and a half later for its portrait of the exotic venturesomeness of the voyages and for its colorful narrative style. We also learn, from her acknowledgments, that Levathes began her work in 1988. Her account of her own travels in China, Southeast Asia, and Africa, her listing of the Ming-era documents available to her then, and the few works of reliable, professionally done history that could serve as background, most of them written decades before, testify that the boom in Zheng He studies had not yet really begun then. Today, the quantity of materials available to an interested writer, whether of the "China's Columbus" variety or of the postcolonial studies sort, or the socioeconomic structural analysis type, is quite extraordinary, especially given the comparatively short period of time that has elapsed.

Beneath the accounts are Zheng He's accomplishments, his seven expeditions, the first in 1405, the last in 1430. Each of the seven fleets Zheng He commanded was a large enterprise for any era; cumulatively they involved thousands of vessels and tens of thousands of men. The fleets visited ports as far away from China as Hormuz, Mogadishu, Colombo, Calicut, and Sanaa, in other words, the modern countries of Iran, Somalia, Sri Lanka, India, and Yemen, as well as ports closer to home throughout the Indonesian archipelago and on the coast of the Southeast Asian mainland.

In offering interpretations of the meaning of Zheng's voyages, the self-conscious present-mindedness of our own discussion has plenty of precedent. At the end of the nineteenth century, Liang Qichao (1873–1929), the great Chinese historian, man of letters, and political reformer, was in exile in Japan, having fled China after a failed political movement known as the

Hundred Days of Reform. Writing in Japan in 1904, Liang saw Zheng as "Master Mariner of the Fatherland," whose achievements could be the inspirational counterpoint to the humiliating defeat China's new navy had experienced in its brief war with Japan a decade before. In the 1930s Chinese scholars were interested in the voyages for what they might reveal about China's relations with Southeast Asia; the inculcation of patriotic sentiment among the overseas Chinese as part of China's resistance to Japan in the 1930s was certainly one purpose of the writings in this period. As for their place in larger world history, it has been observed that, on the one hand, Zheng's voyages could be compared to those of Columbus, Magellan, James Cook, and Vasco da Gama in their nautical prowess, yet, on the other hand, they could be contrasted with those Western endeavors because China was not engaged in wars of exploitation or conquest.[17] Some of China's Zheng He enthusiasts had also noted, but without additional comment, a book published in 2002 by Gavin Menzies called *1421, the Year China Discovered America*. The book represents the high-water mark of Zheng He hagiography, in that it claims that Chinese sailors circumnavigated the globe a century before Magellan, that the Chinese reached both coasts of North America and the western coast of South America in the fifteenth century, and that Chinese mariners had gotten to Australia about three hundred years before Captain Cook did. Even for the most patriotic of Chinese maritime history revisionists, this six-hundred-page volume was too good to be true, and knowledgeable scholars around the world have debunked it.

Nonetheless, in October 2003, China's president, Hu Jintao, when speaking to the Australian parliament, invoked a long history: "Back in the 1420s, the expeditionary fleets of China's Ming dynasty reached Australian shores." But most officially sanctioned Chinese pronouncements follow the more historically agnostic middle ground, celebratory but mostly innocuous. A good example is the compendium of fifty scholarly presentations made at a marathon international conference in 2004 convened by the Jiangsu Province Academy of Social Sciences and published in 2005. This hefty volume tells the Chinese-reading public more than it may care to know, from speculations about the wood used to build the ships to the dress of the sailors and their officers to the analysis of porcelain shards found in many different places. The overall message for the Chinese-language reader is the title of the book itself, which echoes what could very well have been one of Deng Xiaoping's injunctions of the 1980s: *Carry On Civilization, Open Up the World for Peace and Development*.

In noting this revival of interest in Zheng He and his adventures, Richard von Glahn, the preeminent historian of China's monetary history who has done as much as anyone to educate us about the fiscal and monetary complexities of Ming times, has also urged us to turn away from storybook approaches and focus instead on China's maritime history as we would focus on the maritime history of any other important country. This means, in particular, giving up the received moral of the tale, that Ming sea power was China's lost opportunity, that the significance of the story is what did not happen, namely, that the Chinese failed to consolidate their advantages in nautical technology and ceded the Asian seas to the Europeans instead. As von Glahn puts it, "this 'counterfactual,' 'what if' view of things has long inhibited our understanding of the inside of the story."[18]

However, this is beginning to change as at least three important new themes are starting to emerge, each recapturing an imperial memory relevant to China's high politics of the present day. The first derives from the discovery of the Ming commercial revolution and an ongoing reexamination by economic historians of commercial expansion in different parts of the world in the same early modern period. To reduce a complicated discussion to simpler terms, one key issue is this: Did long-distance commerce in Europe develop the same way as it did in China? In particular, what was the role of the state? R. Bin Wong, one of the pioneers of these comparative studies, summarizes the state of the discussion this way: "The new institutional economics offers a bold and simple argument for how states promoted commercial expansion in early modern Europe. Focused on the importance of secure property rights for reducing transaction costs, commerce expands much as an engine burns fuel more efficiently and creates more power when it is well tuned and oiled. Reliable and defensible property rights emerge out of legal systems that specify and enforce the expectations and obligations to parties to contracts; the main contribution of government to commercial expansion is thus in supplying the formal framework that reduces certain types of risks that merchants encounter in their trade activities."[19] But what about China? Could someone imagine something called "commercial expansion with Chinese characteristics?" Or as Wong asks the question: "How shall we compare Chinese and European patterns of commercial expansion?"

Wong's own conclusion is that long-distance trade expanded between the sixteenth and eighteenth centuries in the Chinese empire, but without the same kinds of institutions associated with European commercial expansion. "The state, in particular, played rather little role in ensuring the property rights involved in long-distance trade. . . . But even if this is true, it does not mean that the Chinese state did not play a considerable role in making possible the Smithian growth China experienced over the six-teenth through eighteenth centuries."[20] What, then, did the Chinese state do? Many things but, first and foremost, "it secured centralized rule and supplied peace and security over far vaster spaces than any European state, a rule that covered not only a large country like France, but the equivalent of several Frances, supplying the key public good required to promote com-merce over long distances."[21]

Wong offers other thoughts about the early modern period that rever-berate in debates of the present day. "We can consider the different agen-das and achievements of states in China and Europe to parallel or similar economic effects. . . . The differences in political economy at the two ends of Eurasia remain significant, but however different their motivations or intentions, it seems likely that the Chinese state did at least as much to pro-mote private sector commercial growth as European states did."[22] There is no need to read too much into this area of inquiry nor even to take sides in the argument. It is enough to say that it is one part of a larger discussion of Chinese exceptionalism; in this particular case, whether modern economic activities follow only one set of sociopolitical-economic rules, or different sets of rules, and whether seemingly similar activities carried out in widely separated societies will lead the nations of the world ultimately to the same place or to different places.

The second important theme also derives from the closer attention given to the Ming-era chapter in China's maritime history but looks beyond its economic and commercial significance to its strategic and military impli-cations. As we have seen, the first phase of interest had to do with these voyages as but a footnote in world history, one of history's might-have-beens. Then the voyages were folded into an effort to draw attention to the maritime component of China's economic history and to the structure of global economic relations generally. And, from time to time, the voyages have also been seen as a way of reinforcing patriotic sentiment within the Chinese diaspora, an always important element in the politics and com-merce of modern China.

But beyond these there is now a growing interest in looking to these episodes for insights into China's strategic outlook and to what they can contribute to the creation of a twenty-first-century strategic vision for the country. Americans can understand this progression by remembering how we think about the six Apollo manned landings on the moon between 1969 and 1972. We invoke them now as a great national achievement, a point of patriotic pride, a tribute to the nation's scientific and technological prowess, but mostly as a metaphor for what can be accomplished in other fields. A great achievement has now become a political cliché: if we can send a man to the moon, why can't we organize ourselves to do this or that? And yet the moon voyages, in the historian's mind, are also inseparable from American Grand Strategy in the Cold War; indeed, they would never have happened without it. Besides demonstrating militarily useful technology, the voyages displayed a capacity for national mobilization and organization and were designed to be seen by the rest of the world as a demonstration of the inherent superiority of the American way of doing things—much as Zheng He's patron, the Yongle emperor, put it in his day when he said: "Let all within the Four Seas be edified."

Accordingly, if we look at Ming naval activities from a comparably broad perspective—that is, how they inform various aspects of a Grand Strategy—we can imagine that the Grand Strategy of the Ming Empire was even grander than we have previously thought. For example, Hsaio Hung-te of Australia National University's Faculty of Asian Studies encourages us to look at these episodes from a genuinely global perspective or, at least, a perspective that includes all of Eurasia, and to test the records of the Ming era against documentation in other countries. "Relevant Chinese classical books of the Yuan, Ming, and Qing dynasties carry implications of sino-centrism, prejudice, territorialism, and confusion between tribute and trade. But resources from different countries can be used to appraise the historical works and documentation of the Ming dynasty and the early Qing dynasty, in order to analyze the real situation of international relations in the early Ming period."[23] Hsiao draws connections between Mongol power, the empire created by Timur (i.e., Tamerlane, 1336–1405) in Southwest Asia, Ming imperial expansion into Southeast Asia, and the interactions among them. He hypothesizes that one of Zheng's early expeditions represented an effort to establish a maritime connection to Timur's empire that bypassed the old Inner Asian land routes, perhaps to secure a military alliance for common action against the Mongols.[24] Conversely, Timur's armies had brutally occupied Delhi in 1398, and his fearsomeness should certainly have been well known in the Ming court of 1409. Indeed, in the last year of his life Timur contemplated an invasion of China. To interpret Zheng He's voyages as somehow caught up in this Eurasian geopolitical triangulation may make the expeditions seem to be quixotic examples of Ming strategy, but they are hardly more so than the search for the Northwest Passage that consumed

Western mariners, or even Columbus's idea that one could reach the East by sailing west. In any case, Hsiao theorizes that the so-called mysterious curtailment of Ming naval activity was a logical development as the threat from Inner Asia grew and construction of the Great Wall intensified.[25]

However historians thrash out the interpretation of arcane documents in several different languages, what makes an approach of this kind interesting to us today is precisely the putative connection of Chinese strategic thinking to a sense that there was larger balance of power that affected China, not just the balance closer to home in the Eurasian heartland. Zheng He set out on his last expedition in 1433, and Hsiao lists for us some of the relevant things going on in the world about that time. In 1434 the first Portuguese caravel rounded Cape Bojador, off the coast of farthest West Africa. In 1444 a Thai army forced the Khmer to abandon Angkor Wat. Constantinople fell to the Turks in 1453. Bartholomew Dias reached the Cape of Good Hope at the southern end of Africa in 1488, Columbus reached the Caribbean in 1492, and Vasco da Gama sailed around Africa and reached the coast of India in 1498. The rest, as they say, is history.

Geoffrey Wade of the Asian Research Institute of National Singapore University has provided us with a more focused, but far deeper and detailed, examination of the Zheng He voyages in particular. Wade's close examination of Ming diplomatic records allows him to offer a convincing argument that these were in fact "military missions with strategic aims."[26] He sets them against the backdrop of what he calls Ming land-based military colonialism, especially expansion to the south, which began very early on. For example, what is now the northwestern part of Yunnan province, the Mongols' base for expansion into Southeast Asia, was gradually integrated into the Ming imperium in the 1380s, and the inhabitants were thereby able to benefit from the emperor's munificence by contributing taxes and by being subject to both military conscription and corvée labor levies.

The Yongle emperor, Zheng He's patron, expanded Chinese influence deeper into Yunnan and also into Vietnam. Like Khubilai Khan in the 1280s, he launched a full-scale invasion of Vietnam in 1406, which Wade recounts in a way that provides illuminating details about Ming naval and amphibious capabilities:

Boat-borne forces set sail from Nanjing. They landed in southern China and joined forces with other forces in Guangxi. These included 95,000 troops from Zhejiang, Guangdong, and Guangxi, and an additional 30,000 auxiliary forces; another 75,000 cavalry were deployed from Yunnan, Guizhou, and Sichuan.... In late 1407, [part of Vietnam] became Ming China's fourteenth province and remained so until 1428, when the Ming forces were driven out.... Colonization began almost immediately. By 1408, the Chinese had established 472 military and civilian offices.... Within two years, three maritime trade supervisories had been created.... This was a clear indication of the desire of the Ming to control maritime trade to the south and exploit the advantages of economic control.[27]

Wade has studied the Zheng He naval missions of the next thirty years and places them in the context of similar Chinese imperial expansion, though not colonization and annexation as such.

These missions were intended to display the might of the Ming, bring the known polities to demonstrated submission to the Ming and thereby achieve a *Pax Ming* throughout the known world.... The military forces dispatched needed to be both huge and powerful.... The various missions comprised between 50 and 250 ships, making them huge armadas by any scale, which stayed away from China for several years.... The number of personnel who accompanied these missions varied, the larger ones carrying between 27,000 and 30,000.... These forces would have been equipped with the best and most advanced firearms available in the world at that time.... To enable these great fleets to maintain the *Pax Ming* in the immediate region and sail through the Indian Ocean to Africa it was necessary to create staging posts in what is today's Southeast Asia. These depots were established at Malacca and at the northern end of the Straits of Malacca.... The history of the Zheng He voyages is replete with violence as the eunuch commanders tried to implement the Ming Emperor's requirements. Major military actions included an attack on the port of Sumatra ... [and] the military invasion of Sri Lanka, the capture of a local ruler, and his being carried back to the Ming court.... In 1415, it is likely that Zheng He and his forces inserted themselves into a civil war in northern Sumatra, supported the side that was not hostile to the Ming, and engaged in warfare against the other.[28]

In Wade's summation: "'Gunboat diplomacy' is not a term which is usually applied to the voyages of Zheng He. However, given that these missions were involved in diplomacy and given that the ships were indeed gunboats, with perhaps 26,000 to 28,000 of some missions being military men, this seems the appropriate term.... These missions were also intended through this coercion to obtain control of ports and shipping lanes.... By controlling port and trade routes, one controlled trade, an essential element for the missions' treasure-collecting tasks."[29]

Wade's recapitulation stands in droll contrast to remarks made by Xu Zuyuan, vice minister of communications of the People's Republic of China in July 2004, and which Wade cites on the very first page of his study. For in Minister Xu's version, "these were friendly diplomatic activities. During the overall course of the seven voyages to the Western Ocean, Zheng He did not occupy a single piece of land, establish any fortress, or seize any wealth from other countries. In commercial and trade activities, he adopted the practice of giving more than he received, and thus he was welcomed and lauded by the people of the various countries along his route."[30]

Overall, Wade's findings add new depth to our understanding of the cultural realism that informs China's strategic culture. For just as Iain Johnston's groundbreaking book on the realism of the Ming dynasty's Inner Asian policy was an astringent corrective to fanciful claims, Geoffrey Wade's work has done the same for Ming sea power and maritime policy. Wade also points out how the same documentary material yields insight into the "soft power" side of the equation. The "Veritable Records of the Ming Dynasty" ("*Ming shi-lu*"), like similar materials compiled by other dynasties as raw material for the subsequent official dynastic histories that a successor dynasty might write, are a potpourri of records of day-by-day activities and other official and semiofficial papers. The range of subjects covered is enormous, but they are addressed seriatim, so that modern archivists, bibliophiles, and historians have had to cull through them over decades, before useful topical compendia could become available. Even today, as a historian interested in a particular subject works through the collection, he or she will create a new set of "tabs," a good deed, because others who follow in pursuit of the same subject do not have to begin their own bibliographical data mining ab initio.

In this particular case, in consulting these veritable records in China as a source for the study of Southeast Asian history, Wade noticed a persistent pattern, whereby the dynasty displayed "a desire to dominate politically by using those aspects of culture defined as 'Chinese.'"[31] Ming officials saw themselves as agents of this "civilizing process," which could involve sending teachers overseas, hosting foreign students, offering foreign governments the assistance of Chinese technical experts, sending books of all kinds, and so on. But, "most of the rhetoric centering on China's 'civilizing' role and most of the actions taken on this basis, were intended to assist Chinese political expansion and assimilation."[32] Thus, culture as such can be seen as yet another element of China's strategic culture, standing alongside both stratagem itself and the application of violence.

Withal, the cultural politics surrounding these episodes, whether in the West or the East, have taken their twists and turns down through the centuries. What some have portrayed as heroic adventures in the service of peace others have depicted as cynical forays in the service of conquest. This era of great maritime endeavor that has formed the backdrop of our discussion is easily appropriated, but that is hardly new. For example, Luis de Camoes (1524–1580) is regarded by Portuguese as their national poet. As a literary icon, he is to Portugal what Cervantes is to Spain. Camoes' reputation derives from a long epic poem, *Os Lusiados* (*The Lusaids*—"The Sons of Lusus"). He came late to poetry, for he was a soldier, a sailor, and a world traveler. His epic is patterned on Virgil's *Aeneid*, and he based it on the voyages of Vasco da Gama. The story of the poet's life or, better, the legend of his life, has it that he had to flee Lisbon, that he then lived in Goa, Portugal's enclave on the coast of India, that he then sailed to the Red Sea, and then to Macao, Portugal's enclave on the coast of China.

Camoes began to write his great poem—it was to run to more than two hundred pages—on his way home, but he was shipwrecked off the coast of Indochina, near the Mekong delta. He saved his manuscript, but his Chinese girlfriend, who was accompanying him, perished at sea. He stopped off at Mozambique on his way back to Lisbon, where his poem was published to great and centuries-long acclaim in 1572. Since then, his compatriots have been hailing him as a genius, "a great canonical writer." "He drew from the ocean all the inspiration it contains and passed it on to his readers; in no other poem will one find more perfect pictures." And of the man himself, Vasco da Gama, the sailor whose voyage from Portugal to India and back is the subject of the epic, Camoes the poet is an unabashed admirer: "If there had been more of the world, he would have reached it."[33]

Such adulation from the past is one of the blessings of irrelevance in the present; we can, if we like, argue about the inner nature of Portuguese imperial power, but nobody fears its return. It is gone, and it is never coming back. But da Gama's great Chinese counterpart is another matter. Long thought to be dead, he is now stirring once again; indeed, his imminent return is now widely bruited—and in an overbearing guise, not a poetic one. That can make a great deal of difference. In 1597 the Chinese dramatist and writer Luo Maodeng wrote a popular novel about the voyages of Zheng He, a book usually rendered in English as *The Three-Treasure Eunuch's Travels to the Western Ocean* (*Sanbao taijian xinagji tongsu yenyi*).

We know that Zheng He was accompanied by at least four officials who wrote accounts of the expeditions with titles almost as quaint—*The Triumphant Tour of the Star Raft* and *Captivating Views of the Ocean's Shores*. Luo Maodeng's novel derives from these accounts but, according to the historian Philip Snow, who has actually read these books, the travelogues of the officials were spiced up by Luo with monsters and miracle-working Buddhist monks. There are violent episodes in the novel that, to both jaundiced historians and literary critics of the present day, have the ring of truth, precisely because they depart from the officials' anodyne accounts of peaceable Chinese mariners welcomed everywhere with open arms. So, for one example, Xu Dongfeng, a University of Chicago scholar, finds Chinese cultural imperialism embedded in the novel, because other cultures are presented in ways that strike him as evil, alien, and subordinate.[34] Here, then, a reversal of roles and a transposition of villains: China, once on the receiving end of imperialism, can now be written about, almost offhandedly, as a Great Power like any other power—like any other *imperialist* power.

CHAPTER 4

THE QING DYNASTY AND THE
PAX MANJURICA

In 2012 China will mark the one hundredth anniversary of the abdication that ended the Qing dynasty, the last episode in China's long imperial history. In the normal course of things, the next dynasty would have taken on the task of writing the official history of its defunct predecessor. But there has been no "next dynasty," and thus in this sense the long chronicle of the emperors of China has not been brought to a proper end. Even in the past, when there was a proper dynastic successor, the preparation of the requisite history could take a long time; the Ming had come to an end in 1644, but the Qing did not bring forth the formal Ming history until 1739. Deciding what to make of the successes and failures of one's predecessors on the throne had always been a tricky business. One reason the work often took so long was the need for enough time to pass so that things could settle down and a conventional wisdom emerge. This was especially true in evaluating the Qing, because the consolidation of its control had been a long and very bloody business. Loyalty to the Ming had both a patriotic and a poetic aspect, for, as we know, the Manchus were not themselves Chinese, but a previously unheralded Inner Asian people whose rise in the world was a great surprise. Like the Mongols before them, the Manchus were invaders, not homegrown dynasts like the Ming's founding family of Chinese peasants. The poetic aspect derived from the tragic circumstances of the Ming's demise and, especially, the suicide of the last Ming emperor. So what historians call the Ming-Qing transition is a great story, an inspiration for poets and playwrights.

The great story improved with its telling over time, but firsthand accounts of the great cataclysm are compelling enough. We can read many of them, and some of the more interesting ones were recorded by Westerners, mostly Jesuit missionaries then in the country. Beyond the personal, there were some people in both hemispheres who knew about the cataclysm and understood the global implications that the upheaval would have for all of the seventeenth-century world. When the Manchus came to power, a genuine world economy linking Europe, Africa, South America, and Asia was already in full bloom, and the struggle for power in any significant part of the world could not be separated from the political struggle in China.

It is our comparative closeness to the end of the Qing that makes us more attentive to the pitfalls presented to the Chinese in the writing of Qing history. In the first place, the imposition of foreign rule was always a trauma at the outset, and then an intellectual and philosophical problem. It was an unflattering verdict on things Chinese. In earlier times painful adjustments were made to Mongol rule, but after the restoration of a native Chinese dynasty, the orthodox histories turned away from notions of Chinese-Mongol continuities and adopted a strong anti-Mongol bias.[1] The era of the Qing dynasty was doubly troubling for Chinese; it featured the dominance by not only one but two species of barbarian, the Manchu at its beginning and the Westerner at its end. How were these twin affronts to Chinese dignity to be understood?

While the Westerners of the late Qing have had a prominent place in the story, it is only recently that the Manchus have begun to make an appearance in it as a distinct people with an independent existence. This has been long in coming, not least because the Manchus had good reasons not to call attention to themselves after 1912. Their rule had coincided with the decomposition of the imperial system. Late nineteenth-century revolutionaries had argued for the overthrow of the Manchus because the Chinese saw them as collaborators with the Westerners against the interests of the Chinese as a people. Moreover, according to Pamela Kyle Crossley, "as the new Republic experienced frustration in its efforts to wrest control from the warlords and stabilize the nation's economic and political structures, intellectuals and journalists turned again and again to the Qing period as the source of China's troubles and to the Manchus as representative of the old evils."[2]

The idea of an inherent contradiction between Manchus and Chinese was reinforced during the protracted Sino-Japanese War (Chinese think of their struggle with Japan as beginning in 1894 and not ending until 1945) when Manchukuo, Japan's puppet regime in Manchuria, was nominally headed by an emperor between 1931 and 1945, the man who, as a child, had abdicated in 1912. For Chinese involved in a life-and-death struggle with a multimillion-man Japanese invading army, this was outright treason, and the Last Emperor was routinely denounced at mass rallies. When he died in 1967, he had spent the years between 1945 and 1949 under Soviet house arrest and was then handed over to the new Chinese government, which kept him in a prison camp. He ended his days tending plants in a botanical garden in Beijing. *From Emperor to Citizen*, a ghost-written autobiography presented as if the words were those of the "reeducated" monarch himself, was published in Beijing in 1964. Although we may think of the Dragon Throne as a medieval relic, it is still this close in living memory.

But even in the year of the Last Emperor's death, 1967, an effort to reclaim the achievements of his ancestors had begun. In a 1967 article based on his 1966 presidential inaugural address at an annual convention of the Association for Asian Studies, University of Chicago scholar He Bingdi (Ping-ti Ho, in the romanization in use then) made an argument for Qing greatness.[3] He was then sinology's preeminent figure in the study of early modern China, which added additional weight to his judgments on this touchy subject. He based the Qing's entitlement to greatness on several achievements. The first was the creation of present-day "China" as a geographic entity. The Manchu conquests had added close to a million square miles to the China proper that the Ming dynasty had ruled. Second, various factors in the Qing era led to a rapid rise in population, perhaps to about 300 million in 1800. No matter the country's later travails, the sheer momentum of Qing population growth carried the population forward to its then-level (i.e., 1967) of about 700 million that "when ruthlessly regimented by the most Spartan state in history cannot fail to make its impact felt."[4] He went on to praise the Qing for achievements as varied as greater interregional economic and social integration, the flourishing of voluntary associations, great advances in material culture and the arts, and, most of all, what he called the *Pax Sinica*, from about 1683 to 1800, "a rare century of prosperity and benevolent despotism."[5]

He then praised the dynasty for something that, as it turned out, was to become the core of a major argument that has defined today's revival of interest in Qing-era studies—the relation between the Manchu rulers and their Chinese subjects. "The Ch'ing," He maintained, "is without doubt the most successful dynasty of conquest in Chinese history, and the key to its success was the adoption by early Manchu rulers of a policy of systematic sinicization.... So sinicized were the Manchus that much of what we regard as then orthodox Confucian state and society is exemplified not by earlier Chinese dynasties, but by the Ch'ing period.... When the supreme test came in 1851 with the outbreak of the Taiping rebellion, the majority of the Chinese nation, especially the key social class of scholars and officials, fought loyally for their Manchu masters because the so-called alien dynasty had been, in fact, more Confucian than previous dynasties."[6]

With this formulation He managed to solve several problems for his Chinese compatriots. In retrospect, they could take comfort in knowing that ancestors who had accepted, or even served, the Manchus were not opportunists or cowards, but Confucian loyalists of the best sort. Chinese could now claim the achievements of the Manchus as somehow their own while, at the same time, celebrating a Chinese victory over the Inner Asian conquerors who had once defeated them. But more important, He's notion of deep and profound sinicization as the basis for the premodern Manchu state solved many ongoing problems for the contemporary Chinese state. The republic that came into existence in 1912 had, over time, been successful in laying claim to the Manchu conquests outside of China proper, forging out of what was a Manchu multinational empire a new state that was a Chinese national republic. This was an impressive display of historical legerdemain in the service of the People's Republic of China, but it had been challenged by facts on the ground, such as the armed resistance of Tibetans and Uighurs to the consolidation of Chinese rule in what these peoples regarded as their independent homelands.

These challenges on the ground both fueled, and were fueled by, the appearance of new concepts in the study of the Qing period. The traditional way of imagining China—culturally coherent in its sinicization, politically coherent in its Confucianism, governmentally coherent in its mandarinate, and geographically coherent as One China—came under attack. As the result of careful re-examination of the Manchu era, especially of the theory and practice of Manchu governance, a veritable revolution in Qing-era studies began.

A new generation of scholars, literate not only in Chinese but also in the Manchus' own language and able to examine archives accessible only after the Deng-era policies of openness, saw things in a new way. Now, Manchu rulers were quite self-consciously neither Chinese nor captives of a venerable Chinese-dominated bureaucracy. Instead, the Manchu emperors had an agenda of their own and well-wrought ways of implementing it. They also had a highly developed imperial ideology that departed significantly from the inherited Chinese one. In particular, though the emperor may have displayed a sinified face to his *Chinese* subjects, he did not pretend either to himself or to his many other non-Chinese subjects that he was Chinese. The enlargement of the empire was understood not at all as the enlargement of China as such, but rather as the accretion of ever more and diverse holdings in the Manchus' imperial portfolio. On principle, therefore—but more important, in actual practice—the Manchu emperors did not pursue the sinification of newly acquired possessions; indeed, the emperors often presented themselves as somehow belonging to one or another of those diverse traditions.[7]

These products of New Qing history, as it has come to be called, provide a new way for foreigners to think about the era, but, more significantly, they pressure the People's Republic of China to ponder its own governance of China from the perspective of another, earlier regime, a regime that also governed a place of great size, wealth, power, and standing in the world. And, in so doing, it must confront a model of success that presupposes a cosmopolitan, not a nationalist, outlook, a view that is tolerant, ecumenical, pluralist, and decentralized, not one that is overbearing, racialist, and chauvinistic. Both at home and abroad, both in the civil peace across a vast domain and in the international peace across a vast continent, what may have been at work was not *Pax Sinica* at all, but *Pax Manjurica*.

In academic circles these arguments have been conducted with unusual intensity and even, occasionally, passion. But unlike many academic disputes—the bitterness of academic politics having once famously been attributed to the small size of the stakes—this particular argument has real-world implications, which have been close to the surface ever since historians tried to grasp the significance of the Qing experience. Chen Hsi-yuan of the Academia Sinica in Taipei traces it back to 1914, when the new Republic of China established a Bureau of Qing History. It published a draft history of the Qing in 1927, only to have it banned by Chiang Kai-shek's regime two years later. The project, so his new national government had determined, had fallen under the influence of too many pro-Qing royalists. And two years after that, anti-Manchu sentiment hardened as the last Manchu emperor cast his lot with Japan, China's increasingly belligerent tormentor. It was not until 1960 that the Nationalist government of the Republic of China, now confined to Taiwan, returned to the task.[8]

It is against the backdrop of a worldwide revival of academic interest in the Qing era, but a revival that is in many basic respects a rebuke to present practices of the People's Republic of China, that the Beijing government finds itself in a peculiar situation: the study of one of the greatest, arguably the greatest, epochs in Chinese history may prove highly subversive, precisely because it is very edifying. So it was not until 1982 that a Chinese university began a formal program in Qing studies: Renmin University's Institute of Qing History in Beijing. The institute has now published a trove of monographs and conducted more than three dozen academic conferences. The *Draft History of the Qing Dynasty* itself remained a dormant project until it was finally revived in a conspicuous fashion, by decision of the State Council of the central government in Beijing. In August 2002 it announced an enormous effort to complete the work in time for the centennial of the Qing abdication in 2012. The project will engage four hundred scholars, at least forty of them from Taiwan, and will cost $US72 million.[9]

But early in 2003 the popularity of a fifty-nine episode television series caught the regime totally unaware. The series, called *Toward the Republic*, was coproduced by China Central Television. Midway through the series the government moved against it, censoring the later episodes, but the uncut version circulated on the black market, not only in China but also in Chinese-speaking communities throughout the world. The series was indeed subversive, beginning with the fact that it made no mention at all of "China" but only of the "Qing dynasty." E-mailers and bloggers debated the larger meaning of the series, with some seeing it as an apologia for the current regime, even though the regime seemed not to care for it. But in the opinion of one viewer, "at present there is a trend among intellectuals in China to observe that if Sun Yat-sen (1866–1925) had not carried out his revolution, the late Qing rulers might have, through their existing Westernization program, naturally developed a democratic system without the chaos and bloodshed brought by revolution."[10] Such revisionism from below can only be unsettling to the Communist Party's court historians and to its commissars. In any event the People's Republic will not render an official verdict on the Qing dynasty until a few years after this writing. But when, or maybe if, the verdict does come, it will have great meaning for attentive Chinese and their thinking, for it is now ever more apparent that the modern Chinese state is more a Qing product than has previously been admitted. And, as in the twentieth century, twenty-first-century China's verdict on the last dynasty will tell us a great deal about the state of prevailing Chinese policies and politics.

As of today that verdict will rest, first of all, on an investigation into the deep structure of the *Pax Manjurica* of 1683 to 1796. How did it begin? How was it consolidated? How can it instruct the present? As we have noted, the transition from Ming to Qing rule, the great cataclysm, was violent and wrenching. It was a test of Chinese self-confidence and Manchu ingenuity; it was one of the most important cases of state building that has come down to us. Today we can think of the Manchus as posing something of a revolutionist's challenge to the existing order. As it turned out, they would do more than seize the commanding heights of the old Chinese state; they would also intrude into many established ways of doing things, even as they carried forward many settled practices.

Though the Manchus declared themselves the ruling dynasty of China in 1644, it took another forty years for them to establish that claim incontestably. The decisive episode is known to Chinese as the Revolt of the Three Feudatories, which began in 1674 and ended in 1681. These three feudatories were large independent fiefdoms that constituted the southeastern part of the country; the Manchus had bestowed the territory on three prominent Chinese generals who had defected to them at a decisive moment. The three, however, became increasingly assertive until the then-reigning emperor, Kangxi (1654–1722; r. 1662–1722) decided to crush them, taking personal command of their suppression. It was, in fact, a huge civil war, fought over an area about the size of the southeastern United States and, by some estimates, causing more deaths than all the wars of seventeenth-century Europe combined.

This civil war, like the initial ouster of the Ming, is also noteworthy for what it tells us about a then-revolution in military affairs and the role of foreign technology, tactics, training, and advisers in the rise of the Manchus and their subsequent conquest of China. Nicola di Cosmo of the University of Canterbury has investigated in great detail the role of European firearms during this period of Chinese history. He observes that "the overemphasis placed on the 'natural qualities' of the Manchus as warriors has contributed to obscure the role played by firearms in their conquest of China."[11] In the seventeenth century, Ming armies had begun to deploy firearms along the Great Wall, to defend against Mongols. They used them against the Manchus also, and then in the 1620s the Manchus began to follow suit. As the Ming position deteriorated, the failing dynasty stepped up its efforts to obtain cannons and foreign advisers to train their troops in the use of artillery.

The decisive battles would be fought in the early 1640s. Di Cosmo credits the then–Manchu leader Hong Taiji with instituting "a wide ranging programme of military modernization that focused both on the production of firearms and the creation of a body of specialized troops." Firearms manufacture and training for their use were further integrated into the Manchu armed forces throughout the 1670s and 1680s. Kangxi, particularly, sought the assistance of the Belgian Jesuit Ferdinand Verbiest (1623–1688), then living in Beijing and well schooled in science and engineering, to take charge of cannon casting; at least 240 were ready for deployment against the rebels in the Three Feudatories. Di Cosmo's highly instructive account about the flexibility and adaptability of the Manchu state when circumstances warranted shows the interconnectedness of things even in this early modern time. "The military side of the Qing conquest can be better explained by examining its sophistication than by insisting on the inborn martial qualities of the Manchu soldiers. By weaving together the destinies of Chinese mandarins, Manchu generals, Portuguese cannoneers, European missionaries, and many other people, the history of firearms also links closely the Manchu conquests with the broader current of a world history."[12]

A similar problem of internal security prompted the Manchus' interest in naval warfare, leading to a seaborne pacification campaign against Taiwan that was to bring the island into the empire. Even as the center of Ming loyalism retreated to southeastern China and then crumbled there, many who wished to continue the fight looked to Taiwan as a potential base of operations. The most romanticized figure among them is known in the West as Koxinga (1624–1663) (or Zheng Chenggong, in proper contemporary romanization), the half-Chinese, half-Japanese son of Zheng Zhilong, the shipping cum pirate magnate who had played an important role in the rise of Ming sea power. By the time the younger Zheng inherited his father's network, it reached from Nagasaki to Macao and had made the Zheng family one of the richest in the region, perhaps in the world.

The younger Zheng gained control of Taiwan from the Dutch in 1662, even as his private navy also continued its harassment of ports along the

China coast. Some of these were major military operations, one having reached up the Yangtze River as far as Nanjing. After Emperor Kangxi gained the upper hand against the rebels in the Three Feudatories, he decided that he would subdue Taiwan also, fearing that it could become a permanent base, if not for a Ming reconquest of the mainland, at least for continuing Ming loyalist harassment of the new Qing regime. For as long as organized Ming loyalism survived anywhere, even in the overseas Chinese communities of Southeast Asia, it was a rebuke to the legitimacy of Manchu rule everywhere.

Naval warfare was new to the Manchus. Their navy, hastily assembled for the conquest of Taiwan, consisted mostly of co-opted pirate vessels. Still, by some accounts, Kangxi was able to send a fleet of hundreds of junks carrying thousands of armed men to the island. The Manchu conquest was completed by the end of 1683, and the pirate leaders who had helped Kangxi were rewarded with respectability, the foremost among them receiving the title "Lord Pacifier of the Seas" and a noble rank at the Manchu court. Taiwan became an imperial prefecture in name, but the farming out of local administration and taxation to erstwhile outlaws led to abuses and, finally, to widespread disorder. It was not until the mid-1700s that Taiwan acquired a proper prefectural government appropriate to its place in the Qing imperium. Once again, Manchu imperial aggrandizement had been driven primarily by an internal security challenge. But the pacification of southeastern China and the incorporation of Taiwan into the empire had unwittingly created hostages to fortune, "turning these areas into a key strategic frontier for the Qing state."[13]

In the meantime the costs of the consolidation of Qing power continued to challenge the new dynasty's fiscal policies and placed great strains on the economy. Indeed, economic historians of China record the first half of Kangxi's reign, that is, from 1660 to 1690, as the "Kangxi Depression." Richard von Glahn, in his seminal book *Fountain of Fortune: Money and Monetary Power in China, 1000–1700* (1996), describes the debate about remedies, a debate thoroughly redolent of the arguments of our own time:

> One group of officials held the opinion that a steady influx of silver was essential to maintaining a necessary stock of money. These statesmen accepted the silver economy and, by extension, the integration of China's national economy with the international market as an economic reality, and sought to conform state policies to ineluctable market trends. A dissenting conception was voiced by statecraft theorists who rejected the premises of an integrated

market system. They believed that true prosperity could be achieved only through political decentralization and economic autarky. They revived an atavistic vision of essentially self-sufficient local communities. While not seeking to sever all ties with the national and international markets, they believed that local economies should be shielded from the vicissitudes of exogenous market forces.[14]

Because for a time southeast China and Taiwan, centers of China's maritime trade, were in the hands of the Qing's sworn enemies, the dynasty had placed a formal ban on overseas trade, which had seriously curtailed it. But upon the pacification of both areas, the ban was lifted in 1684, and maritime commercial traffic soared. Thus, China began the eighteenth century, which was to be the defining century of Qing greatness, with this propitious omen of peace and prosperity.

As contemporary Chinese come increasingly to think of Ming-era imperial outreach in the context of naval heroics real and imagined, the Qing Empire is coming increasingly to represent the epitome of a great continental power. The New Qing history, which has focused attention on the triumphant Qing Empire of the eighteenth century and away from the ill-fated reign of the nineteenth, is well established in the West, and it is more and more the touchstone of China's own appreciation of that era. It is also becoming better understood that the People's Republic of China of today is the venerable Manchu Empire as inherited by the fledgling Republic of China in 1912. The creation of that empire—the imagining of it, the way it was acquired, the diplomatic intricacies surrounding it, the governance of its vast territories after they had been acquired—all these are central to our understanding of today's China and today's world.

It is therefore fortunate to have a genuinely magisterial 700-plus-page account of this enterprise, Peter C. Perdue's *China Marches West: The Qing Conquest of Central Eurasia* (2005). "The Qing conquests," he writes, "were a major world historical event. . . . By vastly expanding the territorial reach of the state, the conquests opened up terrain for colonial settlement, for trade, for administration, and for the literary imagination. . . . The expansion of the Qing state formed part of a global process. . . . Newly centralized, integrated, and militarized states pushed their borders outward by military conquest and settlers, missionaries, and traders followed behind."[15]

For the Manchus, it is the enormous scale of their part in this world-wide transformation that astounds. For one example, Perdue describes the logistical requirements alone—armies in the hundreds of thousands to be fed and armed and moved; tens of thousands of horses to be acquired and foddered; coordinated military campaigns across thousands of miles; territorial acquisitions in the hundreds of thousands of square miles. (Xinjiang alone, in its six-hundred-thousand-square-mile enormity, is the size of three Frances.) What should a contemporary Chinese government make of all this? Though Perdue alludes to what this experience has contributed to China's literary imagination—which should hardly be discounted, given how the stories of America's westward expansion have shaped our own sensibility—the greater interest today is in how the western march of the Manchus in the eighteenth century may be shaping present-day China's strategic imagination. For what Perdue describes as "an unprecedented thrust from Beijing into the heart of Eurasia" was in every way informed by strategic design, albeit a design that changed even at the time, and one whose subsequent interpretation has changed since.[16]

In its implementation, Qing strategy was an artful combination of what we today would call both hard and soft power. The Manchu Empire reached its zenith during the reign of the Emperor Qianlong (1711–1799; r. 1735–1796). He engaged in ten military campaigns and in several grand tours of the country so as to solidify the Manchus' grip on power. To the already awesome displays of prodigious military force, Qianlong added comparably awe-inspiring efforts at what the world knows today as public diplomacy. As Perdue recounts, Qianlong sponsored voluminous writings, wrote fifteen hundred poems himself, commissioned countless scrolls and paintings of great battles and victorious generals, and built monuments, temples, and memorials of various kinds—all to create "a public face of the Qing, which glorified its achievements in territorial expansion, while enshrining them in literary works, on paper, and in stone."[17]

The Manchus had also long been at work on an ideology of rulership, which reached its height during Qianlong's reign. Its underlying vision has been described and analyzed in detail by Pamela Kyle Crossley in her path-breaking book *A Translucent Mirror: History and Identity in Qing Imperial Ideology* (1999). Her insights, which have become the foundation for a new understanding of the Qing era, are well summarized by Evelyn Rawski:

This vision of universal rulership, based on the submission of divergent peoples whose cultures would remain separate, was fundamentally at odds with the Confucian ideal of transforming, and culturally unifying, all peoples under a Confucian ruler. . . . The court tried to cultivate each of the "five peoples," Manchus, Mongols, Tibetans, Uyghurs, and Chinese, whom the emperor identified as his major subjects. The languages of the five peoples were officially enshrined as the languages of the empire. The throne commissioned translations, dictionary compilations and other projects to promote each language. Qianlong himself knew Manchu, Chinese, and Mongolian, and studied at least some Tibetan and Uyghur.

. . . But even while they pursued policies of accommodation towards the peoples of Inner Asia, the Qing rulers artfully increased their control over these peoples, and exerted a profound influence on their societies and economies. . . . They restructured the social hierarchy in the peripheries. . . . They eroded autonomous sources of power and prestige to establish the throne as the source of all secular authority.[18]

The extension of a more direct form of Manchu control into southeast China and Taiwan was imperial aggrandizement in the interests of internal security and political legitimacy. Indeed, one can imagine that the sway of the Manchus in that area might have acquired a rather different character if those early Chinese collaborators had not reversed course by deciding to challenge the new dynasty. But the Manchus' major move into central Eurasia is a more complex question. Han Chinese statesmen could have seen it as one way of solving, at long last, the perennial security problems that menacing Inner Asian peoples had for centuries inflicted on the Han Chinese Middle Kingdom. And yet, the long history of Chinese statecraft was not immediately supportive of Manchu policy on this score.

It was one thing to play off the Inner Asian peoples one against another or to secure their general assent to Han Chinese suzerainty in symbolically reassuring ways. But now Manchu leaders of the Qing dynasty were arguing for the incorporation of large expanses of alien territory, inhabited by exotic peoples with unfathomable ways, directly into the empire—except that the machinery of that empire was now in the hands of men whose commitment to the Han Chinese way was more than a little suspect. These were sensitive country-defining and culture-defining questions. As far as Inner Asia was concerned, the Ming dynasty had believed in building walls, not seeking control beyond them. According to Arthur Waldron, the authoritative historian of these Ming-era military policies, strategic considerations were subordinated to a prior issue of whether a Chinese dynasty should define "Chinese" in cultural terms exclusively.[19]

Accordingly, throughout the eighteenth century there was opposition at court to the large and expensive expeditions into the far northwest, and even after these vast regions were pacified, there was ongoing debate, a kind of cost-benefit analysis, about the drain on resources necessary to hold on to them. Han Chinese councilors of state saw no point in wasting the empire's resources on the conquest of barbarian wastelands. The emperor argued back that the incorporation of these new territories would prove to be an economical way of defending the core of the empire in China proper over the longer run.

This was to be a long-running argument, its subtleties reconstructed by James Millward in his detailed study of the Qing Empire in Central Asia.[20] In the nineteenth century, as the dynasty came to be menaced by challenges on its maritime frontier, there was a reversal of positions. The core Manchu leadership, though hardly pleased by the erosion of Qing influence in the far northwest, seemed resigned to it, given the need to focus on seaborne threats. But now it was Chinese officials who began to argue for shoring up Manchu imperial power in the region. In this revised view, if only the territories were properly governed—that is, governed in the traditional Chinese way, not in the looser Manchu way—China as a whole would somehow become stronger in the face of the seaborne threats, not weaker. These men, as Millward puts it, became advocates of "nothing less than the political, demographic, economic, and even ecological remaking of the Western Regions in China's image."[21] Later on, this argument between advocates of continental defense and maritime defense would crystallize the debate about national security in the last quarter of the nineteenth century.

While we have used such terms as *strategic culture* and *Pax Manjurica* to aid our discussion of Qing behavior, we must now ponder the connections between the High Qing era and the present day and try to understand how those wars and the debates about them, like the ancient military classics and the exploits of earlier dynasties, are becoming part of China's strategic tradition, a twenty-first-century work-in-progress. Predictably, there is lively debate about this question, and the discussion here begins with provocative hypotheses put forward by Peter Perdue in advance of his magnum opus about the Qing's Central Asian conquests. Perdue argues that "Qing strategy was radically different from Ming even though both faced a similar situation on the northwest frontier, because the elite was different: solely Han for the Ming, and a tricultural coalition of Manchu, Han, and Mongol for the Qing.... The background of elites does matter, and substituting one elite for another produces different behavior."[22]

Perdue attributes the difference between Ming and Qing strategy to a different understanding of what was "foreign" and what was not. "Ming strategists thought in terms of disconnected crises and threats produced by alien forces over which they had little control. The Qing, however, promoted incorporation of non-Han peoples, using a combination of ritual, economic, and material techniques, [but] those they could not incorporate, they exterminated. . . . The Ming dynasty was locked in a defensive stance," but, Perdue continues, "by 1800 all the major states on China's border had either been exterminated, forced to sign treaties after their fortresses were destroyed, or enrolled as tributaries. China's greatest historical enemies, in the Qing view, had been included inside the realm of civilization for the first time as submissive dependents instead of alien plunderers."[23] Perdue continues:

> Both the Republic of China of 1912 and the People's Republic of China of 1949 consider themselves heir to this much larger Qing realm. Yet this imperial conception left an awkward legacy to the new Chinese nation-state, based on narrower definitions of identity in the twentieth century. Even though Chinese nationalists were anti-Manchu, they supported the territorial boundaries inherited from the Manchu emperors. Redefinition of the Chinese state's identity by the frontier conquests made it impossible to give them up, but transforming identity from imperial to national made it difficult to justify keeping them. . . . These contradictory impulses defined the persistent paradoxes of Chinese nationalism: it is simultaneously a protest against Western and Japanese imperialism and a reassertion of imperial claims over non-Han peoples; a vision of a multiethnic state that presumes Han dominance; a claim to continuity with "5000 years of history" which in fact rests on the contingent conquests of the eighteenth century.[24]

Beijing has promised a new official view of this by 2012, when the People's Republic will publish its own version of the history of the Qing. Much can change before then; indeed, much has already changed. The Qing history project has occasioned the opening of new imperial archives in both the Chinese and Manchu languages and the publication of previously unavailable documents of all kinds—collections of local histories and gazetteers, Late Qing treatises on geography and politics, newspapers and magazines of the Late Qing era, and new textbooks that appeared toward the end of the dynasty as educational reforms began to take hold. Scholars in China are producing a steady stream of new papers and longer monographs that exploit these materials. Obviously, there is no way to know in advance the cumulative effect of these efforts, but the argument is moving ahead. Thus, the historian Gao Zhao has combed through these documents and writings and has put forward a way of understanding the complicated continuities between the Qing dynasty's view of China and the views of China that came to the fore in the twentieth century.

It appears that not only did the Manchus have a sophisticated approach to the incorporation of previously "outside" peoples into the "inside," that is, "China," they also succeeded over time in broadening the definition to include a larger number of people within "China," conspicuously including themselves as a kind of protective camouflage against growing anti-Qing sentiment in the late nineteenth century. For, as we know and as the Manchus of the time certainly felt, the republican movement was emphasizing the racial difference between Han Chinese subjects and Manchu rulers. But in Gao's understanding, "one might say that while Sun Yat-sen won a political victory over the Qing rulers, the Qing dynasty enjoyed a geographical and ideological victory, having defined the form of the emerging post-revolutionary Chinese state. Thanks to the rise and spread of 'greater Chinese nationalism,' the official Qing view of *China* as a multiethnic entity has persisted into the twentieth and twenty-first centuries, contributing directly to the construction of the modern Chinese national identity."[25]

But this was for the future. With the death of Qianlong in 1799, his heirs had every reason to believe the *Pax Manjurica* that was his legacy would continue on. The next emperor did not have the benefit of data now available to us, but he could have sensed it—that, on the edge of a new century, China's farmers were feeding about 30 percent of the world's population; that China's artisans and craftsmen and merchants were generating a gross national product about five times that of Britain and France combined; that the court's fiscal revenues were growing dramatically; that of the ten cities in the world with a population of over five hundred thousand, six of them—Beijing, Nanjing, Yangzhou, Suzhou, Hangzhou, and Guangzhou—were in China.

Qianlong himself, about to abdicate lest he, unfilially, reign longer than his grandfather Kangxi (r. 1662–1722) was well pleased. "I have reigned more than sixty years," he said in 1795, "so that the Four Seas are forever pure and all the regions of the world have been transformed by Chinese culture. . . . My virtuous reputation has spread far and wide . . . and I have always treated Chinese and foreigners as one family. . . . This dynasty views all people of the world with equal benevolence."[26]

Rhetorical flourishes aside, and however the Communists who run present-day China decide to cope with the inherent strategic ambiguities and questions of identity bequeathed to them because of the Manchus' solution to *their* national security problems, the People's Republic is happy to embrace the conspicuous material legacy of the Qing court. During the course of the eighteenth century, the emperors built up a summer capital that became renowned in the West as Jehol and is now referred to as Chengde. It was a vast pleasure dome with palaces, temples, hunting grounds, and large gardens, not so different from Samuel Taylor Coleridge's reverie about the Great Khan's Xanadu: "Twice five miles of fertile ground / With walls and towers girdled round / And there were gardens bright with sinuous rills / Where blossomed many an incense-burning tree / And here were forests ancient as the hills / Enfolding sunny spots of greenery." In its way, Chengde was the Manchu Empire in miniature, as if designed to be a model of it, with the diversity of the empire represented in the varied architectures of its buildings and also of its grounds. Chengde is located about seventy miles north of Beijing. It sits within about 140,000 acres enclosed by a wall, and the Imperial Summer Villa occupies about 1,500 acres. In the heyday of Manchu rule, Chinese were not allowed to enter this exclusively Manchu preserve. Though Han Chinese have a long memory for such slights, the People's Republic of China has nonetheless, since the early 1990s, worked to secure World Heritage Status for the site, which it now enjoys. Whatever the critics of an earlier time may have said about the place as an embodiment of imperial extravagance and decadence, Chengde is now a national treasure, with a government-funded institute dedicated to its study, preservation, and restoration.[27] And it is now also a place that stimulates extensive and provocative study by cultural and architectural historians all over the world as it also inspires practitioners.[28] In at least this one important respect, the Qing imperium still continues "to edify guests from afar."

Within a generation, this great Qing Empire would enter a sustained crisis that would bring about its decomposition and, finally, its collapse. This is not what one would have expected. For the longest time the collapse of the Qing dynasty and, with it, the end of the imperial system in China were attributed to deep obtuseness and arrogance, to a lack of interest in the outer world, of which it was said to be deeply and dangerously ignorant. For all the subtle strategy, deft diplomacy, powerful military forces, and effective governance—not to mention the Qing emperors' near paranoia about enemies real and imagined, nearby and far away—the dynasty failed to discern the mortal seaborne threat of the rise of the West. The dynasty's presumed nonchalance about the world beyond its borders is still, today, accepted by many as a matter of course, but we must still wonder. For at the beginning of this great crisis, the Qing dynasty had been in the world, and had been an important part of the world, for a century and a half. How did the West achieve this degree of strategic surprise?

Roberta Wohlstetter, who wrote the definitive book about the Pearl Harbor attack, *Pearl Harbor: Warning and Decision* (1962), went on to expand our understanding of inattentiveness and incomprehension in the face of life-threatening dangers. It is not only preparations for a sneak attack that may go undetected. There is another kind of attack, one that unfolds over a long period of time, an attack that in one way is plainly visible and apparent—obvious, even—yet that remains unappreciated. Wohlstetter, calling such events in history "slow Pearl Harbors," stated: "A change at any given time may seem innocent enough but, over time, those changes add up and can ultimately spell disaster. . . . The problem is that after each small change, even hindsight is not very clear."[29]

So not a rare phenomenon, and yet its presence in early nineteenth-century China still seems improbable. China's long intellectual tradition is filled with examples of spirited curiosity about almost everything, from accounts of foreign travel to pharmacopeias. The history of science and technology in China is one of intricacy and innovation. The venerable tribute system, whatever its limitations as a means for conducting foreign relations, had kept China conversant for centuries with developments in Asian countries. Certainly, beginning in 1500, China was playing a large role in a genuine world economy; Chinese ships not only were involved in distant expeditions like those of Zheng He but also, on a routine basis, carried on an enormous trade in South and Southeast Asia. Reviews of the debates at court during that era show an impressive sophistication among Chinese officials about the international contacts necessary for China's own prosperity. And it is also reasonable to assume that dynastic records of trade and diplomacy available to scholars in our own time were even more accessible to those who lived closer in time to their creation. The Qing dynasty's official history of its Ming predecessor was completed in 1739 after compilation, collation, and analysis of a mountain of Ming-era documentation.

Even in the late seventeenth century, close upon the Qing's initial consolidation of power, its councilors of state sought revenue from maritime commerce to finance successive emperors' ever more ambitious expeditions into the central Eurasian heartland. Given all of this, would not the Qing court have had at least some inkling, say, of British and French activities in India? Having seen firsthand how earlier rivalries among the Spanish, the Portuguese, and the Dutch affected important places in that part of the world—Taiwan, Japan, the Philippines, Indonesia—would not the Qing court take some notice of the entry of other European nations into this competition? After all, during the seventeenth-century civil war in southern China, when the Qing ascendancy hung in the balance, there had been at least one dramatic intervention into China's internal affairs by a European maritime power—the Dutch East Asia Company's effort to integrate anti-Qing pirate organizations into its own attack on China. Why not another?

Today's scholarship is still at an early stage in its understanding of the history of China's consciousness of the outer world during this epoch—how it was shaped and what accounted for its defects and lapses. Looking at this question from the perspective even of nearby Southeast Asia, John E. Wills Jr., who has been a student of this era in China's foreign relations for more than thirty years, finds that

> it was not China alone that stood on the verge of great changes in 1800, for there were Eurasia-wide changes in state and society, all of them driven by the growth of commerce, productivity, and population. Somehow, China was being drawn into this ferment, a ferment triggered by internal changes more than by European intervention as such, and yet, because it was happening over time, a sense of crisis was long in developing.
>
> ... The Qing rulers had quite a bit of good information about developments in 'tributary states' but did not know what to make of it. They were hampered by the crucial defect of the 'tributary system' as a structure for the management of foreign relations, the absence of a resident delegate of the Qing in a foreign capital, charged, to add to the old pun, not only with lying abroad for his country but with spying abroad for his country. ... Chinese traders and Chinese living in growing settlements outside the country also knew a lot, but their knowledge, often by their own choice, did not find its way to the Qing government. ... These weaknesses were among the many reasons why the Qing rulers, immensely capable of information gathering

in the midst of major reform efforts, in Xinjiang, in the salt administration, and much more in the early nineteenth century sensed so little of the major changes that were coming toward them out of the South Seas.[30]

This unrecognized threat is customarily viewed as a function of military power and commercial penetration. Yet, in retrospect, it may be that the truly subversive character of the West lay in the subversive ideas it brought with it, some of which turned out to be well suited for joining forces with a very old homegrown tradition of heterodox ideologies, which had long fueled rural discontent and frequent antidynastic violence. This had been true for more than a thousand years. Buddhism itself was a foreign import, and in subsequent centuries adherents to its millenarian strain had created secret societies and armed sects that, in turn, fomented violent uprisings, often with devastating effect. Accordingly, this was a familiar kind of threat to internal security and national security and, when joined to Ming loyalism, had plagued the Qing dynasty from the late seventeenth century on.

But no such mixture had ever been as combustible or so dynasty threatening as the Taiping ("Great Peace") Rebellion of the mid-nineteenth century, one of the largest and most devastating uprisings in world history. It was inspired by one Chinese man's interpretation of Christian faith. In 1837 a certain Hong Xiuquan from Guangdong, aged twenty-three, read Chinese-language Protestant pamphlets and, afterward, understood himself to have visited heaven. His vivid recollection of his journey had powerful effects. He came to believe that he was a son of God and the younger brother of Jesus Christ. He set out to give a systematic presentation of his vision both theologically and politically and came gradually to regard himself as the founder of a new earthly order for China. His following grew and came to include men with natural gifts for military operations. Hong began to capture important cities in the central regions of the country, enabling him to implement a Sino-Christian theocracy committed to constructing an earthly utopia, "so that all can live together in perpetual joy, until at last they are raised to heaven to greet their Father." It was a complex system, often arbitrary and brutal, socially communal, and extremely puritanical. (It would be much studied later by the Chinese Communist Party.) At its apex was the Heavenly King, as Hong now styled himself. It was to take the Qing almost fifteen years, until about 1865, to suppress this movement. It was the largest civil war in the history of the world. Tens of millions were engaged on both sides of the struggle; casualties ran to the tens of millions, and the collateral destruction, by all eyewitness accounts, was enormous, so "the distress and the misery of the inhabitants were beyond description." The Heavenly King himself died in the summer of 1864, and Qing forces recovered Nanjing, the Taiping capital since 1853, soon thereafter. It was a murderous reoccupation of one of China's great cities. The Qing pursuit of the retreating Taiping remnants was equally relentless and unforgiving. Against this, were not the demands of the Westerners for lower tariffs but a nuisance to hard-pressed Manchu officials, otherwise occupied?

Perhaps the Manchu court should be forgiven for thinking that if it could survive the Taiping wars, it could survive anything. Nonetheless, it has since fallen to historians to assess whether the years that remained to the Manchus should be read as an old story of a doomed dynasty in its death throes, or as the first chapter of a new story, Moribund China's transformation into Modern China. It is important to understand that a pervasive sense of the inadequacy of Late Qing reform efforts was at the heart of Chinese politics from the latter part of the nineteenth century onward. It not only fed the ultimately successful republican movement that overthrew the dynasty in 1912, but it also contributed, as China's problems multiplied, to a progressive radicalization of Chinese politics throughout the first half of the twentieth century. Indeed, a sense of the failure and futility of the Late Qing era and, even more so, of the early republic, added legitimacy to the argument for wholesale revolution as the nation's only plausible salvation.

Changes in contemporary understanding of the High Qing period are now part of the country's strategic tradition and therefore part of the consciousness of the men who now run the Chinese government. It remains to be seen whether a new and ongoing reevaluation of the Late Qing period and of the ill-fated republic, a revisiting that still lags the reinterpretation of the High Qing but that is starting to gain on it, will have comparable consequences. However, there are many issues that still will need to be resolved, especially how best to evaluate the dynasty's ability to make the conceptual transition from the old way to a new way of thinking about politics, strategy, and diplomacy. For all its awesome destruction and its tortured psychological reliance on a syncretic ideology mainly foreign in origin, the Taiping Rebellion was a recognizable national security threat, not fundamentally different from others that had arisen in the past to disturb the *Pax Manjurica*. Thus, the defeat of the Taipings did not require a new way of understanding the sources of national power or how to preserve it. Western imperialism was another matter; its theory and practice needed to be investigated, because China had not seen anything quite like it before.

Indeed, the Qing Empire, having barely overcome a massive internal threat to its survival, almost immediately faced what would be recognized today as a classic strategic dilemma. Other nations could not help but sense the Qing's weakened condition after the debilitating Taiping wars and thus began to create fundamental, structural risks to the Qing Empire in a way that foreign inroads earlier in the nineteenth century had not. In the far northwest, Muslim separatists, backed by Russia, gained control of a substantial portion of Xinjiang, thereby rolling back some of the Qing's eighteenth-century empire building, and Russian forces were operating in the Ili River valley. At the same time, pressure from Rising Japan forced the Qing to relinquish its claims to the Ryukyu Islands and to accept a growing and subversive Japanese presence on Taiwan.

The naval historian Bruce Swanson, drawing on an analysis of Qing documents by Immanuel C. Y. Hsu, has neatly summarized the intense debate at court during 1875 between those who favored raising a large army to send to the northwest and those who favored acquiring modern warships to defend against Japan on the seacoast. Those in the "maritime faction" argued, first, that the closeness of Beijing to the coast made maritime defense more important than northwest frontier defense. They further maintained that Xinjiang was a valueless wasteland and a drain on the empire's finances. In that the officials of the maritime faction were almost all Chinese from the coastal provinces, they also took pains to say that withdrawal from Xinjiang would not dishonor the Manchu emperors who had conquered the place, because such a withdrawal would contribute to a real strengthening of the empire over the long run. The continental faction countered that the loss of Xinjiang would unhinge the entire Qing position in Inner Asia, for Mongolia would be next, thereby menacing the metropolitan province and, ultimately, the capital itself. Their argument relied on an assessment of the comparative dangers. The continental faction believed that, in the end, the Western maritime nations were interested in China's trade, not its territory, but not so the Russians. Drawing on an ancient distinction in Chinese medicine between a rash on the skin and a disease of the vital organs, one Chinese official put it this way: "The maritime nations are like a sickness of the limbs, far away and light, but Russia is like a sickness of the heart and stomach, nearby and dangerous."[31] In the end, the emperor opted for a renewed, ultimately successful campaign in Xinjiang, using money previously set aside for naval modernization to pay for it.

The maritime faction would in time be heard from once again. As if in anticipation of the crises of the 1890s, it had been developing a maritime-centered view of the history of the world, much at variance with the traditional Inner Asia focus of Chinese historians. It was not that China was ignorant of the maritime world, but rather that hitherto there were not sufficiently pressing reasons to develop ways of thinking about national security that took the maritime world as their point of departure. The appearance of such threats would, however, lead to what Jane Kate Leonard has called "China's rediscovery of the maritime world." Geostrategy had been the missing concern, and it was supplied by the Chinese scholar and official Wei Yuan (1794–1856) in his *Illustrated Treatise on the Sea Kingdoms*, published in 1842, the year of the Opium War. In Leonard's words, "Wei discerned that Western naval power was the spearhead of the Western drive into maritime Asia and that it had, as its ultimate intent, the domination of Asian maritime communications and trade. He viewed this prospect with alarm because it threatened the stable bonds of trade, tribute, and overlordship that had knit together maritime Asia for centuries. He believed that the breakdown of these bonds would create threatening conditions for China."[32]

Within ten years of the Central Asian crisis of the 1880s, it was becoming clear that the continental faction's then relatively benign interpretation of the West's territorial ambitions in China needed revision. Here, it is not necessary to delve into the intricacies of late nineteenth-century intra-European rivalries that set off a scramble for concessions and leaseholds that then bid fair to transform the treaty-port system of Western access and privilege into something else entirely, a regime that could, in time, turn China into a multinational version of India—first, by establishing "spheres of influence," then by "carving up the melon" outright. This was a threat that not even the farsighted Wei Yuan had anticipated.

How had it come about? In its own way, it had originated in the efforts of Europeans and Americans to understand the rise of the West. New concepts emerged to help explain it—social Darwinism, finance capitalism, imperialism. But the notion that seemed to have the most purchase in the chanceries of the major powers was a body of ideas that had coalesced into a doctrine known ever since as "navalism." In 1890 a hitherto unknown instructor in naval history, Alfred Thayer Mahan (1840–1914), published *The Influence of Sea Power upon History, 1660–1783*. This was more than an ordinary case of a man having met the moment. Almost immediately, Mahan's book became a worldwide sensation; was soon translated into the principal languages of the world, East and West; became required reading for diplomats, military officials, and their sovereigns and presidents; and was taught in the world's war colleges. It also grabbed hold of public opinion in a way that led to the founding of navy leagues all over the world, urging that Mahan's vision become national policy.

The purely military component of Mahan's ideas would not have impressed a professional solider or sailor as especially novel. Indeed, his ideas about how to *fight* at sea seemed to be an application of what Carl von Clausewitz had taught about how to fight anywhere—by concentrating one's force and applying it decisively against the enemy at a critical place, a place not always obvious or easy to find. But Mahan's real interest was not a mode of warfare as such, but rather what made for greatness in a nation. Unlike many, he embraced America's post–Civil War industrial society and was a thoroughgoing internationalist who believed that international trade made nations rich. And to this combination of industry and trade, a great nation needed to add up-to-date military technology, especially naval technology, to defend its inherently necessary worldwide interests by being able to project power.

China, now acutely interested in understanding what made the West tick, became a close observer of the West's own efforts at self-understanding. What if Mahan were more than a mania? What if he were right about what made for wealth and power in the modern world? Then China's national security agenda would have to become far broader and deeper; it would have to address the creation of power overall. It would no longer do merely to purchase weapons and ships, however necessary in the short term. There needed to be a change in the way China did things, but first there needed to be a change in how China thought about things.

That change would have great and lasting effects, but none greater than the scrapping of the core curriculum that for centuries had been the common experience of the nation's political leadership. For centuries the civil service examinations, the sole route into the leadership, had required mastery of a curriculum of the classics, properly interpreted. But the value of such a classical education, once the way to wealth, power, and prestige, was coming to an end in late Qing times, and the habits and institutions that it had propped up reached the end of their useful life. The system was abolished in 1905. "A vast institutional apparatus of compounds and buildings populated by examiners, candidates, copyists, proofreaders, and guards had vanished," writes Benjamin Elman in his monumental history of the system.

"Gone were the hopes and dreams of millions of young and old men from villages, towns, and cities who had sought official fame and fortune. A cultural regime that had thrived in its late imperial form since 1450, perished. Also lost in the demise of the civil examinations was the cultural confidence that the dynasty and its elites were united in their efforts to maintain public order, imperial prestige, and literati learning."[33]

Indeed, one can regard this event in 1905 as the single most important milestone in China's journey from the traditional to the modern. As no one other thing could, it ratified what had become the painful consensus among thoughtful people in China and throughout the entire Chinese world: a new intellectual regime, already under construction but not yet completed, would have to consolidate its power before the country's recovery of national power could begin in earnest. In the century since then, the struggle over what would replace the "cultural regime that had thrived in its imperial form since 1450" would determine the shape of everything else that has happened.

Just as the recent scholarly recasting of the High Qing period has led to a transformed sense of its relevance to the present day, there has also been a comparable process at work that has the potential to reshape the contemporary understanding of the Late Qing period as well. In general, this process for the Late Qing is not as well advanced as that for the High Qing, but it is making rapid progress. A generation ago the Late Qing era hardly seemed worthy of study at all. It was seen as just another on that long list of false starts leading to dead ends that made the victory of the Communist Revolution inevitable. Nothing less would have done, could have done, in transforming China from traditional to modern. Indeed, at that time, revolution was the very definition of modernity, and nothing modern could be achieved without it.

But even those interested in the past must take life as they find it today. No doubt, there are many who are disappointed, even embittered, by the direction of socioeconomic events in China these past twenty-five years and who are even more distressed that the search for what explains it is leading us back to some dull Chinese establishment, and not to a more interesting mélange of anarchists, romantics, and revolutionaries. But China, which invented the idea of a constant interaction between *yin* and *yang*, has given us an analogous way of reading its modern history. Merle Goldman reminds us of her fellow historian Philip Kuhn's basic distinction here:

> Two major strains exist in modern Chinese history. One was established by the Taiping Uprising, a millenarian movement whose founder was influenced by a combination of traditional Chinese apocalyptic thinking and Christian fundamentalism. He and his followers attempted to establish a heavenly kingdom on earth, where everyone would be equal, but the leaders would have absolute authority. Mao comes out of this utopian Taiping tradition and the older chiliastic tradition of peasant rebellions in China's premodern history. The other strain Kuhn points to is the self-strengthening movement launched by late nineteenth-century reform officials who sought, by means of economic and technological development and authoritarian rule, to modernize the Chinese economy in order to make China competitive with the West. . . . The Deng reforms have finally fulfilled the wish of China's reformers since the late nineteenth century to make China rich and powerful. . . . Deng, much more than Mao, made possible the attainment of the reformers' century-old dream of making China once again a great and prospering nation.[34]

The idea that we can better understand contemporary China by restarting history in the Late Qing era may nettle some historians still in the grip of an older conventional wisdom, but it is downright dangerous to the men who run China today. Once again, in Goldman's words:

> China's present leaders assert that democratic institutions and Western values are alien to their history and culture. Yet this assertion reveals an ignorance of their own modern history and culture. The local self-government and civil society that slowly emerged in late twentieth-century China had begun earlier in that century. . . . Inspired by reforms in the West and in Japan as well as by the sense of threat of Western imperialism and internal disintegration, reform-minded elites and officials at the beginning of the twentieth century promoted self-government at various levels of society. They saw wealth and power deriving not only from economic development but also from people participating in local government and assuming political responsibility. . . Despite the elitism of the early reformers, they sought to create an active citizenry involved in state-building. The idea was to empower local people and imbue them with a concept of citizenship that tied individuals to the state. By replacing the traditional leadership of local

elders with a system legitimized by the vote of the people in local elections, reformers believed they were taking the first step toward creating a more stable political order.[35]

The stark distinction between Dengist success and Maoist failure is of the sort with which we introduced this book. And because both we and China's leaders have before us the evidence provided by our own eyes, both we and they will not be able to avoid committing the sin of present-mindedness by imposing today's outcome on our reading of yesterday's Late Qing era. For, until very recently, the study of modern China could not help but be informed by a master narrative whose climax was the founding of the People's Republic of China in 1949. All roads seemed to lead to Beijing's famous Tiananmen Square and Mao Zedong's proclamation of China's new order. How else could the historian tell *that* story? As everyone knows, this is how China's political struggles during the first half of the twentieth century resolved themselves.

But today's China has not turned out to be what it was assumed to be or projected to be even twenty-five years ago. What then is it? Where did it come from, and how did it get here? These are the questions that lie beneath another ongoing revolution in the academic study of modern China—the evaluation of the last years of the Qing. That era, once a dead end, is now being transformed into a quite lively beginning, with advances in politics, commerce, and culture that prefigure the China and the Greater China—Hong Kong, Taiwan, and Singapore—we see today.

If the High Qing bequeathed a vision of empire that can inspire China's present leaders by its eighteenth-century imperial sway, the Late Qing has left to them a set of blueprints for the recovery of that grandeur in the twenty-first century. But there is a risk in it, and that risk is the notion central to Late Qing reformers who (to draw upon Merle Goldman's phrasing of it) saw wealth and power deriving not only from economic development but also from people participating in local government and assuming political responsibility. These reformers sought to create an active citizenry involved in state building by replacing the traditional leadership with a system legitimized by the vote of the people.

We have come to this understanding during the last decade of scholarly effort focused on uncovering previously unsuspected links between Late

Qing China and the China of today. One productive area of inquiry has been social history, especially the adaptability of older intermediate social organizations to modern activities. For centuries, lineage trusts and lineage estates had been a way of preserving the capital of a family as a whole, against the claims of individual family members. In the late nineteenth and early twentieth centuries such agrarian-based trusts started to become a foundation of industrial activity and, later, industrial holdings. Though we think of China as preeminently a family-dominated society, we also know that Late Qing social life was, in the words of social historian Carsten Herrmann-Pillath, "ordered by a plethora of institutions that transcended the family. . . . In the Late Qing, there were corporate structures emerging out of the family, becoming the societal framework of an institutional foundation for a more complex economy. . . . Late Qing China was an extremely complex society of migrants and sojourners. . . . Activities took place within the framework of an informal customary law, independent of the state, but formalized and binding. . . . Core family contracts were very often used to prevent conflicts from emerging, and to settle obligations for the future. . . . In this sense, traditional China was a contractarian society to a degree perhaps even greater than Europe."[36]

Some of these points are concretely made in recent case studies of the history of Chinese business. Madeleine Zelin has reconstructed the history of a major part of one of China's most important homegrown industries, salt making, from the early 1800s to the 1930s. She portrays these merchants of Zigong, in Sichuan province, as technological innovators, agile marketers, capable managers, and astute capital raisers, all without benefit of well-developed government rules and regulations. A kind of independent, self-governing industry grew up. It did its part, but it could not survive constant political instability, internal violence, and international wars—the things against which a well-run state is supposed to guard.[37] Kathryn Bernhardt and Philip Huang, who specialize in the study of this period, have reported "how the opening of local archives to Western scholars in the 1980s provided a basis for the re-examination of past assumptions about civil law in Qing and Republican China. . . . We can say now with confidence that those who assumed that the formal court system of the Qing dealt little with civil matters were simply wrong. . . . These newly available records also permit us to raise new questions and to contrast actual legal practice with its representation in the code. . . . The evidence argues for a fundamental reconception of the Qing legal system."[38]

The larger case for focusing on the Late Qing as segue to Chinese modernity, as also put forward by Rebecca Karl and Peter Zarrow, is a case for turning received wisdom on its head. They explain that among scholars in China who study this period, there is a debate about the balance that should be struck between radicalism and conservatism in explaining the course of China's modern development. "This confrontation marks a move away from the 'particularism' of Chinese socialism to the universalism of non-socialist globalized capitalist modernization and development. . . . It is the similar context of China's encounter with two global capitalisms— that of the nineteenth century and that of the late twentieth century—that renders [the reforms of] 1898 so full of meaning today." Focusing on the late nineteenth century necessarily marks a turning away from the older view of the seedtime of Chinese modernity, the so-called May Fourth Era of the 1920s. That era, so Karl and Zarrow point out, had too narrowly constrained Chinese history by defining all of China's past as a stagnant traditionalism.[39]

We in the West see in developments like these the emergence of Civil Society, that cluster of private institutions that mediates between an impersonal state and a society of individuals. In this respect it is not too far-fetched to see the relatively nonviolent end of the Qing dynasty—its abdication in February 1912 in favor of the new republic—as a consequence of the growing presence of moderating and calming institutions during the dynasty's final decades. The end of the Qing, though hardly bloodless even at the time, still cannot compare in death and destruction to the end of its great predecessors, the Song and the Ming dynasties. For there was, by 1912, a network of narrowly elected provincial assemblies and a national assembly, and a sense that subjects were on the way to being replaced by citizens. All this helped make the denouement of the Qing era more of a proverbial whimper than a bang. The last century of Qing rule had indeed been beset by the extraordinary violence of the Taiping Rebellion and the Boxer Uprising. The decades after the Manchu abdication would see year upon year of internal violence and international war.

But the final moments of the Qing ruling house were quiet ones, a rare recess of civility. In the best high Edwardian way, the Qing dynasty negotiated itself out of existence. Its last regent signed the Act of Abdication of the Emperor of the Great Qing. Under its terms, the Qing house retained ownership of some of its palaces and property and was enrolled on the public dole, entitled to an annual stipend from the Republic of China.

America's minister in Peking, William Calhoun, was properly guarded in his report to Secretary of State Philander Knox: "The revolution was comparatively easy; it had no opposition; but now the great strain, the great test, of the [republican] movement has come."[40]

This is the case that supports Late Qing revisionism in our own time. But there were reasons why people at *that* time were not impressed. The many advances that now seem momentous in retrospect did not deter the radicalization of successor generations, for whom only the most radical of solutions would do. Nor did they have an opportunity to re-examine core questions that would serve to create the Late Qing's century-long reputation for futility. The epitome of Late Qing failure, both at the time and today, is China's twin defeats in naval battles in the Sino-French War (1884–1895) and the Sino-Japanese War (1894–1895), "which historians have used to prove the failure of self-strengthening reforms after the Taping Rebellion." These defeats, as historian Benjamin Elman writes, "transformed official elite and popular opinion, which shaped the emerging national sense of crisis among Han Chinese."[41] As part of his much larger history of four centuries of science in China, Elman sets out "to refute the received wisdom concerning the late nineteenth-century developments in science and technology."[42] His discussion is another reminder that changing perceptions of success and failure—both those that are contemporaneous and others that are the product of historical analysis a century later—can have profound effects on the strategic imagination and the grand designs of governments.

Elman builds his refutation of the received wisdom about the naval defeats in great detail and with a close examination of Chinese shipyards, the warships they built, and the base of knowledge created to support the effort to produce a modern navy. "The rise of new arsenals, shipyards, technical schools, and translation bureaus, usually undervalued in the 'failure narratives,' should be re-considered in light of the increased training in military technology and education in Western science available to the Chinese after 1865."[43] In this respect, Elman offers the underappreciated fact that "a decade before anything comparable in Meiji Japan, many [Chinese] literati and artisans saw in Western learning and the modern sciences an alternative route to fame and fortune."[44]

The main issue is whether China lacked the scientific and technological capability to support a modern navy, or whether the defeat of the Late Qing navy in battle is better attributed to other shortcomings. Elman's assessment of the actual achievements in science, technology, and engineering direct him to an alternative explanation, one offered by military, political, and diplomatic historians, who see the failures as those of organization, tactics, unreasonable expectations for diplomacy, and the imposition of domestic political requirements on the command structure and the deployment of naval forces.

In any case, the defeats really happened, and what Elman calls "the refraction of China's self-strengthening reforms into scientific and technological failure" had long-term psychological effects on Chinese politics. But a less appreciated, but very powerful, consequence over time involved the attitude of many Western friends of China—educators, diplomats, missionaries—who had contributed mightily to building the edifice of self-strengthening in China. They, too, were caught up in feelings of pessimism, gloom, defeatism, and futility about mere reform.[45] Decades later, many of them would show a tolerance of Chinese radicalism, even of Maoism itself, which would have political effects all its own. But, in the twenty-first century these older debates have been overtaken by China's restarted history. The centerpiece of the Late Qing's modernization effort was the renowned Jiangnan Shipyard, established in Shanghai in 1865. It became one of the major arsenals of the world, and its own history mirrors China's, having been occupied by foreign enemies, then nationalized, then partially privatized. In 2003 the Chinese government announced that the historic facility would be dismantled and its prime Shanghai location turned over to real estate developers. It will be replaced by a new $4 billion facility a few miles away on Changxing Island at the mouth of the Yangtze, part of a plan to make China into the world's leading shipbuilding nation by 2015.

And yet, for all this, the historical terrain that is the Qing dynasty remains as treacherous as ever. In January 2006 the Chinese government shut down a popular weekly review, *Bingdian* [*Freezing Point*]. The magazine's offense was printing a long analysis of Chinese middle school textbooks, a study that had been written by Yuan Weishi, a professor at Zhongshan University in Guangzhou. Yuan criticized the one-sided treatment of several nineteenth-century events that, in the official version, attributed all the fault to the foreign imperialists but that, in Yuan's view, were far more complicated than that. Yuan was particularly critical of the textbooks' version of the Boxer Uprising of 1900, viewing the Boxers solely as national heroes and anti-imperialist fighters. "But the textbooks," he wrote, "do not mention that the Boxers were hostile to modern civilization, that they cut down telephone lines, destroyed schools, demolished railroad tracks, and murdered foreigners."

Yuan went on to equate China's official treatment of this and other episodes to Japan's whitewashing of its own modern history, seeing both as crude attempts to inflame nationalist passions. And, for good measure, Yuan also drew a direct line from the Boxers of 1900 to the "violence," "xenophobia," "anti-imperialism," and "antiforeignism" of the Red Guards during Mao Zedong's Cultural Revolution in the 1960s and 1970s.[46]

Meanwhile, the government's own scholars still remain hard at work on the Qing dynasty history promised the country by 2012.

CHAPTER 5
THE PROLETARIAN DYNASTY OF CHAIRMAN MAO

Contemporary China's changing understanding of the country's modern history begins with Mao Zedong's proclamation of the People's Republic of China on October 1, 1949. Until not too long ago, it was the final destination of older historical interpretations and the point of departure for newer ones. Here was another cataclysm, not only in China's modern history but also in the history of the world, a great event among the other great events of the twentieth century. The victory of the Communist Party of China was unanticipated. The party had begun with a single cell in Shanghai in 1921. It had been paralyzed by endless intra-party disputes about doctrine and tactics. In 1927 it was driven deep underground by Chiang Kai-shek's (1887–1975) new national government. Its rural-based remnants were chased all over the country—the so-called Long March, in the party's official parlance—and it was only the full-scale invasion of China proper by the Japanese in 1937 that gave the party a new lease on life. When full-scale civil war resumed between the Nationalists and the Communists after the surrender of Japan in 1945, the Nationalists appeared to be by far the stronger combatant. Hence, their rapid collapse was unanticipated by the world at large.

In 1949 the administrative remnants of the Nationalist state, its army, and Chiang himself fled to Taiwan.

At the level of day-to-day politics in the United States, the explanations for this reversal of fortune quite naturally focused on the end game, the day-to-day maneuvering during and immediately after World War II and how it may have affected—or even actually *effected*—the Communists' victory. At the same time, sinologists and historians began combing through China's long history to find the People's Republic that had to have been gestating there for many centuries. How was it that China—the Middle Kingdom, isolationist, xenophobic, culturally imperious—had proved so receptive to the radical, and foreign, political ideology of Bolshevism? What did it mean to see great May Day parades in Beijing's Tiananmen Square that featured gigantic portraits, not only of Mao Zedong, but of conspicuously un-Chinese-looking men such as Marx, Engels, Lenin, and Stalin? And what about the totalitarian structure and methods of New China? Such questions required a new understanding of what it may have meant to be Chinese or even whether the new regime in Beijing was Chinese at all.

Throughout the first half of the twentieth century, well-intentioned Westerners thought they had found in China's long history many things that predisposed the country toward Western-style democracy—a focus on affairs familial and local, not national; Confucian governance, whose beau ideal of the public official was a cultivated man of letters; a political culture that disdained the military arts, teaching that "one did not make nails out of good iron, nor soldiers out of good men"; a growing cosmopolitan elite, Ivy League graduates fluent in English, able to use the post–World War I weapons of law and diplomacy to defend China's interests.

For one important example, as historian William Kirby has since pointed out, "the story of Chinese diplomacy in the Republican era is one of stunning accomplishments from a position of unbelievable weakness." The new republic had only the shakiest of titles to a huge piece of real estate. In fact, "no Chinese empire had been so big for so long as the Qing realm of the Manchus. The first decade of the twentieth century was full of portents of its dissolution. But the amazing fact of the Republican era is that this space was not only redefined as 'Chinese,' and as the sacred soil of China, but also defended diplomatically to such a degree that the borders of the PRC today are essentially those of the Qing, minus only Outer Mongolia. The Qing fell, but the empire remained. More accurately, the empire became the basis of the Chinese national state. This was perhaps the greatest accomplishment of Republican diplomacy."[1] Moreover, as Kirby points out, these men were also successful in recovering the country's internal sovereignty, so that Mao's New China inherited a state unencumbered by extraterritoriality and foreign concessions.

These were the same men who were China's face to the larger international community. Between 1912 and 1945 they had maintained an intricate pattern of international alliances and affiliations within a constantly shifting, and always dangerous, international environment. They had negotiated the agreements that recognized a weak and anarchic China as one of the world's major powers nonetheless—a veto-holding permanent member of the United Nations Security Council and a founding member of the General Agreement on Tariffs and Trade (the predecessor of today's World Trade Organization). Yet overnight, they had become adept at the peculiar international practices and even stranger jargon of the Soviet-led Communist World. How could this have happened?

New China's internal arrangements resembled those of Stalin's Soviet Union, leading to a search for the origins of what today we might call totalitarianism with Chinese characteristics. Chairman Mao had praised China's first emperor, and so his methods and philosophy in the third century BC became an obvious starting point. China's first unifier had embraced Legalism as his governing doctrine. Unlike the Confucians who embraced what might be called limited government, moral edification, and the training of a governing class of men whose high standards and proper conduct would inspire, not coerce, the Legalists were followers of the third-century BC political philosopher Hanfei, who had a much different outlook: "The intelligent ruler will use but two handles to control his ministers and two handles only. The two are chastisement and commendation. To inflict death or torture upon culprits is called chastisement; to bestow encouragements or rewards on men of merit is called commendation." The first emperor embraced this outlook to the point of ordering the burning of Confucian books and the burial alive of Confucian scholars.

The Western concept of Oriental Despotism, traceable to the way ancient Greeks distinguished their polity from that of the Persians, was also brought into play. The idea had figured conspicuously in G. F. W. Hegel's (1770–1831) views about the progress of history and, via Hegel, became influential in different stands of Marxism. Marx himself had once written of an Asiatic mode of production, neither wholly feudal nor wholly capitalist, as the characteristic mode of social organization of some Asian countries. This idea, in turn, got caught up in intra–Communist Party disputes and power struggles. Some of Stalin's critics used the term *Asiatic Society* to describe the bureaucratized collectivist police state he had actually established in Russia under the guise of socialism. Both the notion of an Asiatic mode of production and the subsequent controversies about it served also as the basis of bitter academic arguments about Agro-despotism and Hydraulic Society, concepts put forward by the German sinologist and historian Karl Wittfogel.[2] Wittfogel, himself a survivor of both Nazi imprisonment and intra-Socialist sectarianism, had thrown yet another apple of discord into the acrimonious ongoing debate about totalitarianism as such—whether Hitlerism and Stalinism were really the same thing; whether Chinese totalitarianism was the same thing as Soviet totalitarianism; indeed, whether either Stalin's Russia or Mao's China were totalitarian at all. In large part, of course, these high-toned academic stances were placeholders for political positions about the proper conduct of the Cold War.

The argument about the Chineseness of Mao's China also entered into an evaluation of its strategic outlook and foreign policies. Almost immediately, the new regime undertook what was essentially the reconquest of Xinjiang and Tibet, both of which had slipped into a loose relationship with Chiang Kai-shek's Nationalist government, otherwise occupied in its life-or-death war with Japan and, after that, in an equally fateful struggle with the Communists. Both Xinjiang Muslims and Tibetan Buddhists forcibly resisted liberation, which *they* understood as the imposition of Han Chinese dominance, pure and simple. Less than two years after its founding, the People's Republic intervened directly in the Korean War to save the otherwise-doomed North Korean regime of Kim Il-song (1912–1994), father of the current North Korean dictator, Kim Jong-il. After the truce in Korea was signed in 1953, New China stepped up its already important logistical and diplomatic support to the Communist Viet Minh, led by Ho Chi Minh, in a successful effort to end French rule in Indochina. New China also had close ties to a Communist insurgency in the Philippines; was conspiring with the Communist Party of Indonesia, leading to an audacious coup d'état attempt in 1965—"the year of living dangerously"—which led to the deaths of hundreds of thousands of ethnic Chinese; and had operational links to Communist organizations operating in Thailand, Burma, Laos, and Cambodia. Indeed, Maoism, as a doctrine, was the inspiration for the ideology of the murderous Khmer Rouge.

Why was China doing these things? Was it acting in concert with, or at least as the junior partner of, the Soviet Union? Was it asserting some uniquely *Chinese* national interest, hoping to revive what had once been China's dominance in Asia? Or was it asserting more of an ideological interest, a *Communist* one as such, or perhaps only a uniquely *Maoist* one? Some answers—but even more questions—soon appeared in the form of a statement from China's highest-ranking military official.

On September 1, 1965, then–Chinese minister of defense Lin Biao published a seminal article in the newspaper of the People's Liberation Army to mark the twentieth anniversary of Japan's defeat in World War II. Lin had been the commander of one of the PLA's four field armies and had commanded the decisive operations of the late 1940s in the north of the country that had led to the rapid collapse of the Nationalists. Lin would go on to be designated by name, in one version of New China's constitution, as "Chairman Mao's closest comrade-in-arms and his successor"—before dying under mysterious circumstances, perhaps in a 1971 airplane crash.

Entitled "Long Live the Victory of People's War!" Lin's article attributed the Communists' success in their war against the Nationalists and their decisive (in Lin's view) role in the defeat of Japan to the military theories of Mao Zedong. In developing concepts of People's War and Protracted War, Mao had, so Lin maintained, solved the problems of revolutionary strategy and tactics in a historical epoch dominated by the increasingly frantic (because it was doomed) actions of the imperialists on the one hand and the weak-kneed capitulationist stance of the Khrushchev revisionists in control of the Soviet Union.

But the article was to become renowned by offering China's prescription for the revolutionary transformation of non-Western societies and how that transformation could then be applied on a global scale to change fundamentally the world's balance of power. In a tribute to the Communist Party of China's establishment of its rule in China, Lin argued that just as China's peasants had surrounded their country's cities from the countryside, so too could a World Countryside of Maoist states surround the World City of advanced industrial societies and thereby initiate an entirely new era in world affairs. This was not a modest proposal. It was a grand design that placed New China at the center of the whole world, a world-transforming China, a China beyond the ambitions of even the most megalomaniacal of the great Chinese emperors. These prescriptions and prophecies had an electrifying effect. The world now had before it, to use some of the catch phrases of the day, "China's blueprint for world domination," "Mao's Mein Kampf . . . chilling and Orwellian."

The reactions were of different kinds. The first was Pekingological, that is, an analogue to Kremlinology. Pekingology was the term applied to the work of China watchers who were trying figure out what was going on inside the tightly sealed society of China, and the even more closed upper reaches of the Chinese government. Pekingology was an activity within the provenance of modern political science, not traditional sinology. A Pekingologist tended to see Lin's article as the tip of a political iceberg—the bulk of which was, by definition, invisible—but was thought to consist of some combination of bureaucratic and personal rivalries, intra-party debates, arguments about fundamental strategic policies, and disputes about doctrine and policy within the Communist International.

Lin's article appeared in September 1965; in December Pekingologists learned of the purge of the chief of staff of the People's Liberation Army (PLA), the hapless Luo Reiqing. General Luo, denounced as a traitor and a spy, was thought to be an advocate of a more modern approach to China's defenses, even an heir, one could say, to the maritime faction of the late nineteenth century. He looked toward the American buildup in and around Southeast Asia and was impressed, perhaps too impressed, so far as the continental faction of the PLA was concerned. This was also a time when China's relations with the Soviet Union were deteriorating much faster than its relations with the United States; a large Soviet military buildup in Central Asia, and also in the then-Soviet satellite of Outer Mongolia, had already begun. These presumed tensions inside China's military were of great interest to U.S. strategic and military planners, then trying to calculate the limits of Chinese tolerance for, and capability to thwart, growing American power in Southeast Asia.

There was also what may be called a sinological reaction, a search for the roots of Maoist doctrine in China's long political and cultural history. Since Mao was known to fancy classical Chinese strategic and military doctrine, there was a revival of interest in the Old Masters, especially Sunzi—born in the sixth century BC and, therefore, a contemporary of Confucius—and in Master Sun's canonical text, *The Art of War*. (Indeed, a generation later, the Sunzi revival shows no signs of abating, as the thought of the master has migrated from the general staffs, the military academies, and the war colleges into the business schools. "If Sun Tzu had been an entrepreneur, this book would have been written centuries ago," enthused one reviewer of a recent manual of business strategy.) There had been a translation of Sunzi's book back in 1910, done by the British diplomat Lionel Giles (son of Herbert Giles, himself a British diplomat, known for his translations of Chinese literary classics, for helping to devise the then-prevalent romanization system for Chinese, and for holding the chair of China studies at Cambridge University). The first translation by a man of military background, retired Marine Corps general Samuel Griffith, did not appear until 1963.

Until then, Master Sun's epigrammatic and aphoristic text had seemed remote from actual military problems; now it seemed to be a key to unlocking the very modern military doctrines of Mao Zedong. Sinology also had something to contribute to yet another then-popular mode of conflict analysis, game theory. The games in the West were derived mostly from economics and were purported to be useful in analyzing approaches to high-stakes decision making and negotiations, such as those involving strategic nuclear weapons and intercontinental ballistic missiles.

But strategists and mathematicians interested in China soon became fascinated by a different game, a board game called *weiqi*, the same game known in Japan as *go*. The game is played on a grid, and the players vie to control territory on the board by placing their pieces, or stones, in slowly unfolding patterns, the final shape of which is not supposed to be readily apparent. Unlike the pieces in chess, the stones are of equal power, and the art of victory inheres in devising strategies of encirclement, and then counterencirclement, of the opponent's stones. The winner is the player who ends up controlling the most territory. It was widely bruited that Mao Zedong liked to play it.

In 1969 Scott A. Boorman published *The Protracted Game: A Wei-Ch'i Interpretation of Maoist Revolutionary Strategy*. Boorman was much more than a hobbyist. His book was based on an undergraduate thesis at Harvard. (One of his teachers was Thomas Schelling, a pioneer who linked economics and game theory to diplomatic bargaining and nuclear strategy; for this work he would belatedly receive the Nobel Prize in Economics in 2005.) Boorman's impressions of China had been shaped by occasional collaboration with his father, Howard Boorman, himself highly regarded for organizing and editing the three-volume *Biographical Dictionary of Republican China* (1967, 1968, 1970).

In an analytical tour de force, the younger Boorman contrasted a series of *weiqi* grids with maps of China at different times to argue that the moves of the Communist forces reflected sound *wieqi* strategy, analogous to the way a master of the game might deploy his stones. In doing this Boorman was also building on views of Chinese national character and Chinese strategy that he and his father had previously put forward:

> Chinese strategy is pre-eminently manipulative. Western strategy is
> chiefly mechanistic. Although oversimplified, this dichotomy symbolizes

a fundamental defining characteristic of Chinese national character: the contrast between the direct and the indirect approach to conflict resolution. Chinese military strategy, for example, seeks to manipulate an entire set of variables left almost untouched by its Western counterpart: the enemy commander's mind, his self-image, his face; the view of the situation and of its objective potentialities; the psychology of the opposing army; and so on. By contrast, Western strategic thought is far more oriented to the objective situation: given such and such troops, such and such road conditions, and such and such deployments, we can concentrate our forces at point P to annihilate enemy unit Q and break through the position.[3]

Here then, in a succinct statement, was the summation of the case for the Chineseness of China's strategy, for the need to understand its particularities, not its conformity to some universally true set of strategic principles.

At the same time, it was also possible to represent Maoist strategic behavior as connected both to China's own traditions and to strategic traditions in the West. For example, Alistair Iain Johnston's analysis of Mao's strategy—his penchant for violence, for the offensive, for his oft-stated conviction that violence is the final arbiter of conflict, for his famous aphorism that "political power grows out of the barrel of a gun"—cannot be surprising to either a Chinese or a Westerner. "The predominant Chinese strategic tradition does not differ radically from key elements in the Western *realpolitik* tradition. Indeed, the Chinese case might be classified as a hard *realpolitik* one, sharing many of the same tenets about the nature of the enemy and the efficacy of violence."[4]

Yet, figuring out how analyses like these could be applied in the real world to the actual conduct of diplomacy and war was more a task for the sinologist than for the political scientist, who could be called on to address actual Chinese behavior at a more human level. In this respect, the requisite data were more apt to be found in the subtleties of Chinese literature, philosophy, and art than in the hypotheses of social science. About this time, for example, when it was thought that much could be learned from a China-specific game of strategy, Westerners became aware that one of Asia's homegrown literary geniuses had written a tour de force that used a famous game of *go*, one that had actually been played in 1938, as a metaphor not only for the vicissitudes of personal life but also as a rumination on the rise and fall of nations.

The great Japanese writer Kawabata Yasunari's (1899–1972) acclaimed 1954 novel, *The Master of Go*, appeared in English translation in 1972. Kawabata had won the Nobel Prize for Literature in 1968, which gave the book a reception in the United States that it otherwise would not have had. The novel is based on an actual event, the last game played by a venerable *go* master against the most formidable of the younger players in the country. After a contest that took six months to complete, the older master was finally defeated, and he died about a year later.

The novel's verisimilitude originates in the fact that Kawabata had been working as a journalist in the late 1930s and had covered the epic contest as a reporter. Its appeal derives from its evanescence, its fatalistic brooding that the old must give way to the new, and the decrepit to the vigorous. For Kawabata himself, and for his Japanese readers, the story had an allegorical aspect as well, for it was also to be read as an account of Japan's defeat in World War II, a country worn down after a needlessly prolonged exercise in futility. And yet the central figures remain the players themselves, their stoicism and stamina, their capacity still to see nuance in an ancient game and, therefore, the possibility of hitherto unused ploys, even after centuries of play.

For Westerners interested in understanding how this same ancient game might inform the strategic behavior of Mao Zedong's Rising China, it was more than merely a peek into the mindset of actual players. And in a few simple but elegant sentences, a master of prose captured the appeal of the strategic game both to spectator and player alike. "In the world of competitive games, it seems to be the way of the spectator to build up heroes beyond their actual powers. Pitting equal adversaries against each other arouses interest of the sort, but is not the hope really for a nonpareil? 'The Invincible Master' towered over the board. There had been numerous battles on which the Master had staked his destiny, and he had not lost one of them. The results of the contests before he gained the title may have been determined by accidents and shifting currents. But after he became the Master, the world believed he could not lose, and he had to believe it himself."[5]

Perhaps this explains why the metaphor of China's strategy as a game of *weiqi* writ large is so powerful and enduring. It may lie dormant for a while, but it is there to be revived in periods of anxiety about China's intentions toward the rest of the world. It was one of the ways we in the West tried to decrypt the operational code of Maoist strategy during the first twenty or so years of the People's Republic—until the improvements in China–United States relations that began with President Richard Nixon's 1972 visit to Beijing. But now there is another Rising China, one that purports to adhere to a course of Peaceful Rise, not one of People's War. Is there an essential Chineseness that connects them?

Meanwhile sinology, again trying to hold its own against the onslaught of the social sciences, opened another front in the debate over the Chinese-ness of Maoist strategy. This was an effort to connect the ethos of Maoism to an old Chinese literary tradition, the vernacular novel. Of these, four stood out as "the extraordinary ones," all of them written during the late Ming era. Of these, two were relevant, one known as *The Romance of the Three Kingdoms*, the other known in English by three different titles—*The Water Margin*, or *The Outlaws of the Marsh*, or *All Men Are Brothers*—depending upon the translator's preference.

The *Three Kingdoms* is set in the Three Kingdoms period, AD the third century, when the Han dynasty was crumbling. The story is near-incomprehensibly complicated as the rivalry for power is played out. One of the major heroes of the novel is Zhuge Liang, a wily strategist and itinerant counselor of warfare—a latter-day Sunzi, if you will. The literary scholar Andrew Plaks gives us a fine summary of the novel as repertoire of Chinese warfare in that day, the way of war celebrated in Mao Zedong's military writings: "preliminary skirmishes, confrontation of armies in full battle ar-ray, a whole range of more crafty acts of war—ambushes, surprise raids, defections, holing up in fortresses, laying of sieges, burning of supply de-pots, and even more devious types of stratagems: fake surrender, counterfeit messages, luring the enemy with beautiful women."[6]

Another literary scholar, Andrew West, has expanded understanding of the role this novel has played as a practical guide to warfare in China by describing how the Manchus, in their earliest years in Beijing, arranged for a translation of the *Three Kingdoms* from Chinese into their own Manchu language. Indeed, the translation was considered a matter of great impor-tance in the Qing court, and it appeared in 1650, six years after the Manchus officially proclaimed their dynasty in 1644, but years before securing their nationwide grip on the Mandate of Heaven.

West speculates that the Manchus did this because they wanted to iden-tify themselves with rebels against bad government—a fine Chinese tradi-tion—the better to legitimize their own replacement of the Ming dynasty. In any case the translation of the novel was given priority even over the translation of the Confucian classics as a way of demonstrating the Man-chus' respect for things Chinese. The decree that ordered the work main-tained that "this book can serve as a model of exemplary conduct for loyal subjects, righteous worthies, filial sons, and chaste women. It can also serve as a warning against treacherous subjects who harm their country, and bad government which leads to disorder." Because the book was also a primer in military tactics, it was useful to the Manchus in analyzing popular resistance against them and devising means of overcoming it.[7]

The Water Margin, unlike the *Three Kingdoms*, is peopled not with the high and mighty contesting for control of the state, but with outcasts and outlaws, organized into sworn brotherhoods, living in another chaotic time of transition, this one between the collapse of the Song dynasty in the thirteenth century and the consolidation of the power of the alien Yuan. That *The Water Margin* would come to be seen as Socialist realism before its time was made almost inevitable by the title, *All Men Are Brothers*, that Pearl Buck gave to her translation of the work in 1948. Buck, recipient of the Nobel Prize for Literature in 1938, though not widely read now, was once the best-known interpreter of China in the English-reading world. In her understanding of the centuries-long appeal of traditional Chinese fiction, *Three Kingdoms* and *Water Margin* were joined together.

As for *The Water Margin*, it was not for nothing, as she said in her 1938 Nobel lecture—years before the novel would be thought to offer insight into New China—that "the Chinese Communists printed their own edition of it with a preface by a famous Communist and have issued it anew as the first Communist literature of China. The proof of the novel's greatness is in this timelessness. It is as true today as it was dynasties ago. The people of China still march across its pages, priests and courtesans, merchants and scholars, women good and bad, old and young, and even naughty little boys."

And, she continued:

If *Shui Hu Chuan* [i.e., *The Water Margin*] has importance today as a novel of the people in their struggle for liberty, *San Kuo* [i.e., *The Romance of the Three Kingdoms*] has importance because it gives in such detail the science and art of war as the Chinese conceive it, so differently, too, from our own. The guerillas, who are today China's most effective fighting units against Japan, are peasants who know *San Kuo* by heart, if not from their own reading, at least from hours spent in the idleness of winter days or long summer evenings when they sat listening to the storytellers describe how the warriors of the Three Kingdoms fought their battles. It is these ancient tactics of war which the guerillas trust today. What a warrior must be and how he must attack and retreat, how retreat when the enemy advances, how advance when the enemy retreats—all this had its source in this novel, so well known to every common man and boy of China.[8]

In hindsight, we can recognize different layers of meaning in this statement. In the context of the world crisis of the 1930s, it is reassurance from a renowned American sinophile that the Chinese revolutionary movement is a homegrown phenomenon, not some foreign—that is, Russian—import. On the eve of war between the United States and Japan, a war brought on by Japanese aggression in China, it is an appeal to enlist the Chinese Communists as an effective ally with deep popular support. Ten years before the defeat of Nationalists on the Chinese mainland, it is the seed of the prediction that, sooner or later, the innate Chineseness of China will assert itself, and that China will not long remain a passive satellite of Soviet Russia. For grand strategists around the world in the 1960s and 1970s, it is a basic and reassuring conclusion that, for all its international pretensions, Maoist global strategy is self-limiting, not at all cosmopolitan, but irredeemably provincial.

Some of these propositions received a fair test, others not. The Southeast Asian wars of the 1960s and 1970s were thought at the time to be important test cases, but in the end, changes in China's domestic and foreign policies after the death of Mao in 1976 deprived them of their educative value. Under serious duress, the United Sates withdrew from Vietnam in 1975, but some of the dire strategic consequences that some had predicted dissolved amid China's reversal of alliances. It turned against its former Vietnamese ally, and this so-called third Indochina war—"the last Maoist war," in Edward C. O'Dowd's phrase—went on from 1978 until 1991. In February 1979 China sent four hundred thousand soldiers into northern Vietnam in order "to teach Vietnam a lesson," as Deng Xiaoping put it. Such instruction was made necessary because of nothing less than "Vietnamese aggression" against neighboring Cambodia, an ironic use of a phrase that the United States had used to justify in part its own military actions against the Vietnamese Communists.

But the People's Liberation Army did not acquit itself well. It suffered substantial losses, and this short punitive expedition's main political objective—forcing a Vietnamese withdrawal from Cambodia—remained unfulfilled. For years there was sporadic cross-border artillery firing and yet another movement of PLA forces into Northern Vietnam in 1984. This was not the only irony. Just as China's Vietnamese younger brothers seemed to have surpassed their Chinese tutors in the tactics of a people's war, its governing doctrine and Grand Strategy had become an antique, as the United States and China found themselves on the same side in maintaining a balance of power on the Southeast Asian mainland.

What had happened to the feared fighting force that had driven the Americans back from the Yalu on the North Korea–China border, crushed a pro-independence Tibetan guerrilla movement, humiliated the Indian army in 1962 (a trauma from which it has still not recovered), inspired insurrectionists and insurgents throughout the Third World, and held Europe's political philosophers and social theorists in thrall? In Edward O'Dowd's view, the decline began in 1959 when Lin Biao became defense minister, and accelerated thereafter as he and Mao came increasingly to believe in the military efficacy of their political doctrine. As a consequence, "the PLA had been rendered hopelessly ineffectual by the military policies of the Maoist era. . . . The 'Maoist detour' ended in the 1980s, when it became clear that the PLA was incapable of aiding China to achieve its strategic objectives in the Third Indochina War. Real military modernization finally could begin."[9]

The backsliding, when it began, unfolded just as the great Lenin knew it would: "He who says *A* must say *B*," he once had said. The failures of Maoist military theory in actual practice triggered an avalanche; the structural reforms of China's economy that began after Mao's death withdrew the country from the Socialist camp and placed it in the mainstream of international capitalist development. In 1989 the Soviet satellites in Europe also joined in, and finally the Soviet Union itself collapsed in 1991. The world's thinking about China had to adjust to the fact that communism as such no longer mattered, that what we had before us was "socialism with Chinese characteristics," and it was the particulars, the ineffable Chineseness of the place, that we now needed to ponder.

For all of this, it is useful to understand how the High Maoist era, like others in China's history, may have entered into China's strategic tradition. The place to begin is with the nature of China's armed forces, whether they can ever become wholly professional so long as the ruling Communist Party is in essence a Leninist one, as China's still is today. Lin Biao put the case most clearly that, in a state so governed, the army worked for the party, and not for anybody else:

> The essence of Comrade Mao Tse-tung's theory of army building is that in building a people's army prominence must be given to politics, i.e., the army must first and foremost be built on a political basis. Politics is the

commander, politics is the soul of everything. Political work is the lifeline of our army. True, a people's army must pay attention to the constant improvement of its weapons and equipment and its military technique, but in its fighting it does not rely purely on weapons and technique, it relies mainly on politics, on the proletarian revolutionary consciousness and courage of the commanders and fighters, on the support and backing of the masses. . . . All this makes the people's army led by the Chinese Communist Party fundamentally different from any bourgeois army.[10]

Invoking the jargon of his time, Lin also described a template for organizing the world against the major imperialist power—1960s jargon for the United States—not yet the sole superpower of 1990s jargon that it would become: "The peoples of the world invariably support each other in their struggles against imperialism and its lackeys. Those countries which have won victory are duty bound to support and aid the peoples who have not yet done so."[11]

Are there echoes of this nostrum in China's backing of Milosevic of Serbia, or Saddam of Iraq, or Kim of North Korea, or Mugabe of Zimbabwe, or the generals of Burma/Myanmar—a cast of characters well outside the boundaries of polite society? And if it be strategic *weiqi* that is being played by Beijing, what are the implications of the stones China has put down in Sudan, Iran, Tanzania, and Venezuela? Organizing the World Countryside may no longer be the strategy of choice, but do not Africa and Latin America still comprise the soft underbelly of the world's hegemon?

At the end of the twentieth century, Americans seemed to have the satisfaction of knowing that things in China had turned out to their liking and in accord with their preferences: the Radicals had been routed; the Pragmatists were in control; China had opened itself to the world; China was now at last a Great Power, vindicating President Franklin Roosevelt's preferred architecture for the United Nations at the end of World War II. America and Americans could now contemplate the pleasures of living with answered prayers.

CHAPTER 6

THE HISTORY OF THE WORLD AS CHINA'S OWN

For centuries the West has had a stake in China's struggles about its political culture and its mode of governance. In particular, the West believed that a triumph in China by one or another of its major religious or political creeds would tip the balance of power in the world. Thus, in the sixteenth century, Catholic missionaries sought the conversion of China not only in the interests of the Middle Kingdom's lost souls but also in the interest of Christianity as a whole; a Christian China, if one could be brought about, would be the decisive factor in Christianity's worldwide struggle with Islam. Within the Christian tradition itself, the rivalry between Catholicism and Protestantism was, for a while, thought to hinge on which variant of Christian teaching would gain the upper hand in China.

The same was true for the West's secular creeds. In the seventeenth and eighteenth centuries European sinophiles saw in China an enlightened despotism based on right reason that might inspire, and also bolster, the same thing in the West. Later on, Western liberals, Socialists, and Communists believed that the conversion of China to one or another of their creeds would tip the world's ideological and political balance entirely. Lenin himself is supposed to have said that "the road to Paris lies through Peking"; so the prediction that the conversion of China to Bolshevism would shake the entire world was hardly Mao Zedong's invention. In the event, the world took seriously the implications of Mao's call for a new world order based on a kind of Sino-Leninism. Today, with the seeming conversion of China to a belief in open trade and market economics, there is a new situation: for the first time in a long time, the principal countries of the world appear not to be separated by the ideological differences so prominent and dangerous in the twentieth century. And the mere adoption of one or another of the Western creeds by Chinese is but the beginning of a story, for both the introduction of Christianity in the nineteenth century and of communism in the twentieth produced results that neither Western churchmen nor Russian Bolsheviks very much liked.

Thus this book, which can be described as a hypothetical history of the future, is informed repeatedly by these cautionary tales. And Americans are not the only ones who have had disappointments to ponder. Chinese who had sought the collapse of their own imperial system and who thought the solution to their country's problems lay in emulating the great Western nations of the nineteenth century were profoundly shaken by the political, moral, intellectual, and spiritual destruction that was World War I. After that, many Chinese believed that their country's salvation lay in emulating a great rising power of the twentieth century—the anti-West, that is, the Soviet Union. In the twenty-first century, China appears to be betting its future on emulating the anti–Soviet Union, that is, the United States. But what will be the fate of American-inspired and American-led globalization and how will China be affected?

The world has an important interest in how China poses this question to itself and in the methodology it uses to arrive at an answer. China once interpreted its own past in the light of yesterday's failures, but now it is coming to a new appreciation of its past in the light of today's successes. Thus, the past itself will have a future: to speculate about that future is to assess Rising China's sense of the world in which it now finds itself. Just as a century ago, when China had difficulty in understanding what the West called world history and China's place in it, the need to make sense of those same things still exists today. The difference—and it is an important difference—is that today's China is not in mortal danger and thus has the luxury of a more leisurely examination of its prospects. But even without the sense of existential threat, the intellectual competition among interpretations and schools of thought is no less intense, and its outcome no more predictable, than it was a century ago.

The critically important event of the Late Qing period was the abolition, in 1905, of the centuries-old Confucian examination system. For centuries the civil service examinations, the sole route into the leadership, had required mastery of a curriculum of the classics, properly interpreted. But the value of such a classical education, once the way to wealth, power, and prestige, came to an end in Late Qing times, and the habits and institutions that it had propped up reached the end of their useful life.

In this respect the end of the examination system in 1905 was the single most important milestone in China's journey from the imperial to the modern. As no one other thing could, it ratified what had become a painful consensus among thoughtful people in China and throughout the entire Chinese world: a new intellectual regime, already under construction but not yet completed, would have to consolidate its power before the country's recovery of national power could begin in earnest. In the century since then the struggle over what would replace what Benjamin Elman described in *A Cultural History of Civil Examinations in Late Imperial China* as the "cultural regime that had thrived in its imperial form since 1450" would determine the shape of everything else that has happened. The struggle over the future of China's cultural regime can be viewed from different and diverse points of view. Activities as varied as new ways of studying history, or of writing fiction, or of designing and building cities are contributing to the creation of China's visions.

One useful place to begin is with Liang Qichao (1872–1929), the most brilliant and the most formidable public intellectual of his time, and certainly one of the most important men of his era. In the 1890s he was one of China's leading advocates of reform and was forced into a fourteen-year exile in 1899. During that time, Liang Qichao traveled throughout the world—he met once with President Theodore Roosevelt—but he spent most of his time outside China in Japan. Headquartered in Yokohama, he established several Chinese-language journals, which he used not only to rouse China's national consciousness against the then-reigning Manchus but also to introduce the Chinese-reading world to the latest developments in the political and intellectual life of the Western world. He became the single most influential Chinese reformist writer of his day. In his personal politics, Liang began as a constitutional monarchist, but he then had an important role in the new Republic of China. His reputation survived the brutal ideological combat of the twentieth century, and he remains an icon. In the view of Andrew Nathan, a scholar of the evolution of democratic politics in China, Liang Qichao was the intellectual godfather of the program of most pro-democracy political reformers—even those inside China's Communist Party since the late 1970s, including its now-legendary general secretary Hu Yaobang (1915–1989).[1]

Of particular importance is the enormous influence Liang Qichao exerted over the study and writing of Chinese history. In 1902 he published "The New Historiography," a six-part article. He argued for a new historiography, he said, because the new citizens he wanted to help create in China needed one. The new historiography involved a recasting of many subjects, including traditional Chinese approaches to geography, science, literature, and literary criticism. In its simplest rendition, it was a call for China to study the nations of the world so as to understand China's own place in the world, because world history had now come to supersede any one national history.

Liang himself was a polymath of the sort produced every so often by Confucian training, and over time he would change his mind about the methodology and the direction of the new historiography that he advocated. He was a man of great intellectual and physical energy, for the range of his interests and the sheer quantity of his writing were enormous. His prodigious output bespoke his interest in a larger cultural reform—of which the new historiography was to be but one part. For one example, one of the journals he founded was called *New Fiction*, and years before many of his compatriots he called for a literary revolution that would produce Chinese fiction engaged in the ongoing problems of the country. He translated Jules Verne's 1888 adventure novel *Two Years' Vacation* into Chinese. His own failures as a political reformer, Liang once said, had led him to call for a grand rethinking of fundamental Chinese ideas about almost everything.

In this respect Liang Qichao believed that China was indeed in need of a cultural revolution, but of a complex kind. Thus early in his career he wrote to introduce his countrymen to a wide range of Western political thinking and translated several of its canonical texts. He wrote biographies of four nineteenth-century European state builders—the Hungarian Louis Kossuth and the Italians Giuseppe Mazzini, Giuseppe Garibaldi, and Camillo di Cavour. As the twentieth century began, he argued that China should fit its own history into what today's historians now call the enlightenment narrative—that is, an interpretation of the history of the world that argues for the universality of Western values. But by the 1920s Liang would become more interested in what contemporary jargon would term the particularities of China's experience. In this he would be expressing China's post–World War I disillusionment with much of modern thinking about culture, society, and politics. The great Western empires had collapsed and, with them, the credibility of many of the ideas associated with them.

Along with his work as historian, literary critic, and advocate for literary renovation, Liang also tried his hand at writing novels. In 1902, even as he was at work on other projects, he published a political novel, *The Future of New China*, that began with a description of the prosperous China of 1960, sixty years hence. As the literary historian and critic David Der-wei Wang describes it, "the first scene depicts a lecture given by a descendant of Confucius in the seventy-second generation to an enthusiastic crowd of thousands, including students from all over the world. The novel continues on as an instructional political treatise where the virtues of various modes of government are lucidly debated."

Wang also tells us that Liang had intended to write a trilogy, imagining different outcomes for China, based on how these arguments might resolve themselves.

> One volume, to be called *The Future of Old China*, was to describe a dysfunctional China that had refused to change and, in the final volume, *New Peach Blossom Spring*, Liang planned to describe how the descendents of a group of exiled Chinese who, two centuries earlier, had established a flourishing society on an island, return to China and help reconstruct it. . . . The trilogy, of course, was never written; even *The Future of New China* comes to a sudden stop in chapter 5. . . . We know its beginning all at once, but not the middle part that would have bridged the beginning and the ending. . . . The future appears as a magical moment that stands at the other end of history.[2]

Somehow or other, the brilliant and patriotic Liang Qichao wanted China to end up as one of the great nations of the world, but as both a political thinker and novelist, he was stymied about how to get there.

Despite its truncated form, *The Future of New China* inspired other novels, akin to scenarios about the future of China. One such was *New China*, by Lu Shi-e, published in 1910. In David Der-wei Wang's description, "The novel depicts its narrator's visit to China in 1950, a prosperous China in every aspect. Advanced industries have long been established; universities are thriving everywhere; women enjoy equal rights; and Tibet has become a province. To the citizens of this 'new China' the social evils of old China sound like nothing but fiction; the only problem that besets them is a surplus of national wealth."[3]

Even better, and also more intriguing from the contemporary Chinese perspective, is Biheguan Zhuren's *New Era*, published in 1908. Once again, Wang's description is worth citing in extenso:

> Set in the year 1999, the novel starts with a panoramic view of China as the supreme world power. By the end of the century, we are told, China will have long been a constitutional monarchy. Central and local parliaments are functioning well; parties with different political platforms are free to express their ideas. . . . Advancements in science and technology have prompted China's triumphant return to its erstwhile world supremacy. Its total population amounts to one trillion. China is no longer an old, decaying, oriental empire, but a new potential "yellow peril" (*huanghuo*) with the power to dominate Western countries. . . .
>
> The core of the novel is a world war. . . . As the war develops, Chinese immigrant workers establish their own country in the western part of the United States. . . . They seize the Panama Canal, a move that shakes the American government to seek an alliance with the European forces against China. . . . Chinese workers in Australia also form their own nation. Upon learning that their other country is waging a war with the Western powers, Chinese from all five continents pledge their loyalty by joining the Chinese troops. . . .
>
> Combat between China and the Europeans takes place somewhere near the Suez Canal. . . . As the war continues, the battlefield moves to the Indian Ocean, then to the Red Sea, and finally to the Adriatic off the coast of Italy. . . . In its epic scale the novel is a maritime version of the Mongol conquest of Europe. Newly invented weapons replace magic tricks. . . . Besides balloons and submarines, which are represented as common military vehicles, the author introduces more than twenty new inventions, such as marine sensors, torpedo detectors, amphibious shoes, high-powered telescopes, electricity repellant clothing, radioactive dust, bullet-proof satin, and various poisonous gases.[4]

In the end, in a decisive battle at sea, a Chinese fleet defeats a European fleet by setting it ablaze. Wang highlights this particular scene's resemblance to a famous episode in *The Romance of the Three Kingdoms*, where an enemy's fleet also meets a fiery doom: *"New Era's* future war is a strange recapitulation of the war in the second century, which decided China's fate for the next century."

In the novelist's mind, science fiction, science fantasy, futuristic literature, vernacular classics, political imagination, geopolitics, strategic planning, and grand designs can all somehow be brought together in one satisfying conclusion. Yet, as Wang emphasizes, "between present and future there is a mysterious time span in which everything about China has been reversed; between now and then, *something* will transform China from a declining empire into a superpower. . . . China's metamorphosis presupposes a marvelous, invisible time machine, capable of turning present things into everything they are not. . . . There is a mysterious gap between the present and the future, and how to imagine the future hinges both on how we look at the present and how we evaluate the past."[5]

That mysterious gap, of course, was to be filled up by the events of the twentieth century. Liang Qichao joined in the practical work of government, serving as minister of finance and as minister of justice in some of the new republic's early, and ineffectual, cabinets. It was a chaotic era, featuring a failed attempt at imperial restoration, a failed attempt by leader of the republican movement Sun Yat-sen to expand his authority, the devolution of political power into the hands of local warlords, and a host of foreign policy problems brought on by World War I. It was, as historian James Sheridan has written, a time when some of the most formative events in modern Chinese history took place. "It was during those years that young China repudiated Confucianism, that Chinese anti-imperialism entered a more intense phase, that the Literary Revolution occurred, that Marxism was introduced into China on a significant scale, that the Communist Party was established and the Kuomintang [Nationalist Party] reorganized, and that Chinese social disintegration accelerated."[6]

Liang Qichao was a member of China's delegation to the Versailles Peace Conference in 1919. The first casualty was China's high regard for Japan as a model for modernization. Japan had inspired Liang, Sun Yat-sen, and many others, and it had also served as China's most important tutor in Western ideas and practices. But Japan was now no longer a friend and an inspiration, but a predator. Similarly, liberal internationalism and international law, which China was supposed to adopt as a replacement for its inherited concept of the world order, turned out not to serve China's interests either; instead, they were used to shore up the West's privileged position inside China.

As Liang traveled widely in post–World War I Europe, what he saw there was a blow to his intellectual self-confidence. As Xiaobing Tang, Liang's most recent biographer, describes it, "contrary to his previous belief in the positive influence of modern intellectual constructs, Liang now evaluated the major social theories and ideologies of nineteenth century Europe far more critically. Liberalism did help to accelerate political reform and economic development, but it also planted the seeds of social disaster for the future."[7]

In his account of his post–World War I stay in Europe, *Excerpts from Impressions of Travels in Europe*, Liang focused especially on the advance of science and the speed of change that characterized modernity and globalization in their early twentieth-century manifestations:

> As a result of the development of science, the organization of industrial production underwent fundamental innovation. Changes were carried out at such a fast speed, and also on such a large scale, that people were always and everywhere at a loss when they tried to make their inner life agree with their outer life. The most obvious example is the drastically opposing ways in which urban life in the present and village life from before are experienced.[8]

In this respect Europe's early twentieth century surely foreshadows China's early twenty-first, and Tang's summary of Liang's encounter with then-modern Europe can serve as a primer, an introduction to what we will find in China today:

> The alienating urban landscape appeared to Liang to be most symptomatic of the modern malaise for a number of reasons: aggregation of a large population throws together people connected not by emotional affinity but by a mere relationship of interest; the inevitable disappearance of landed property gives rise to a sense of perpetual uncertainty and rootlessness; the fluctuation and complexity of social situations demand strenuous attention and lead to mental fatigue and weariness; work and diversion follow upon each other at dizzying speed and therefore both are depleted of any pleasure; and finally, with the public's desire continually stimulated, consumer goods keep getting more expensive and the competition for survival even fiercer.
>
> The disconnection between a fast-shifting public "outer life" and a weakened private "inner life" causes much anomie and anxiety. . . . The emphasis placed on constant change has raised the issue of political and cultural legitimacy. . . .

"New authority" [Liang wrote] has difficulty establishing itself, and yet old authority is abolished beyond restoration. Consequently, the entire society is thrown into skepticism, despair, and fear, just as a ship without a compass caught in a storm and enshrouded with a heavy fog at the same time. No one has any idea of what the future will be like.... The Europeans have had an enormous dream about the omnipotence of science, and now they begin to decry its bankruptcy.[9]

Until his death in 1929, Liang elaborated a political program of his own for the new Republic of China. It resembled what we would think of as moderate or democratic socialism within a strong parliamentary system, an altogether reasonable response from a reasonable man to the problems of his day. Even so, Liang's description of Europe's disintegration prophesied China's future. Modernity itself had separated politically into the opposing camps of Wilson and Lenin and had divided economically into the competing systems of capitalism and communism; culturally, modernity more than merely divided; it shattered. Whether by deep structural cause or only by emulation, China splintered in the same way, and its opposing camps also spent decades fighting viciously among themselves for supremacy.

Attentive Chinese of every political and philosophical stripe were affected by the collapse of the nineteenth century's version of the modern and the global. Some changed their opinions; others became more confident in the ones they held. Thus, while those who had rejected the traditional way now fought among themselves to decide what modern was supposed to mean, the traditionalists and the unreconstructed Confucians, who had resisted the new cultural and educational consensus represented by the abolition of the centuries-old imperial examination system in 1905, felt their predictions had been confirmed. They, too, entered the post–World War I debate. They argued that China, having mindlessly aped the West, had overcommitted itself to things Western and was now itself falling apart as the West was.

A leader of these so-called traditionalists or neo-Confucianists, Liang Shuming (1893–1988) felt emboldened enough to assert the universality not of Western values but of Confucian ones. "I see the pitiful condition of the Westerners who, desiring spiritual restoration, are running all over searching.... Should I not guide them to the path of Confucius? I also see Chinese slavishly imitating the shallowness of the West and some of them mistakenly studying Buddhism.... Should I not guide them to the best and most beautiful of lives, the Confucian one?" Indeed, Liang believed that Western culture had played out its role and that "future world culture will be a revival of Chinese culture. . . . Humankind will turn from an epoch of material want to one of spiritual unrest." This, he was convinced, would produce "a decisive basic change for Western culture, which would follow completely the Chinese road."[10]

As we now know, things in both the East and West were to get far worse before they got better. The dilemma of modernity became a triangular battle involving the seemingly overmatched liberal followers of Wilson, Hitler's following throughout almost all of Europe, not merely in Germany (and in Latin America, the Middle East, and Asia also), and Stalin's following, one even wider than that. China's twentieth-century political history was a proximate analogue; even as these doctrines acquired "Chinese characteristics" they would lose nothing of their virulence.

These divisions have now receded, and a more benign understanding of modernity has appeared today, not so very different from the late nineteenth- and early twentieth-century version. It is a consensus, but is it only an interim one? If we look forward from the Late Qing era of the 1890s, we are pointed toward a globalism and a modernity of stability, peace, progress, and philosophical and cultural homogeneity. But if we look backward from the early Republican period of the 1920s, we see a failed globalization scheme and a discredited modernity.

Leaders in Rising China must decide in which direction they are pointed at the beginning of the twenty-first century. For that, they will need once again to begin with the study of world history as it is understood in their own time and with the study of China's own history, a history that is increasingly the product of a new historiography, still in progress.

CHAPTER 7

CHINA'S CONTINENT AND THE WORLD CITY

One of China's greatest and far-reaching discoveries in the nineteenth century was that the world was no longer what it had once been thought to be. China was hardly alone in having to readjust its most basic sense of things, for this was a problem for the entire non-Western world. The West had also gone through similar conceptual crises, and the world history that the West presented to the world in the nineteenth century was just the latest iteration in a long series.

Classical historians such as Herodotus, Thucydides, Polybius, Livy, and others had developed a sense of what belonged in the world and what did not, and whether the story of any one great nation or empire was the story of everything, or only a part. Judeo-Christian historians understood history and its purposes as the unfolding of God's plan for all human beings and, therefore, for the entire world. Historians during the Renaissance revived Europe's interest in their classical predecessors and used their accounts of Greek and Roman times as manuals of instruction for the conduct of then-modern politics. At the same time, the geography of history expanded enormously as Europe established new relations with empires and cultures all over the world. The world history of Jewish prophets, Greek and Roman historians, Christian theologians, and Renaissance writers grew to incorporate what we now know as the world, including a New World that became linked to the rest of it during the sixteenth century.

The West's sense of the world changed once again as ideas about the Enlightenment and Progress began to inform the West's study of its own history and the world's history. The enormous shift in the world's balance of power during the nineteenth century seemed to validate the West's ways of thinking and acting, and the globalization of the early twentieth century imagined world history as only a further elaboration of the then-regnant political and philosophical order. But then World War I put such notions to rest, making it seem that teleology—the purposeful direction of world history—needed a thorough re-examination. World history thus became the provenance not only of historians but of writers, theologians, philosophers, sociologists, and artists. Generally speaking, the optimism of the nineteenth century was superseded by a gloomier outlook, sometimes called Spenglerian, after Germany's Oswald Spengler (1880–1936), author of a hugely influential book, *The Decline of the West* (1918). Even so, world history remained a popular topic, and practitioners of it—like Britain's Arnold Toynbee (1889–1975), author of a twelve-volume history of the world that appeared between 1925 and 1961—could become world-renowned celebrities for a while, before disappearing into now near-total obscurity.

The historian who best embodies the link between that bygone era in the understanding of world history and today's understanding of the same words is the American (though Canadian-born) William H. McNeill (b. 1917). McNeill began working on a one-volume history of the world at about the same time as Arnold Toynbee was putting the finishing touches on the last of his twelve volumes. McNeill, as he was to put it later, "turned Spengler and Toynbee on their heads." In the first place, the very title of his magnum opus—*The Rise of the West: A History of the Human Community* (1963)—played off Spengler's vision of the West in decline. Second, his view of the relationship between the great civilizations of the world was diametrically opposed to theirs. McNeill believed that "both had erred in asserting the independence of civilizations, which made external influences seem relatively incidental." McNeill was a so-called diffusionist, "who focused from the start on points of contact between civilizational centers and the resultant stimuli produced by cultural diffusion."[1]

McNeill's book comported well with the spirit of the time; it was widely praised by professional historians and was also very successful in the publishing marketplace. (It is still in print.) From his vantage point of the late 1950s and early 1960s—that is, in the midst of the Cold War—McNeill saw a world that, despite its profound and threatening rivalries, was in fact moving toward greater integration; unlike the post–World War I pessimistic generation, his own post–World War II generation was well situated. "The dangers and complexities of the day," he wrote—a reference, no doubt, to the advent of thermonuclear weapons—"oppress the minds of many sensitive people [but] foresight, cautious resolution, and sustained courage have seldom counted for more.... Our world assuredly lacks neither dangers nor the possibility of failure, but it also offers a theater for heroism such as has been seldom or never been seen before in history.... Men some centuries from now will surely look back on our time as a golden age of unparalleled technical, intellectual, institutional, and perhaps even of artistic creativity.... Life in Demosthenes' Athens, in Confucius' China, and in Mohammad's Arabia was violent, risky, and uncertain; hopes struggled with fears; greatness teetered perilously on the brim of disaster. We belong in this high company and should count ourselves fortunate to live in one of the great ages of the world."[2]

In the spring of 1990, McNeill published an essay titled "The Rise of the West after Twenty-Five Years," the first article in the inaugural issue of a new journal, *Journal of World History*, that he had helped found. The essay was also printed in a new edition of his book. Three of his observations are relevant here. First, in looking back on his treatment of the period between AD 1000 and 1500, he noted how "new scholarship since 1963 has pointed the way to a firmer and better understanding of what was going on in the Eurasian world," leading him to realize that he "had overlooked the ultimate disturber of world balances in the era itself: that is, an efflorescence of Chinese civilization that raised China's culture, wealth, and power to a new level, far outstripping all of the rest of the world for a period of four or five centuries."[3] He would later describe in his autobiography how he came to understand, as one example of the power of the "trans-Eurasian market" that China had created, that even "the rise of towns in medieval Europe was best understood as a distant offshoot of far more massive commercialization taking place in China and along the shores of the Indian Ocean."[4]

McNeill's second self-criticism is that "the book is flawed simply because it assumes that discernibly separate civilizations were the autonomous social entities whose interactions defined history on a global scale. . . . The central methodological weakness of my book is that while it emphasizes interaction across civilizational boundaries, it pays inadequate attention to the emergence of the ecumenical world system within which we live today."[5] Finally, he said that he had also come to think that the global cosmopolitanism that he had described as a post-1850 phenomenon had begun centuries before that.[6]

In the 1990s McNeill's notion of "the emergence of *the* [emphasis added] ecumenical world system" comported well with that decade's sense of itself. With the collapse of the Soviet Union and the acceleration of capitalist-like growth in both China and India, the world as a whole seemed to have reached an agreement about the once divisive contest between East and West. Called by some the "end of history" or by others only a "holiday from history," this sentiment encouraged some world historians to develop new concepts that would subsume everything that had gone before.

The West is still the one part of the world that continues to generate different ways of understanding the whole world. Oftentimes, such intellectual constructs correlate with political preferences and are therefore invoked in support of various policies and programs. Some of them reflect enduring sentiments about the nature of things. We know that a generation ago certain readings of world history were put forward to buttress calls in the 1970s for a new international economic order as an alternative to the world economic system of liberal, internationalist capitalism. One of these, world systems theory, once part of the critique of liberal capitalism pre-1991, has taken on a comparable role in the present. Its major creator and advocate, Immanuel Wallerstein, maintained that capitalism could not exist without a world economy to sustain it, and in this particular world system, the strong—whether states, peoples, or individuals—would always do better than the weak, given that the capitalist world economy has as its basic requirement the unceasing accumulation of capital above all else.

Wallerstein did not like this system then, nor does he like it now. Accordingly, he and like-minded thinkers would like to see these arrangements eventually run their course, after which history will replace them with something new and maybe even better. Their analytical task is to discover whether analyses drawn from history and the social sciences can reinforce that hope, or at least be seen as reinforcing that hope. One can be discouraged by the near term, yet optimistic when thinking in longer-range historical categories. Thus, Wallerstein believes that the capitalist world economy has been in serious crisis since about 1968 and that the crisis may continue on for another fifty years or so before the system's inherent contradictions transform it into something else.[7]

Presumably, a farsighted people—or governments—should plan accordingly. For some, however, such theorizing, especially its focus on commerce and economics, is far too narrow and, moreover, too old-fashioned in its vocabulary. According to them, world history as such must now give way to global history, the study of the things that have produced globalization as we know it—a globalization that is but a way station en route to dramatically new modes of economic, governmental, and cultural organizations on the planet. In all of these schema, older notions about economic, diplomatic, and political history, even nations themselves, are thought to have been superseded by new sets of human relationships—whether to the biosphere, or to the world at large, or to what may be only imagined communities.

People are now encouraged to think about things like macrohistory, megahistory, and metahistory, or just plain "big history." In 2004 David Christian, who coined the latter term, published a 600-plus-page exposition of the subject called *Maps of Time: An Introduction to Big History*. William H. McNeill wrote an effusive foreword to the book, which, he said, "unites natural history and human history in a single grand and intelligible narrative . . . a great achievement . . . analogous to Isaac Newton and Darwin. . . . It starts with the Big Bang 13 billion years ago . . . 4.6 billion years ago, planet Earth formed and soon became the seat of more complicated processes, including life in all its forms. . . . Human societies became uniquely capable of concerting common effort and later of expanding into varying niches of the ecosystem around each of them, and which by now surround all of us in a single, global system."[8]

There is intellectual history here also—the twentieth century's effort to connect advances in the natural sciences to the work of historians and social scientists—that is, to find similarities between patterns of transformation in the natural world and patterns of transformation in the societal world. Thus, in Christian's view, "in the early universe, gravity took hold of atoms and sculpted them into galaxies. . . . By a sort of social gravity, cities and states were sculpted from scattered communities and farmers." As these communities became denser and more complicated "social pressure rose until in a striking parallel with star formation, new structures suddenly appeared together with a new level of complexity."[9]

Of course, this is hardly the first grand narrative that has been put forward to explain everything. It is reminiscent of many such in the twentieth century, but it is not gloomy. Nor does it make a twenty-first-century case for so-called chaos theory. Instead, Christian's main achievement, in the opinion of McNeill, is his "discovery of order amid the 'endless waltz of chaos and complexity.' [*Maps of Time*] is a historical and intellectual masterpiece.... It is a magnificent synthesis of what scholars and scientists have learned about the world around us in the past hundred years, showing how strangely, yet profoundly, human societies remain a part of nature, properly at home in the universe despite our extraordinary powers, unique self-consciousness, and inexhaustible capacity for collective learning."[10]

In this respect all Great Powers, whether rising or already risen, must decide whether the future should be understood in the light of these newer visions, or whether the future is better understood by assuming the ongoing relevance of more traditional ways of thinking about the world. One part of the difficulty is expressed by Arif Dirlik, who believes that "globalization entails the end of Euro-American-centered history." He is very happy about that, but he nonetheless also thinks that "globalization and localization are different aspects of the same processes that produce different results according to different historical circumstances," and that both "homogenization" and "heterogenization" can be occurring at one and the same time.[11]

China is coping with these issues once again. On May 31, 2006, the Hong Kong magazine *Phoenix Weekly* published a long interview with Zhou Chunsheng, a professor at Shanghai Normal University and the editor and chief planner of a new set of high school history textbooks.[12] The magazine, widely circulated throughout Greater China, had sought out Zhou to respond to the complaints of Shanghai teachers who had been told they would be using a new modern China history text in the upcoming semester. Indeed, upon examination, Zhou and colleagues' *Modern Chinese History* presented a new rendition of Modern China's experience, placing it not into an old Western-derived scheme—classical Marxism—but into a newer Western-originated scheme—the so-called *Annales* made famous by one of its most accomplished practitioners, the renowned French historian Fernand Braudel (1902–1985). To be sure, there was more than a little of Marx in Braudel; he had emphasized material civilization and had rejected traditional narrative history in favor of grand analyses of the large units of civilizations, especially one he called the Mediterranean World. During the course of his own career and, later, because he had trained and inspired many disciples, Braudel wielded an enormous influence on the research and writing of history in the West during the late twentieth century.

Braudel, to be sure, was also well known in China, but his infiltration into the high schools of Shanghai was not what one would have expected. How did it happen? Zhou Chunsheng, himself a great admirer of Braudel, explained that the idea for a new modern history text dated to 1999 and that he had been placed in charge of the project by the Shanghai government. He acknowledged that he appeared to be an unlikely candidate for the assignment, for his own specialty was European intellectual and cultural history; indeed, he had made his reputation inside China as an authority on the history of the West's civilization, not China's. In any case, under the leadership of the Secondary School Textbook Group of Shanghai Normal University, it took Zhou six months to gain approval for the "guiding principles" of the project and another two years for him and his colleagues to do the actual writing and editing. The new modern China text began to take shape in 2001 and was put into test use in fifty Shanghai secondary schools in the autumn of 2003.

Whatever the workings of local and national politics that lay behind the initial test-marketing and the subsequent decision to use the book throughout the system beginning in the autumn of 2006, Shanghai's high school students will now have before them—at least for a while—a story of modern China with a moral very different from the one taught their parents. The older hagiography of Qing-era peasant rebellions, once taught as precursors to Maoism, are given short shrift. Mao himself is given but cursory mention. Dynastic history, and even national history, are now subsumed into world history. What matters now, in this new rendering, is China's acquisition of "knowledge of the world," "cultural exchange and conflict," "the era of the global economy," and "the present reality of civilization and its future." The "narrative thread," as Zhou describes it, is not the old Marxist/Maoist progression of primitive to slave, to feudal, to capitalist, to Socialist society, but rather the progression from agricultural to industrial, to postindustrial society. In this story, then, China is no longer leading the world into a new Socialist age but is itself joining a world historical process larger than itself, and into which, by implication, it will ultimately be dissolved. Thus, this particular dispute about teaching China's modern history in Shanghai is not about the past at all; it is a debate about what will become of China in the future.

So far as China's leadership is concerned, a simpler way of stating the question is whether China is becoming more like the rest of the world, or more different from it; whether the ongoing changes in China, which are transforming the country into a rich and powerful force in the world, are also creating a China fundamentally different from the place that existed when its rise began twenty-five years ago; whether the present shape of the world presents something new—or at least new enough—so that the country's strategic culture and strategic tradition should be adjusted to accommodate it; whether, in sum, the world is working in accordance with some inherent tendency toward disorder, or whether in fact the world is moving toward ever-greater order amid that "endless waltz of chaos and complexity."

These are not unprecedented questions. In fact, in their own way, they track the questions posed during the nineteenth and early twentieth centuries when visions—later to prove chimerical—also dominated the debates among China's political and cultural leaders.

As it happens, when it comes to trying to fit China into some great scheme of things, the West has a far longer and richer experience than does China itself. The West has been at it for almost a thousand years, and it has been a millennium of mood swings. There was the visit of Marco Polo to the Beijing court of the Great Khan in the thirteenth century and the Italian's lavish praise of every facet of life in China. During the Renaissance, China's aura grew brighter still, as China's interest in scholarship, the arts, and its own classical learning were highly regarded. For one example, Gregory Blue describes the writings of Giovanni Botero (1544–1617) best known as a critic of Machiavelli's political doctrines. For Botero, "China was the model of prosperous urban culture, based on the skill of its artisans, its internal waterways, and its access to the sea. . . . The political wisdom of the Chinese was shown by the fact that unlike certain European states, China placed limits on expansion and refrained from pursuing a course of unbridled aggression."[13]

European *sinophilia* continued throughout the seventeenth century and into the eighteenth. Competing belief systems in Europe sought to enlist China either as an intellectual ally or a real one. For a long time the Roman Catholic Church found no irreconcilable contradiction between traditional Chinese teachings and Catholic ones and therefore imagined that China could be made a part of the Catholic world order. Other Europeans believed that China's political philosophy and its practice of Confucian statecraft placed it not in the transnational church of faith, but in the transnational

Empire of Reason. Yet, as Blue remarks, "anyone who studies the evolution of ideas about China is soon struck by the radical reversal of Western judgments about almost all aspects of Chinese culture which took place from the mid-eighteenth to the mid-nineteenth century. . . . The shift seems to have resulted not so much from any new empirical knowledge about the country, but rather from changes in Western perspectives."[14] The West was doing very well in the world and associated success anywhere with Western ways of thinking and acting. Thus, like both Catholicism and reason before it, liberalism, capitalism, and later modernity all saw a place for China in a world order of *their* making. Similarly, those who sought the overthrow of capitalism worked hard to bring China into *their* preferred world order, the world of proletarian internationalism.

How was a bewildered Chinese *literatus* or statesman supposed to make sense of these competing claims? Millions of Chinese in the mid-nineteenth century had embraced the eschatological Christian vision of the Taiping Rebellion, and millions more later accepted a utopian Communist vision proffered by Mao Zedong. Today, hundreds of millions of Chinese have accepted commercial capitalism with an enthusiasm that surpasses any in the world. Even so, China's embrace of Western-created visions of the world has often produced great disappointment and oftentimes anxiety and fear.

Yet the ambivalence and unpredictability seemingly built into China's modernization was detected early in the twentieth century by one of the great masters of fiction in the Late Qing era, Zeng Pu (1871–1935). Just as we saw how one kind of imaginative writing could lay out a happy future for China without ever describing how the country was going to get there, other writing could, on balance, accept the necessity of modernization, and even its desirability, and yet worry that Western ideas might produce something else entirely once planted in the ground in China. Zeng's masterpiece *Flower in a Sea of Retribution* [*Niehhai hua*, also known in English as *Flower(s) in a Sea of Sin*] was published in 1905, to great critical acclaim and commercial success. Writing in 1928—about a quarter-century later, during the cultural and political turmoil of the 1920s—Zeng offered a characteristic understatement: "The core meaning of this book consists of my view of how during the thirty years [i.e., 1868–1898, the years depicted in the novel] our China went through a huge transformation from new to old, consisting of one part cultural development and one part political change. Phenomena both alarming and pleasing occurred in this period one upon the other."

Here then a modern Chinese writer's invocation of a *yin* and *yang* pairing for his own time, this one an ongoing interaction between alarm and pleasure. Theodore Huters, a literary historian who has made a careful study of *Flower in a Sea of Retribution*, has elaborated on it, pointing out:

> One of the most striking things about the novel is the prominence given to the presentation of the foreign. . . . This figuration of a world that is at once beyond China but which has also become profoundly imbricated with Chinese society is highly complicated. . . . Part of this complexity arises out of a sharp awareness that indigenous knowledge would be lamentably insufficient in the new international age, and yet there is a profound ambivalence about what the coming of the West means for China. . . .
>
> In the novel, Western ideas, no matter how noble and practical they have proved to be on their native terrain, never seem to work out once they are imported into China and grafted on to the preexisting Chinese way. When these Western practices come to China, for all the inevitability of their presence, they somehow come to embody a crudity and an amorality that cast doubt on the desirability and even the stability of Chinese participation in the Western-dominated new world order. . . . Something about the Chinese context renders the universality of Western ideas problematical.[15]

China's literary imaginings of a hundred years ago are preparation for encountering some contemporary Chinese examples of what political scientists today call the law of unintended consequences. William McNeill could take the gloomy world historical outlook of Oswald Spengler and turn it on its head, and in today's China one of the defining conceits of Mao Zedong's has also been turned upside down. Mao's vision for both China and the world was expressed as a prediction—and an exhortation to the World Countryside—to surround the World City.

Instead, the Chinese city and the World City have taken the offensive, not merely surrounding the Chinese countryside and the World Countryside, but rapidly destroying them. This reversal of roles will have an enormous influence on the shape of any grand vision for China's future that comes to be developed by China's leadership.

The reversal is, first of all, important for its influence on the imagery of Chinese urbanization and helps explain why so many millions of Chinese have opted for it, even beyond economic necessity. For example, in reflecting on the history of modern Shanghai, China's most important and most cosmopolitan city, Wen-hsin Yeh describes the notion of "surrounding of the city by the countryside" not merely as a metaphor for a tactic of guerrilla warfare, but also as a shorthand way of expressing Mao Zedong's ambition to overcome Shanghai's Western-derived reaction and decadence with the revolutionary and modernizing force of scientific socialism.

Yet Shanghai, once rejected by millions of Chinese as the embodiment of everything bad that the world had done to China and, worse, as a major weapon that once served Western interests against Chinese ones, is now seen as something else entirely—the incubator and disseminator of the creatively modern, a place that demonstrates China's capacity to comprehend everything included in the contemporary definition of modernity, whether in politics, economics, science, and, especially, culture.[16] But the reversal between countryside and city is important for another reason, not just a metaphorical one. Liang Qichao, in his post–World War I disillusionment, imagined modernity's urban future—and, therefore, China's urban future—as exciting and as necessary to China's rejuvenation, but also as unsettling, even nightmarish. Like Zeng Pu before him, he experienced both pleasure and alarm.

Today, as a clearer vision of that future comes into focus, what does it presage for the twenty-first century? As China rises, it is being transformed, becoming something very different from what it was when its contemporary rise began. It has thus become a New China yet again, and in its own way, it is experiencing a new Great Leap, that is, a profound remaking of society. The difference is that the Great Leap of the 1950s had as its objective the radical remaking of China's *rural* society into a new kind of rural society. That is not the intention nor the design of what is happening today, even though rural China is being fundamentally, even radically, remade. Rather, as Chinese journalists Zhou Qun and Lin Yanhua (among many others) report: "Whether in scale or speed, China's ongoing urbanization is unprecedented in human history. In the past decade, China's cities expanded at an average rate of 10 percent annually. From 1978 to 2004, China's urbanization rate rose from 17.9 percent to 41.8 percent and its urban population increased from 170 million to 540 million. By the middle of this century, the country's urbanization rate will rise to 75 percent or so in order to support its overall modernization process. China will complete in just a few decades the urbanization process which took western developed countries three to four hundred years."[17] In the next twenty years alone, Chinese cities will probably absorb more than 300 million new migrants from rural areas.

The implications of this prediction are daunting—requirements for housing and otherwise providing for an additional urban population in China equal to the current population of the United States; economic growth sufficient to absorb many millions of new urban workers; enlarged supplies of water and electricity; new transportation networks. The capital requirements are by themselves immense; the challenge to established methods of governance is unprecedented; and the implications of all of this are far from obvious.

What has happened only thus far has been enough to provoke uneasy brooding about the future. The photography critic Christopher Philips has described how some Chinese photographers are documenting today's rapid urbanization, thereby creating a contemporary visual record of the realization of Liang Qichao's early twentieth-century forebodings about urban China:

> "Drastic urbanization" is a term often used to describe the extraordinary wave of demolition and construction that has swept through the country since the early 1990s. During that period, China's economically booming cities have added an astonishing 20 million new inhabitants each year, with no slowdown in sight. . . .
>
> In response to the resulting strains placed upon the infrastructure of Chinese cities, grandiose renovation projects have been launched, which typically commence with the wholesale leveling of "dilapidated" areas—that is, the remnants of the historic urban fabric. . . . Cities which were once quite architecturally distinct are becoming almost indistinguishable, as generic megastructures, both commercial and residential, rise on the rubble of local building traditions. The speed and blithe efficiency with which the traces of the country's urban past are being erased have led critics to predict that the signature urban form of twenty-first-century China will be the city without memory.[18]

And if this were not enough, the countryside—according to all reports—is also in great disarray, increasingly unproductive economically, unstable socially, and in a surly mood politically. The rural system of publicly provided social services is increasingly dysfunctional—nonfunctional in many places. In response to these conditions, the central government, early in 2006, promised massive new investments for rural reconstruction. This suggests that rural China will now begin to live through yet another dramatic transformation of its own.

These phenomena, in city and countryside alike, are changing the nature of the realm—changing the very sense that Chinese have of their own country—and thus requiring China's leadership to ask whether the means for the defense of the realm must also change accordingly.

In Yuan, Ming, and Qing times, a great capital was called into being because a great dynasty wanted to make a statement about its own magnificence. As a byproduct of such efforts to overawe the population, a set of economic and trading relations grew up around the great city, as if also by decree, for these relations would not have arisen otherwise. In this one respect the history of a city like Beijing displays the penchant to "place politics in command," long before Mao Zedong coined the phrase. The appropriation of Beijing by the People's Republic of China is only the most recent example. Beijing as a capital goes back to Mongol times, but it reached its zenith when it was the nerve center of an enormous Manchu empire. It served as the capital of the new Republic of China from its founding in 1912 until 1928, when the new Nationalist government of Chiang Kai-shek moved the capital to Nanjing (Nanking). The new governing powers in Beijing set out to transform their old imperial city into a suitably new republican metropolis. "Beijing needed to break down the cumbersome structures of the past," as urban historian Madeleine Yue Dong has noted,

> and adopt a network of metal rails and asphalt streets distinguishing a thriving, industrialized city. An important motivation was the creation of a new spatial order that would train imperial subjects to become Republican citizens.... The Chinese nation-state needed to establish itself as modern and at the same time secure the "distinct Chineseness" of the new nation. To live on in continuity with the imperial past would imply "stagnation"; yet inability to claim the past would indicate a lack of "civilization."[19]

Beyond the fact that there was a new national capital to the south after 1928, Beijing was further isolated from the rest of China as Japanese influence expanded throughout the 1930s. Manchukuo, Japan's puppet regime in Manchuria, was portrayed as a successor state to the Qing dynasty with the Last Emperor as its nominal head, and was thus connected to Beijing, the old Qing capital. The connection was both metaphorical and real, in that Beijing also lived under Japanese occupation from 1937 until the end of World War II.

Beijing thus had a troubling dossier. It had more than its fair share of collaborators with the Japanese—who, in addition to their other sins, had worked to promote nostalgia for the old Chinese imperial way of doing things. Beijing's commitment either to Chinese republicanism or, especially, to Chinese communism was suspect. In any case, Mao Zedong decided that Old Beijing would be New China's capital rather than, say, having its capital in a different city or building a new capital city from the ground up as other great dynastic founders had done in their time. There would be no Chinese version of Abuja, Brasilia, Canberra, or Washington, D.C.

As Wu Hung, a student of Beijing's history, describes it, the juxtaposition of old and new, of political statements and practical purposes, immediately became contorted:

> How could this old city be transformed into the capital and a shining symbol of New China? Two different solutions were soon caught up in heated debate. A group of conservation-minded architects envisioned building an administrative centre west of old Beijing [but] an unlikely coalition of left-wing Chinese architects, Soviet specialists, and Western-trained urban planners of modernist bent argued for locating the government in traditional Beijing. . . . Mao himself decided to locate the government's offices in the old city, thereby insuring the inevitability of the destruction of old Beijing. To Mao, such concerns were relevant, because revolution meant destruction and transformation. . . .
>
> To welcome the new millennium, Jiang Zemin, who had succeeded Deng Xiaoping in 1989, constructed the mammoth Millennium Altar. But instead of putting it in Tiananmen Square, he placed it in Beijing's new urban space. . . . Jiang's architectural legacy will also include the National Theater. . . . After an intense international competition, which went three rounds and lasted a year and a half, the top leadership finally made a decision in July 1999. The design that Jiang approved was by the French architect Paul Andreu, who proposed building a shiny egg of glass and titanium, encircled by a large pool, and entered through an underwater tunnel. . . .
>
> The great difference between Jiang's vision for a "socialist monument" and Mao's became unmistakable. . . . By constructing an ultra-modern structure next to the Great Hall of the People, Jiang connected himself to the Mao era while simultaneously separating himself from it.[20]

In this, there is a blending of both a traditional Chinese way and a modern Western way of making great things happen, that is, from the top down. A small group of likeminded men have a vision, and a grand design flows from it. Whether by inspiration or coercion, the requisite resources are mobilized, and the project is completed. That project may be a great city, but it is also the entire world in miniature; it brings together ideas, attitudes, and ways of doing things that are intended, sooner or later, to be expanded, first on a national and then on a truly grand scale. This is the story of China's urbanization in the twentieth century—prior to the dramatic departures in social and economic policies after 1978.

In the first eight decades of the twentieth century, Chinese had before them the example of the imperially decreed, awe-inspiring, and monumental metropolis. But political requirements changed, and it was believed necessary to bring into being cities that would embody the spirit of the new age—democratic, scientific, and modern. A famous example was the small city of Nantong, on the north bank of the Yangzi River, about seventy miles upstream from Shanghai. In the 1890s, it was still a backwater town, but in the ensuing decades it was transformed under the guidance of local Chinese scholar-businessman Zhang Jian. He, and other members of the local elite, not only caught the spirit of the modernizing Late Qing era, but they also realized that they could cement their own influence and bring in outside capital in the bargain.

In his detailed study of the history of Nantong—essentially a textile-producing company town—from its founding until its effective demise around 1930, Qin Shao describes both Nantong's founding vision and its implementation:

> The plan was to transform a country seat into a cosmopolitan city by opening its ancient walls, providing paved roads, importing mechanized clocks, electric street lights, and Western-style buildings. . . . A Zhang Jian–controlled shipping company offered discounted fares to visitors; famous opera stars performed in Nantong; national and regional conferences were held there; tour guides containing statistics, photos, blueprints and maps were published; film companies were created. . . . By the late 1910s, Nantong was recognized as an outstanding model of modernity. . . . Liang Qichao called it "the most progressive city in China." . . . Its success was an inspiration for an alternative path to China's urban-centered, foreign-dominated modernization. . . . Nantong became a tourist attraction. . . . John Dewey made a stop there in 1920.[21]

The Nantong vision was, in the end, the response of a local conservative elite that had been the product of generations of Chinese habits of governance. In the early years of the new republic, the roots of visions for the renovation of China came from other places. Sun Yat-sen himself (1866–1924), the founder of the new Republic of China, was in no sense a product of Old China; rather, as his most recent biographer, Marie-Claire Bergere, describes him, "he was a pure product of maritime China, the China of the coastal provinces and the overseas communities, open to foreign influences." He was educated in Honolulu, later trained as a physician, and was also a Christian. "The education that the young peasant received in missionary schools initiated him into the modern world and aroused in him a desire to give China a rank and role worthy of it in that world."[22]

Sun built his first political base outside of China by organizing overseas Chinese around the world. Like the world-famous Chicago urban planner and architect Daniel Burnham (1846–1912)—the creator of modern city planning who had become well known in China—the Father of the Chinese Republic did not believe in making small plans. In 1919 Sun published his own vision for China, *A Plan for National Reconstruction.*

> With the passion of a demiurge, Sun modeled the future China, recommending "gigantic methods," wiping from the map whole towns, cutting across 100-kilometer-wide loops to rationalize the course of the Yangzi, and making provision for "the establishment of a direct rail link between Zhili [the province of Peking] and Capetown [South Africa]."
>
> These plans were supposed to be realized thanks to the reconversion of the industry of the United States and the European powers, which, with peace restored, would devote 25 percent of their erstwhile annual war budget to financing Chinese modernization.[23]

Sun's plan also imagined the Three Gorges Dam, a million miles of highway, and a national rail network. For being the father of such grandiose national blueprints, he would become a heroic figure in Communist as well as Nationalist China.

Sun Yat-sen sent his only son, Sun Fo (1891–1973), to study at the University of California and at Columbia, where he became interested in urban planning. Upon his return to China, the younger Sun published a paper on the subject, arguing that China's future lay in cities built and administered on Western scientific principles; he thought that traditional Chinese people who lived in such cities would be transformed into modern Chinese people. His father arranged for him to become mayor of Canton

(Guangzhou today) in 1921, but like the rest of the Nationalist Party's hierarchy, he followed Chiang Kai-shek north in 1927 to Nanjing, where he became minister of railways.

The new Nationalist government established in Nanjing had as its aim the physical as well as the cultural remaking of China. According to the leading historian of China's republican era, William C. Kirby, "If, in Shanghai, modernity could be defined as the 'material transformation of everyday life,' Nanjing was consumed with the industrialization of *national* life. . . . The new government planned to 'reconstruct' China to make it modern. A gleaming capital would rise out of the mud alleys of Nanjing, a city twice destroyed in the previous century."[24] Within a year of the founding of the regime, as Kirby recounts it, a team led by an American-trained engineer had produced a detailed plan. It called for a new airport, modern water and electrical systems, a new ring road to circle the city, new railroad connections, a new government district, twelve new parks, and many tree-lined avenues, along which seedlings imported from France were planted.[25] For all this, in 1937, the city that was supposed to become the Paris of the East was instead immortalized as the site of one of World War II's signature atrocities.

The next new national government, that of the People's Republic of China, continued the Chinese tradition of making large political statements through the design and redesign of its capital and also of other large cities. But China's great cities, upon deeper study, turned out to have another role. Their deep structure was first noticed by the pioneer in the study of China's urban history, G. William Skinner (b. 1925–2008). "Fairly early in my research on Chinese cities," Skinner wrote in 1977,

> it became clear that in late imperial times they formed not a single integrated urban system, but several regional systems, each only tenuously connected with its neighbors. . . . The region they jointly defined coincided with minor exceptions to a physiographic unit. I eventually came to conceive of urban development—the formation of cities and the growth of their central functions—as a critical element in regional development, the processes whereby regional resources of all kinds, social, cultural, as well as economic and political, were multiplied, deployed with greater effectiveness, and exploited with increased efficiency.[26]

In another essay Skinner commented: "In late imperial China, field administration was designed not only to promote social order and foster the well-being of the populace but also—and more importantly—to ensure the regular flow of revenue, to defend the various parts of the realm against internal and external enemies, and to prevent the concentration and consolidation of local power that might pose a threat to imperial control."[27] In Skinner's understanding of how these systems actually worked, he distinguished between the weak power structure represented by the imperial bureaucracy and what he called the informal parapolitical systems on the local scene that attended to those aspects of governance not focused on the court's overriding concern with revenue and defense. "In this variable division of labor, the tasks of the informal parapolitical system included resolving civil disputes and maintaining local order; apprehending and punishing criminals; dispensing famine and disaster relief and other welfare services; promoting education and supervising institutions related to imperial examinations; constructing and maintaining public works; and licensing and regulating certain semiprofessionals and businessmen."[28]

In the generation since Skinner introduced these and related concepts to the study of how China "really works," his ideas have become building blocks for a more expansive analysis. Skinner had looked on the nine macroeconomic regions that he had delineated primarily as physiographical entities, that is, as products of China's natural geography. Thus created, they were not contingent on the vagaries of international trade, or on changing *ideas* about the origins of, and the generation of, real wealth. Today, even as observers of Chinese economic behavior remain very much interested in "real" regions, they also think in terms of what we can call "virtual" regions, that is, a regionalism that is the product of shared economic activity and a shared outlook about it. Thus, the macroregions first discovered by Skinner have now become much bigger, literally and metaphorically. In the past the analytical focus was the relation of regions, one to another, inside China. Today, the focus is on the relation of the various regions, not to each other, but rather to the outside world. To borrow some current jargon, the regions are no longer regions of China as such, but transboundary regions, created and defined by activities that transcend existing political borders. These new and rapidly growing transnational macroregions are functioning entities; each one has an internal cohesion of its own, a cohesion that separates it from its immediate neighbors and, more important, from its national government.

This important transformation is too easily hidden behind the off-putting academic argot about the "reification of bounded space" or "theoretical emplacement" or "embeddedness of subjectivity" that is often used by specialists to describe this phenomenon. Indeed, in China real changes are happening so rapidly that they are outpacing even the ability of economists, sociologists, anthropologists, and geographers to invent neologisms that purport to describe them. However, to invent some new jargon based on more familiar catchphrases, G. William Skinner described an "urbanization and regionalization with *Chinese* characteristics;" now the task is to describe a "Chinese urbanization and regionalization with *global* characteristics."

The suddenness with which China reversed course at the end of the 1970s and the unexpectedly rapid and successful transition to the new way—all its profound problems notwithstanding—should make us wonder in retrospect whether China was as oblivious to worldwide intellectual debate as it appeared at the time. Throughout the 1970s economic growth came under attack, and much dissatisfaction was expressed with what had happened in the Third World during the 1960s and early 1970s. One approach was to reject the notion of a so-called international division of labor. In a series of conferences and studies, the various arms of the United Nations called for self-reliance and advocated the weakening of, if not the severance of, a country's ties to the world economy and to multinational corporations. "This implied," as economist David K. Y. Chu put it, "that countries should adopt territorially-based, autonomous development."[29]

From this there arose such concepts as *agropolitan strategy* and *ecodevelopment*. It is certainly fair to call this a Leftist critique of the liberal, capitalist, international economic order. But the Left was far from united on the matter. In another context, in the 1970s so-called world systems theory was developed and propounded by Immanuel Wallerstein. His ideas were hardly designed to buttress the then-existing world economy, but he did not believe in economic isolation as a solution. Instead, Chu states, "his work projected a new role for cities as part of the larger historical movement of industrial capitalism. The new world system production of markets would be spatially articulated through a global network of cities—the world cities. Life in these cities would reflect, to a considerable extent, 'the mode of their integration into the world economy . . . ; the mode of world system integration . . . will affect in determinate ways the economic, social, spatial, and political structure of world cities and the urbanizing processes to which they are subject.'"[30]

Thus an argument for ending traditional Maoist self-reliance by restarting China's international economic activities could be construed as a perfectly respectable Leftist position, even if it were not the dominant Leftist position in the world of that day. An intra–Communist Party debate over whether, in effect, to reintroduce a form of capitalism into China could readily be construed as nothing but an argument among good Communists, with not a single capitalist roader among them.

In the event, the main premise of the post-Mao reforms, famously known as "socialism with Chinese characteristics," was that future economic development would be driven by reconnecting China to the world economy. The rapid urbanization of both the coast and the hinterland has been the result. These new agglomerations could not survive were they ever to be severed from the international economic networks that sustain them. Chinese urbanization and the regionalization that it anchors have thus moved beyond the local and even the intra-Chinese to become, according to Alan Smart, "the visible tips of icebergs of social networks that extend around the world."[31]

Though this outward-reaching process is farthest advanced in southeast China anchored by Hong Kong and Guangzhou, it is no less the reality in the Yangzi delta anchored by Shanghai. Less remarked on, but part of the same development, are southwest China's ongoing integration with mainland Southeast Asia, the Greater Mekong Subregional Economic Zone; northeast China's meshing with Japan, South Korea, and far eastern Russia; and even the transborder economic integration of northwest China's Muslim region with the countries of Central Asia.

As this process continues to accelerate, these emerging transboundary regions, though not themselves states in a traditional political or juridical sense, nonetheless begin to take on some attributes customarily ascribed to states. Sometimes, for example, they have a name—like Greater China—or sometimes the common characteristics, akin to a national identity, are attributed to them. Thus, in many places, and especially in today's China, as Carolyn Cartier observes, "there are collisions between the historic norms of nation-state governance and the new realities of transboundary and transnational processes."[32] Indeed, as she also notes, the famous slogan "one country, two systems," which Beijing used to describe its formula for reestablishing Chinese sovereignty over Hong Kong, is in fact an acknowledgment of the inability of China's existing political system to cope with this phenomenon. In fact, even the megacities in China proper are governed under novel arrangements; the six largest ones have become Special

Municipalities, having the status of provinces, but also some attributes of what we would call regional authorities.

The irony, and the challenge, to a national government that seeks to devise grand visions that incorporate China's growing power, is that the very growth in that power creates ever greater disaggregation. This, in turn, is leading to an ever-growing recognition that the political system needs adjusting to reflect these changes, and that the adjustment will have to come at the expense of the power of the national government. Two systems may not be enough. It may be that the better formula, to borrow again from Carolyn Cartier, is "one country, all kinds of systems." Such a notion, she thinks, "may be read as a postmodern alternative to the modern state system." For example,

> analysts concerned with the future of Taiwan have suggested that China adopt a policy of "one country, four systems," in order to recognize the differences in political culture between the mainland and Taiwan. . . . In a twist that prioritizes differences in political systems, suggestions for a "one country, five systems" model included autonomy for Tibet. . . . [In 1999] former Taiwan President Lee Teng-hui wrote about China as a system of seven distinct economic regions. In this model, Taiwan is its own region. The other six are Tibet, Xinjiang, Mongolia, Northeastern China, Northern China, and Southern China. . . . President Lee defined the seven-regions model as an administrative approach that would redistribute the power of the central government, but not create separate sovereign systems.[33]

From the point of view of the actually existing People's Republic of China, these are not primarily questions of public administration or of bureaucratic organization; they are strategic issues of the highest order. The empire that the People's Republic inherited from its Manchu predecessors was not primarily the product of a public administration mindset either; it was the product of strategic calculations. The very nature of the continental empire constructed by the last dynasty had planted within it a strategic challenge to *any* successor regime. Well before world maritime society even began to tug on the continental empire, that empire contained strategically significant, *internally* generated stresses. Today, Chinese regionalization is based on powerful networks of personal connections that extend beyond Beijing's current political reach. Organization theorists and management experts call this a problem of the span of control. Strategic analysts also need to study it on their own plane.

Once again, some inherited ideas need to be turned upside down. For example, students of China know that local affinity, loyalty to native place, and connection to family, clan, and ancestral home are important components of traditional Chinese civilization. These are reinforced by language and local dialect and by geographical variation across the country. The political history of regions and localities is also important, especially in modern times. After the overthrow of the Manchu dynasty, for example, a locality might claim for itself the mantel of Ming loyalism, that is, loyalty to the preceding ethnic Chinese ruling house. That was a shrewd thing to do in 1912. After 1949 a locality might claim for itself an old allegiance to the Communists, and that would have been a shrewd thing to do also. Localism has always been understood as a source of resistance to overbearing central authority, whether in imperial times or in the twentieth century. Such localism persists in China, even beyond emerging macroeconomic regionalism. But localism in the post-1980 era of Opening Up and Reform has been manifesting itself in unexpected ways. It used to be something that complicated the internal workings of China's polity. Now, counterintuitive as it may seem, Chinese localism is aiding in the expansion of the country's foreign ties.

To be sure, even older localism as a source of resistance to central authority would be enough of a challenge to Beijing's span of control. There now exists in China a huge floating population of workers in the megacities who are clustering by native place affiliations. They are creating urban ghettos, defining themselves by common occupations, and organizing native place associations. But, unexpectedly, there has sprung up a growing relationship between the local and the global; localism is now intertwined with globalism, and the two are fostering each other. There is historical precedent for this seemingly unlikely partnership going back to the Late Qing era, which was another period of Opening Up and Reform. Indeed, some historians now believe that this trend was only temporarily interrupted during the high Maoist era between 1950 and 1976.

Tim Oakes has created the phrase *Translocal China* to help in our understanding of this new development. He points out that traditional appeals to localism or regionalism do indeed seek "to negotiate the tension between provincial autonomy and central power. In so doing, however, they appeal to broader networks of economic power. This is now part of a strategy whereby local [Chinese] elites attempt to promote a cultural identity attractive to global capitalism ... seeking to align themselves with broader forms of political and economic power in very specific ways.... They attempt to position themselves into the pathways of power that circulate throughout China, the Asian Pacific area, and the world."[34]

In this respect, Oakes thinks that "contemporary globalization is not just an expanded version of capitalism, but an altogether new form of capitalism." It has created what he conceives of as a "new local imperative: not to resist the incursions of transnational capital, but to align with those flows." And the reverse is also true: "Local cultural diversity and difference are no longer regarded as obstacles to capitalist development, but have become core features of its expansion." In other words, the traditional Chinese localist outlooks, which might once have been isolationist, antiforeign, and obscurantist, today are creating something else entirely.[35]

Beyond its powerful effects in China, this phenomenon needs also to be appreciated both in an Asian and a worldwide context. Today, there are twelve cities in Asia with populations over ten million, ten of them outside China. Three of these—Tokyo, Osaka, and Seoul—are in East Asia; two—Jakarta and Manila—are in Southeast Asia; five—Delhi, Bombay (now Mumbai), Calcutta (now Kolkata), Dhaka, and Karachi—are in South Asia. These cities, whatever their varying degrees of economic development, technological sophistication, and organizational effectiveness, are now the critical nodes in their native countries and in these regions, and they are increasingly connected to other expanding megalopolis areas around the world, whether in the First World or Third World.

The writer and commentator Martin Wolf took the occasion of the death of the renowned urban historian Jane Jacobs (1916–2006) to recapitulate the long argument among economists and economic historians about the roles of nations and cities respectively, and how they in turn fit into an even larger scheme of things.

> [Jacobs's] best book, *Cities and the Wealth of Nations* (1984), was nothing
> short of a direct challenge to Adam Smith's *Wealth of Nations*. Smith, Jacobs
> argued, was wrong: cities, not nations, are the sources of development.
> Nations are merely "political and military entities." Once we "try looking
> at the real economic world in its own right rather than as a dependent
> artifact of politics, we cannot avoid seeing that most nations are composed
> of collections or grab bags of very different economies." Above all, according to Jacobs, "We cannot avoid seeing, too, that among all the various types
> of economies, cities are unique in their abilities to shape and reshape the
> economies of other settlements, including those far removed from them
> geographically." Cities, not countries, Jacobs insisted, are the constituent

elements of a developing economy and have been so from the dawn of civilization.[36]

Jacobs herself was not averse to following her own arguments where they led. She coined the term *transactions of decline* to describe how the productive wealth generated in cities was siphoned off by national governments to subsidize failure in other parts of the country. In the early 1980s she viewed both the Soviet Union and China as governments that "depended to an extreme degree on transactions of decline to hold the political unit together"; she saw in both places "the spectacle of old empires still holding together at all costs . . . the end products of huge and tenaciously preserved sovereignties."[37] As things have turned out since then, the Soviet Union imploded in a failed effort to hold itself together, whereas China has pulled itself out of this particular death spiral, at least for a while.

All this, Jacobs thought, argued for a "multiplicity of sovereignties" as the most economically rational arrangement for economic relations over large territories; she regarded such an "expedient division of sovereignty" as far preferable to transactions of decline. And the logical outcome of it all—which, to be sure, she herself described as a utopian fantasy—was a league of great cities on a global scale. "If unhampered trade with one another were all that cities needed to flourish, a single world government would be the economic ideal, and all the great empires of the past as well as those of recent times would have remained splendid environments for cities. But they didn't."[38]

More prosaically, Aprodicio Laquian, who has spent decades studying urbanization—and especially the new Asian megalopolis—as an interconnected local, national, and international phenomenon, finds that, in its present manifestation, these developments are inseparable from globalization. Individual nations awkwardly attempt to get out of the way of globalization and yet operate in its midst at one and the same time. According to Laquian, "The increasing role of transnational corporations, the construction of new trading blocs, the globalization of economic and socio-cultural development, and the persistence of international debt, all find expression in these cities. . . . As international trade, global finance flows, cross-border manufacturing, offshore industrial investment, outsourcing of production, and the use of advanced information technology encompass more and more countries, these urban centers have turned into crucial hubs of development in a global network of settlements, even as they have remained important engines of economic growth in national development."[39]

But, at the same time, Laquian continues, "a particularly disturbing effect of globalization in many cities in Asia has been the resurgence of particularistic movements, based on religion and on cultural and ethnic identities. Globalization is supposed to erode primordial loyalty and identification with family, clan, tribe, linguistic group, or religion. This is supposed to occur more rapidly in cities that are more exposed to globalization. However, even a quick look at what is happening in many Asian mega-urban regions reveals that religious fundamentalism and identification with ethnic enclaves are on the rise."[40]

And there are still other complicated and interrelated phenomena. In the network of global cities, each has more in common with a counterpart far away than with the nation in which it is situated. Hence, such places, tied together more by business, trade, and finance—even in the use of English as their common language—evince a desire to form, de facto, a league of their own. Yet they also wish to participate in nation building inside their respective homelands; indeed, they aspire to direct it, and thus, even if they are committed to patriotic purposes and to their nations' aggrandizement, they weaken the sway of the national governments' authority at the same time. They may yet end up in a Jane Jacobs–type transnational municipal league in spite of themselves.

We do not know how these various tensions will resolve themselves. We in the West like to think, as Laquian does when he cites Aristotle's famous remark that "city air makes men free," that "city regions may play a very important role in the spread of norms of democratic governance, the values of environmental protection, social justice, and human rights. . . . It is that commitment to *civitas*, the right to citizenship in a free community and assuming responsibility for actions that uphold the common good, that makes citizens' involvement the keystone for city-region development."[41]

The possible effects on the strategic outlook of China's leadership, political and otherwise, must remain a central consideration. Those leaders, as does everyone else, see before them an enormous transformation in degree throughout Chinese society—indeed, in societies all over the world. At what point should they, and we, begin to consider that, cumulatively, the change has become one not merely of degree, but of kind?

Since 1991 the world's sense of itself has changed in many ways. So far as academic study was concerned, the reorganization of the world following upon the collapse of the Soviet Union changed not merely political boundaries but also scholarly ones. For one example, what was once thought of as Eastern Europe essentially disappeared, and what was once thought of as Central Asia reappeared in an entirely new guise, that is, as a strategically relevant area in its own right. This in itself was not surprising, because it is the kind of thing that routinely happens after great upheavals. As the geographer Kären Wigen reminds us, this redrawing of intellectual boundaries was hardly unprecedented; before World War II, some of the areas that became the basis for area studies were once European colonial empires.[42] Accordingly, one question today is how, or even whether, the upheavals of our own time should actually shape the analytical frameworks we use to explain them.

In Kären Wigen's account, scholars of all political stripes were discontented. "The Left wanted to do away with traditional area studies because it thought they helped further the strategic interests of the United States. Mainstream social scientists criticized area studies for focusing too much on a region's particularities and not enough on more universalistic models. And even traditionalists were becoming unhappy with their centers for regional studies and their ever-growing bureaucracies for becoming overly regionalistic and insufficiently supra-regional."

One suggestion that emerged in the late 1990s from this frothy debate was the use of the ocean as the foundation of regional analyses, thereby regrouping area studies around maritime basins. In this way the relations among the littoral societies are in the foreground and the connections among them become the key concern. To use the academic jargon, "this was a move away from static 'trait geographies' in which East Asia, for example, was defined as the land of ideographic writing, Confucianism, chopsticks, and the like, toward 'process geographies' in which regions could be conceptualized as both dynamic and interconnected."[43]

These notions have implications for historians and students of culture, but they can also have meaning for those looking for insight into appropriate national strategic and military doctrines. China's history contains many examples of important connections between the country's coast and the world, and the effects of those connections on China's hinterland. Twenty-first-century globalization certainly marks an enormous change in degree in both sets of effects. China's urban transformation is itself instructive about a key difference between this era and previous ones, namely, that the growth of cities today is the product of, and is now inseparable from, China's integration into the world economy.

That the change in degree has become a change in kind has been well understood since the late 1980s, acknowledged in ways both ordinary and melodramatic. China's urban-maritime-global coming of age was affirmed in the famous six-part television series *He Shang* (River Elegy), broadcast in China in 1988. The film offered an astringent portrayal of China's isolationist eras and the disasters wrought by the Maoists' attempt to deal with them. None of this was stated literally, of course. Instead, viewers watched the great Yellow River flow into the sea leaving the "Yellow River culture" behind and entering the "blue ocean culture" that connected China to the other cultures across the sea. The Communist Party, in its customary way, acknowledged the correctness of the documentary by subjecting it to relentless denunciation. Several of those associated with the production fled the country.

"What strikes the geographer about *He Shang*," writes Carolyn Cartier,

> is the dramatic way in which landscape images were made to tell the full sweep of imperial and national history. In contrasts between the landed river empire and the mercantile coasts, the series suggested the dynamic possibilities of urban maritime cultural economies. It also evoked the challenges and opportunities posed by a globalizing cosmopolitanism—one that brings the West and its cultural-economic complex along with it. The seriousness of the reaction to the series was based in part on an understanding that China had once produced a material and cultural civilization unprecedented in world history. The challenge for China's leaders is to acknowledge China's cosmopolitanism as an integral part of that history.[44]

The computations of China's State Statistical Bureau provide a more prosaic way of making the same point. China's economy, once isolated and striving for autarky, is now built on large imports and large exports. Foreign trade, which accounted for 10 percent of gross domestic product in 1978, rose to 30 percent in 1990, and to 70 percent in 2004. Hundreds of thousands of enterprises of every size and description, all created by foreign investors, engage in trade and manufacturing that presupposes China's continuing links with the outside world. With large-scale movements in materials, funds, technologies, and human resources, China is more sensitive than ever to international politics and market changes. China is now dependent on foreign suppliers for necessary raw materials; it imports about 40 percent of its oil, half of its iron ore, and a vast assortment of other primary products. It is, in particular, a voracious consumer of forest products, and as agricultural lands are turned into four-lane highways, China will become more reliant on the international market for its food supply. Withal, China's trade is now worth more than $1 trillion and is growing, and the lion's share of that moves across the Western Pacific.

This, then, is China's contribution to, and its role in, what has come to be called *Pacific integration*. Its visible indications are economic and cultural, but its deep structure is strategic. Indeed, the structural strategic foundation for these arrangements—the necessary condition—is hegemony. As Paul Blank points out, naval hegemony in particular has been critical to ongoing Pacific integration for centuries. "The arrival of the Spanish on both sides of the [Pacific] basin in the sixteenth century initiated the process of integration. . . . It established Spanish silver and the Spanish dollar as a medium of exchange throughout the [Pacific] basin. . . . The search for raw materials and new markets in the context of industrial capitalism stimulated the settlement and integration of the Pacific under British hegemony. . . . This included the expansion of the China trade, the settlement of Australia, and the exploitation of new opportunities created by the independence movements in Latin America. . . . New commodities and products created new markets which were then linked by steamship, railroad, and telegraph with each other and with the Atlantic economies."[45]

The replacement of British naval hegemony by American naval hegemony is an oft-told tale. However one explains the origins of the naval rivalries of the nineteenth and twentieth centuries, it is undeniable that, in the end, they contributed mightily to the globalized and wired world of the twenty-first century. As Jon Tetsuro Sumida, a naval historian, points out, the technological and organizational sophistication of modern navies and the skilled manpower that operated them were "the precursors of the large industrial organizations which dominate the economies of the modern world. . . . Navies generated fundamental breakthroughs in computers and related electronics, and were a major contributor to the information revolution. . . . Finally, major navies were components of a transnational system of naval security that fostered the growth of international trade. Naval supremacy, therefore, had two faces—as an agent of great power rivalry to be sure, but contrarily as a force that encouraged international cooperation and the emergence of a global economy."[46]

Thus, whatever may be said about the decline of the nation-state in our global era, and however much traditional components of national power may be "deconstructed" by many contemporary students of world affairs, there remains a recognized need for strategic hegemony. That need may be acknowledged only reluctantly, quietly, and tacitly, and spoken of only sotto voce—but it is a need, nonetheless. *Whose* hegemony—whether *some-body's* or *something's*—may in the end not matter, *if* one can be confident that the happy results of the present arrangement will continue on during some yet-to-be-described new dispensation. But in the meantime, this is a predicament for any rising power that may in fact have hegemonic aspirations—whether it be China, the international community, the United Nations, a coalition of nongovernmental organizations, or a planetwide cartel of the richest multinational corporations. How is any transition to be arranged? How can it happen without destroying the actually existing ecumenical system of the day?

For China, this is a great and grating irony. The success of China's great project of national renovation depends, in the last analysis, on a world arrangement that remains reliable and predictable only because of American strategic hegemony. Does China crave a strategic independence that it can achieve only by becoming, in its own right, the maritime hegemonic power—the world's navarch and, therefore, the archon of the maritime World City? If so, is there any realistic prospect that China can do that? Has it already concluded that there is no such realistic prospect? Or does the Chinese leadership believe that such a goal is indeed achievable, even as it must superintend an epochal national transformation and govern an already enormous and increasingly fractious continental empire?

Some decades from now, even after Rising China has become Risen China, acquiring control of the World City will be a formidable task, comparable in its own way to Chairman Mao's vision of a China-based transformation of the entire structure of world politics. But gaining control of the World City, and then governing it over the longer term, is not at all like gaining control of the World Countryside and then governing it. After all, explicit in the Maoist countryside strategy was its reliance on violence. There could be no Peaceful Rise of Chinese power; such a thing could not even be imagined. Nor would patience alone—the mere conduct of China's daily business as usual—lead to dramatic changes over time.

In today's world, however, China's Peaceful Rise seems both a theoretical and practical possibility. China's patience and persistence—time on task by a busy population of more than one billion—could achieve in a mundane manner what grandiosity and violence could never attain. In this, the counsel of patience is reinforced by the West's own prognostications about China's great future—so long as it stays on its current path. In this, we sense a traditionally Chinese view of things. And yet China's imperial memories—the great achievements that make them memorable—are alive in the modern milieu precisely because the creators of those great empires were not content to wait. China's greatest political leaders always pushed the pace.

In the meantime, China continues to build its great cities into real and symbolic representations of its present rise in the world. Both China's commercial capital, Shanghai, and its political capital, Beijing, are in the midst of transformations unprecedented not only in China's history but also in the history of the world. In Shanghai its selection as the site of World Expo 2010 has become the pretext for an acceleration of what is already a huge building boom. "By the standards of recent urban projects in the West—the so-called Big Dig in Boston, say—the scale of what the city is undertaking is astounding. . . . A 2,000-plus-yard-long stretch of the waterfront is being razed and redeveloped. . . . Nearby, there will also be a modern passenger ship terminal; the world's fastest commercial train service—a high-speed magnetic levitation line from Shanghai's international airport—will be extended to Hangzhou, a city 100 miles to the southwest. . . . The airport is adding a second terminal whose futuristic design is to complement the original terminal, designed by the French architect Paul Andreu. . . . Shanghai already boasts 4,000 skyscrapers, nearly twice as many as New York, and plans to add 1,000 more in the next decade."[47] Even the model of New Shanghai, on display at the city's Urban Planning Exhibition Hall, is on a grand scale. "The urban planning museum is Shanghai's monument to its future. The centerpiece is a 600-square-meter model—the size of two tennis courts—that shows what Shanghai will look like in 2020."[48]

And in Beijing, an international event has also touched off major urban projects. On July 14, 2001, the International Olympic Committee announced that it had selected China's capital as the site of the 2008 summer games. (For the first time, it also allowed two members of the international committee to host events in the same Olympics, when it subsequently permitted Hong Kong to serve as the site of the equestrian events for the games.) For the government of China, this was the culmination of a long effort to secure the games and what they symbolized for China's new status in the world. Serving as the Olympic venue had been important to other nations that had wanted either to introduce themselves or reintroduce themselves to polite international society—a kind of debutantes' ball for nouveau riche counties. Berlin's hosting of the 1936 Olympics had become infamous for that. More recently, Tokyo's hosting of the games in 1964 had served as Japan's final reintroduction to society, marking the end of its probation. The 1972 Munich games were designed to do the same for Germany, but athletic competition and political symbolism were overshadowed by a still-notorious terrorist atrocity. The 1988 games in Seoul were a symbolic introduction to the rise of Asia and to the Pacific century. In 2008 China planned to indulge in the self-display of an *arriviste*, but on a grand world stage. Indeed, it had hired the American film director Steven Spielberg (later to resign in protest over China's support of the government of Sudan) and his Chinese counterpart Zhang Yimou to produce and to stage the opening and closing ceremonies of the games.

The significance of this to China can be seen not only in its worldwide diplomatic effort to secure the games but also in the elaborate construction plans the Olympics have brought forth. Olympic Beijing has become a major statement and, therefore, like the plans a decade ago to rebuild Berlin after German reunification, or the debate in the United States about what should replace the World Trade Center buildings and what memorials should mark the attacks of September 11, 2001, it has engaged passion and politics. For, as Deyan Sudjic, director of the Design Museum in London, has pointed out,

> In recent years, it is architecture more than any other aspect of contemporary culture that has touched the rawest nerves. . . . It was architecture that Saddam Hussein used to consolidate his grip on Iraq. And it was architecture that the Serbs and the Croats deployed in the first stages of their bloody battle over the division of the former Yugoslavia. Both sides marked out their territory by building churches: steel and glass modern for the Catholic Croats; neo-Byzantine in so-called traditional stone and tile for the orthodox Serbs. . . .
>
> Architecture matters because it lasts. . . . It matters because it is big, and it shapes the landscape of our everyday lives. But beyond that, it also matters because, more than any other cultural form, it is a means of setting the historical record straight. . . . Arguments over architecture are arguments over how a society understands its past and its values. Until those arguments end, architecture will never cease to incite.[49]

Billions of dollars have been invested in upgrading telecommunications and transportation infrastructure throughout the country, but it is the Olympics-inspired major renovations in Beijing that displayed post-Mao

China in a way it has not been displayed before. A new fifteen-mile-long boulevard was constructed between the Olympic Park north of the city and the Forbidden City and Tiananmen Square in the center of the city.

To help design the new boulevard, urban planners in Beijing's municipal government hired the German urban planner and architect Albert Speer Jr., son of Albert Speer, Hitler's personal architect. Some saw an eerie resemblance between the new Beijing North-South axis being created by the younger Speer, and the North-South axis once planned by the elder Speer for Hitler's New Berlin, which was to be called Germania.[50] The main argument, however, has been between traditionalists and modernists. Over the past several years, there have been growing complaints from practicing Chinese architects that the city's signature projects are being designed almost exclusively by Western firms. For example, the new headquarters of the country's largest government-owned bank is a project of Skidmore, Owings and Merrill of New York. A Dutch firm won the competition for two new buildings for CCTV (China Central Television), the state-owned broadcaster—one to serve as its headquarters, the other to serve as a cultural center and also to include a large hotel. The headquarters building, skyscraper though it is, is also renowned for its radically untraditional appearance and the difficulties its shape presented to the people who actually built it. And, the new National Theater, that egg-shaped structure with a titanium skin that is adjacent to the Great Hall of the People and is the work of French architect Paul Andreu, finally opened for business in April 2008.

The 2008 Olympic projects afforded the present government of China an opportunity to revamp the nation's capital, an opportunity at least the equal of any of the great capital builders in Chinese history. Nor was the government in Beijing alone in seeing the potential for signature building projects against the backdrop of the Olympics. In 2004 ground was broken for a five-building complex to house a new American embassy. Also the work of Skidmore, Owings and Merrill, it rides Beijing's modern architecture wave; it now represents America's official version of modernism in China's capital. It was completed so as to be noticed, for the President of the United States would be able to dedicate the new embassy during his visit to the Olympics.

But if China's billions of yuan of new construction are supposed to alert us to Rising China's preferred definition of itself, the signals are mixed at best. On the one hand, the government has undertaken a major effort to refurbish many traditional sites in Beijing and environs in anticipation of the Olympics. The most conspicuous of these is the multiyear plan of restoration within the Forbidden City. But the Olympic facilities are far more conspicuous for being "cutting edge." The centerpiece of the Beijing games was the new National Stadium, dubbed the Bird's Nest, because of the startling intricacy of its appearance and construction. It was the product of collaboration among three architectural firms—Swiss, British, and Chinese. It set the avant-garde standard for stadium design and construction throughout the world and also attracted attention from builders because it was unprecedented as a high-challenge engineering project. As one of the design and engineering firms, Arup and Partners of Britain, described the project in its own promotional literature: "inspired by randomness in nature, and patterns found in Chinese-style 'crazed' pottery typically found in Beijing markets, there are, in fact, several layers of patterns that the eye does not pick up on the stadium's apparently random structure. The very irregular nature of the structure meant looking for new methods of designing structural steel sections."

The National Stadium was hardly an anomaly. One of its codesigners was also a member of the winning team that designed the swimming and diving venue, quickly dubbed the Water Cube. The contest for the latter was a hard struggle, at least according to Arup and Partners:

> The competition, which was judged by a panel of international architects, engineers and pre-eminent Chinese academics, commenced with submissions from ten international consortia and also involved a public exhibition and vote.... To arrive at the building's structural design, which is based on the natural formation of soap bubbles to give a random, organic appearance, we used research undertaken by two professors of physics into how soap bubbles might be arranged in an infinite array.... This U.S. $100 million premier recreation centre will have five pools, including one with a wave machine and rides that are six times the size of an Olympic pool. There will also be an organically-shaped restaurant area carved out of the bubble structure.

Thus, the nationalistic and patriotic energies embedded in Beijing's hosting of the Olympics came to be expressed in an internationalist idiom. Yet it is far from obvious how this seeming contradiction should be interpreted. In one respect, it is just the latest example of one facet of China's interest in the modern; for a century and a half China's desire to be modern and up-to-date has indeed been expressed by what has been built there. But this has not been its sole manifestation. In culture, and in politics especially, the modern has also come to China in the form of murderous ideologies and blueprints for renewed Chinese imperialism. Moreover, there has always been a dangerously fine line between what seems to be modern and what actually turns out to be decadent. That line is even harder to detect in a country like today's China, which is being "deconstructed" and "reconstructed" at a rapid pace, and which is thus vulnerable to all the dangers that thinkers and writers like Liang Qichao and Zeng Pu called to their countrymen's attention one hundred years ago.

Still, there are signs of balance and accommodation in the implementation of the modern in today's China. If new buildings can be said to tell us something about the kind of China under construction both literally and figuratively, then the career of prominent Chinese architect Yung Ho Chang (Zhang Yonghe) is an illuminating illustration. His father, also an architect, designed the Chinese People's Museum of the Revolution (1960) on Tiananmen Square, but he was somehow able, even during the Cultural Revolution, to send his son to study in the United States. The younger Chang graduated from the University of California at Berkeley and later taught at the University of Michigan and Rice University. In 1993, he returned to Beijing, where he opened his own firm and also became chairman of the architecture department at Beijing University.

The architecture critic Daniel Elsea, who has paid special attention to ongoing developments in China, thinks that Chang's work

> stands in contrast to the flamboyant airports, concert halls, museums, office campuses, and stadia that non-Chinese architects are designing in China; Chang's projects are pared-down and intimate, and concern the fields of education, the arts, and civic building. While Chang is doing some work in Beijing, most of his designs are in the "other" China—the provinces—where the vast majority of the country's population lives, and which are largely left out of China's relentless economic growth. . . . He has become the first Mainland Chinese architect to work overseas, with a publishing house in Paju, Korea; a public housing project in Gifu, Japan; and the temporary Chinese national pavilion at the Venice Biennale.[51]

Chang's internationalism is now both a style and a career. In March 2005 he became chair of the School of Architecture of the Massachusetts Institute of Technology, but he also spends part of his time tending to his firm in Beijing and to its ongoing projects in China, Japan, and Korea. He will continue, he says, "to fuse the universal modern and the Chinese."[52]

For all of this, the Communist Party of China, the People's Republic of China, the Beijing Municipal Administration, and China's Olympic

Committee remain exasperating patrons. Arthur Labow, a writer who has been following the fate of some avant-garde architectural projects in China, has described how

> innovative foreign architects are often in the dark, frequently blindsided by forces they never anticipate or fully comprehend. Even the identity of the true decision maker can remain mysterious. Everywhere in the world, not only in China, the struggle to realize a design is vulnerable to forces outside the architect's reach: the budget shrinks, the program changes, the financing collapses, the building code alters, the client reneges. In an authoritarian and secretive state that is trying to spur capitalist initiative without relinquishing government control, however, these calamities occur with less warning or transparent reasoning. "It's like two walls in front of each other," one of them says. "You have no clue what really happens, what are the dynamics really."
>
> ... Both the reigning government bureaucrats, who respond to social and political pressures, and the newly ascendant capitalists, who try to anticipate market conditions, make sudden and seemingly capricious decisions. Their explanations are incomplete and unconvincing.[53]

It is in competing visions of the world's urban civilization that the future of China's national policies will be found. China finds itself at the leading edge of unprecedented urbanization and must decide how to cope with its consequences. Paying the costs of its own advances at home will affect China's capacity to pursue grand ambitions overseas—even as the advances at home are based on, and therefore require and compel, more and deeper international involvements. We may have become used to thinking of some fundamental tension between "domestic" and "foreign" policy, but it appears as if China's domestic policy has become its foreign policy; the two are becoming inseparable.

In the hundred years of Chinese foreboding about the consequences of following the dao of modernity, there has been no shortage of grim forecasts. It is now for China's contemporary leadership to decide how frightened it is of what it has wrought. The social scientists in China's growing network of think tanks will find no shortage of dire predictions to bring to their patrons' attention. They might, for one example, pick up a typical example of the new literature of urban dystopia and summarize it, as journalist Pepe Escobar described Michael Davis's book *Planet of the Slums* (2006) in May 2006:

> Davis sees the future as a realist, not as an apocalyptic visionary: "This great dragon-like sprawl of cities," he says "will constitute the physical and demographic culmination of millennia of urban evolution. The ascendancy of coastal East Asia, in turn, will surely promote a Tokyo-Shanghai 'world city' dipole to equal the New York–London axis in the control of global flows of capital and information."
>
> ... But most of all, the dire consequences of the hypercity explosion will be inevitable: appalling inequality within and between cities and, as far as China is concerned, the terror gripping their urban experts—the unbridgeable gap between small inland cities and coastal hypercities. Nobody yet has examined in full the implications of China ceasing to be the predominantly rural society it has been for millennia.[54]

All this can be made to seem scarier still as speculation about China's urban future takes off from the urban present of megacities throughout the developing world. They are, as Davis portrays them, "the radical new face of inequality, a grim human world largely cut off from the subsistence solidarities of the countryside as well as disconnected from the cultural and political life of the traditional city. . . . This is the edge of the abyss, the new Babylon . . . based on an architecture of fear and a culture of the absurd. . . . The future of warfare lies in the streets, sewers, high rise buildings and sprawl of houses that form the broken cities of the world."

The People's Republic of China, the product of a rural insurgency, has shifted its base of operations. Having left the Countryside to its own devices, the Communist Party's rule is now bound to the City that it once regarded as its mortal enemy.

CHAPTER 8

A PEACEFUL RISE AND MEMORIES OF VIOLENCE

A century ago a few of China's most brilliant and insightful thinkers imagined a stellar future for their country—a China that is now under construction before our eyes—but none of them envisioned the details of the intervening hundred years, the actual events that would occur between then and now. From the perspective of 1905, neither utopian philosophy nor religious conviction nor science fiction provided even a hint of the horrific occurrences of twentieth-century history. And no pessimist—no prophet of dystopia—could even have begun to foresee them either. To re-examine great eras in China's past is to inspire speculation about how those imperial memories could inform China's national politics and Grand Strategy today. Far more recent developments in both intellectual and political history—in both China and the West—will also lead to speculation about *their* influence on China's emerging sense of today's world.

If we think about the formulation of Grand Strategy as intellectually creative activity—that is, as an imaginative activity ultimately not very different from any other activity that seeks to imagine the future—we should infer that a strategic vision is no less the product of the cumulative experience of any country than is a literary vision or an artistic vision or an architectural vision. Indeed, in certain fundamental respects each one of these visions not only informs the others but each, in its own way, feeds into the completion of the others. Put more simply, each of them can tell us something useful about the others.

In China today these visions can be wildly different from each other, even as they are all the products of the same history of the same country. In this respect a Chinese leader who seeks to draw exclusively on the triumphant episodes of the past as practical and inspirational templates for what can be achieved in the future is not the sole entrant in a competition for control of the popular imagination. There is a competing vision that is far less ambitious; it draws on horrific memories of the past, not uplifting ones. The competition between these two in today's China is, in and of itself, a fundamental strategic datum. It is another case of the age-old struggle between culture and politics in China, and it could very well serve to constrain great societal and political plans for national power and national aggrandizement.

To understand how a test of wills of this kind may come to unfold in China, we need to look beyond history itself—that is, beyond the study and writing of history—and examine other kinds of writing that are shaping China's sense of its past situation and its future possibilities. Such a discussion can conveniently focus on a single theme: to paraphrase yet again that too frequently quoted sentence from the *Communist Manifesto*, there is a specter haunting China, and it is the specter of violence. As David Der-wei Wang strikingly points out:

> One can hardly read modern Chinese history without noticing a seemingly endless brutality. . . . At least one million Chinese lost their lives during the Warlord and Nationalist periods, and more than fourteen million were killed during the Second Sino-Japanese War. More than two million fled China after the Communist seizure of power, while almost five million perished during the same period.
>
> After the founding of the People's Republic, at least thirty million perished during Mao's Great Leap Forward, which was followed by the Great Famine and Retrenchment Period, and an estimated fifteen million were persecuted and executed every year between those famously bloody wars, campaigns, and movements.[1]

And to these, one could readily add the deaths of about one million Chinese "volunteers" in the Korean War and all the civilian and military deaths that resulted from the forcible incorporation into the new People's Republic of China of Tibet and East Turkistan, two parts of the old Manchu Empire that resisted becoming a part of the new Maoist dispensation.

The central premise of Wang's own examination of one cumulative effect of these episodes is that "modern Chinese historiography has not sufficiently addressed the scale of the moral and psychological aftermath of China's violence and pain and that literature, particularly fiction, can be drawn on as a complementing *and* contesting discourse."[2] Wang draws for his central image on a mythical creature of ancient China, the so-called *taowu*, a ferocious monster known for its power to see the past and the future.

Over the ages this monster became identified in China's culture with history itself, but as a supplier of its missing pages, a kind of Greek Chorus that, over the ages, provided unofficial commentary, a necessary supplement to history as written by officials, so that important facts would not be forgotten. It is thus history recorded from the point of view of those on the receiving end—the victims of history, not its perpetrators. The role of the *taowu* was, and remains, to keep alive the memory of outbursts of violence and brutality in China. Just as Standard History and Dynastic History were designed to perpetuate the memory of great achievements so as to instruct the future, the counterhistory preserved for us by the *taowu* provides a different kind of instruction all its own. Thus, the study of history as such can teach us only part of what we need to know.

Nor are the offering of deep explanations for violence and destruction, and the preservation of memories of them, the provenance of intellectuals and poets alone. China, even after a quarter-century of urbanization and globalization, remains the home of more than 800 million peasants. Embedded in their part of Chinese culture, according to Steven Smith, is a sense that "power operates in two separate, yet related, realms, one visible, the other invisible. Between these two, there exist causal links, meaning that invisible powers sometimes produce visible outcomes. . . . In theory, the cosmology of the Party-state was an antithesis of this, since it purported to render the social body amenable to the dictates of reason. In practice, however, the Party subscribed to a worldview that was almost as occult; it assumed that the world of appearances was intrinsically deceptive, masking a hidden world whose nature was dark, cruel and deceptive."

In any case, as Smith further notes:

Since the death of Mao Zedong in 1976, there has been an astonishing
revival in the People's Republic of China of what the government calls
"feudal superstition." The 1980s and 1990s saw a rush to rebuild temples and
ancestral halls, the resurgence of spirit mediumship and exorcism, renewed
interest in divination and geomancy, and the reemergence of heterodox
religious cults, notably Falungong....

This raised questions about the nature of the beliefs and practices that
revived during the era of economic reform. Were these manifestations
of a tradition that had been preserved unscathed in the face of turbulent
socioeconomic and political transformations? Or were these substantially
new configurations of beliefs and practices adapted to the changed power
relations of the reform era?[3]

David Der-wei Wang, in an analogous way, maintains that the persistence of awesome violence across the generations must cause one to ponder: Could history be regarded both as an embodiment and an indictment
of monstrosity? To what extent has the contemplation of history entailed
insight as well as indifference? "Particularly in view of the massive scale
of violence and pain that Chinese administered to China in the name of
enlightenment, rationality, and utopian plenitude, one senses that the line
between understanding and complicity has never been so difficult to discern."[4]

This way of approaching things may seem recondite and impractical,
but it nonetheless defines one of the challenges facing any maker of grand
plans: the first requirement for the organization of a great national project
is what today's academics call a grand national narrative or what used to be
called a great national epic. However, if careful students of contemporary
Chinese culture are to be given credence, the country is still far from the
creation of any such story.

It may well be that China, closer in time to many of the representative
horrors of twentieth-century totalitarianism, is more apt to carry its psychological scars; Hitler died in 1945, Stalin in 1953, Mao not until 1976. At
the same time, as compared to other post-Communist societies, China has
moved further and faster from a brutal Communist/Socialist past to an
intense capitalist/commercialist/consumerist present.

Some outside China might think of this as an inspiriting experience and
wonder why this better-than-expected historical outcome has yet to be reflected in an outpouring of cultural exuberance. Be this as it may, the *taowu*

is alive and well, and its influence can be seen in contemporary China's intellectual and artistic life. Ban Wang, writing in the late 1990s about the relation between politics and history in post-Mao Chinese cultural creation until that time, describes how things appear to many Chinese writers and artists:

> History is the shock that forebodes a horrible and crushing calamity. The foreboding turns out to be devastatingly real: what happened was death, murder, disappearance, some incomprehensible upheaval. . . . History as a series of catastrophes finds a heart-wrenching emblem in Zhang Yimou's 1994 film *To Live*. . . . In this film, some unexpected calamity always lies around the corner; some calamity is always about to fall out of the blue. . . .
>
> The Chinese literary critic Meng Yueh has culled scenes from numerous works of Chinese fiction into a comprehensive vision of Chinese society in the twentieth century. . . . For her, the catastrophe is a nightmare that cannot be fully interpreted and grasped, a darkness that cannot be fully illuminated and redeemed.[5]

Ban Wang also argues for seeing a sharp contrast between this view of history as propounded in writing and art and what it replaced. "Writers were once exhorted to write novels, stories, and plays singing the praises of the great campaigns and movements that the Chinese people, led by the Party, have waged and are still carrying out in breathless and epoch-making endeavor . . . witness the many novels and plays written about military campaigns, massive land reform projects, and large-scale political movements. Even the classical historical novel is often cast in terms of sequences of gigantic and historical events, retroactively signifying and affirming a vast underlying master narrative."[6]

But in the 1990s, by Ban Wang's account, Chinese writers were already displaying, at one and the same time, the influence of modernity in their writing styles, the subjects about which they chose to write, *and* the influence of postmodernity in how they interpreted the actual consequences of modern life. To develop this point in a graphic way, Ban Wang comments on the uses that Chinese writers have made of a famous image created by the legendary postmodern German literary critic Walter Benjamin (1890–1942), an image that has since become an icon for rejection of belief in progress. Benjamin's inspiration was a painting, *Angelus Novus*, by the Swiss artist Paul Klee (1879–1940). After contemplating the angel Klee had painted, Benjamin would later write that what he had seen was a "being with his eyes staring, and his mouth open." He continues:

This is how we imagine the Angel of History, with his face turned toward the past. Where we perceive a chain of events, he sees one single catastrophe which keeps piling wreckage upon wreckage and hurls it in front of his feet. The angel would like to stay, awaken the dead, and make whole what has been smashed. But a storm is blowing in from Paradise; it has got caught in his wings with such violence that the angel can no longer close them. This storm irresistibly propels him into the future to which his back is turned, while the pile of debris grows skyward. This storm is what we call progress.[7]

In this way Benjamin offers a graphic comment on the outcome of modernity in Europe—murderous ideologies such as Nazism and Bolshevism, the mass murders of the Holocaust and the Purges. Yet insofar as many contemporary Chinese writers are concerned, though this may be the end of the story in Europe, it is only the beginning of the story in China; the denouement of China's story has not yet been reached. Thus, in Ban Wang's powerful presentation, even as the Angel of History may usefully serve to instruct Chinese about the past, there are at least three more angels who are now serving to inspire writing about the present and the future—the angels of the fantastic, the schizophrenic, and the grotesque.[8]

There may be something of the melodramatic and even of the histrionic in analyses of this sort, but they feed into an ongoing discussion of the significance of the modern Chinese experience, and they are no less meaningful than the works of academic historians. Li Tuo, editor of the Beijing magazine *Reflections*, places the discussion within the framework of the basic question of China's response not so much to the West but to modernity. He points out that the most recent thoroughgoing critiques of modernity as such began to appear in Chinese writing at about the same time that Deng Xiaoping announced the famous Four Modernizations. To be sure, the reforms were welcomed at one level, but like a hundred years ago, many Chinese thinkers remained skeptical and worried: "China, like other non-Western countries, is already saturated with cultural values associated with modernity. Is Chinese modernization entirely a reprint or a copy of Western modernization? Or does it have its own particular quality, its own particular experience? Do we Chinese have the possibility or necessity to form our own discourse of modernity, or do we open a 'branch office' of the Western discourse of modernity in China?"[9]

Li also finds—and he is hardly alone in this observation—that after 1985, a trend began among writers to write about smaller subjects, rather than larger ones—"experimental novels," "searching-for-roots novels," "new realism," and so on. These writers are, in their way, escapist, even if they see themselves escaping to places more mundane than the fantastic, the schizophrenic, and the grotesque. What ties all of these things together, however, is the contrast with previous eras in Chinese writing when the large and the great and the national and the socially transforming were among the subjects of interest.

How should these particular contemporary developments enter a discussion of China's future national strategy? How does a Chinese political leader incorporate them into his evaluation of China's longer-term capabilities? Is he even aware of them? If he is, does he think they matter? To be sure, Chinese and Americans alike need to understand more about this. But when we turn to contemporary cultural analysis, we discover that it tends to be written in a specialized academic—and very off-putting—jargon. The terminology originated in French or English, and, for Americans, the academic English of cultural analysis must first be translated into normal English before one can begin to reflect on its usefulness for other purposes. Similarly, its translation into comprehensible Chinese is difficult—in a country, let us remember, whose linguists disagree about how to translate even so seemingly harmless an English term as "stakeholder."

For example, contrived phrases such as "politics of marginality," or "poetics of hybridity," or "global contextualization," or "local articulation," or "mimetic realism," have been applied to the post-1980 Chinese cultural and literary scene, as has been a discussion of the relationship between "geopoetics and geopolitics." What could this mean? It means in the first instance, as David Der-wei Wang has written, that the production of Chinese writing is now widely dispersed over China, Taiwan, Hong Kong, Singapore, and in the worldwide Chinese diaspora. The overseas writers, many of them exiles, are increasingly influential; "they show fewer symptoms of an obsession with China" but instead feel "compelled to ponder the consequences of choosing nationalist causes over individual quests."

> The new diaspora of Chinese literature is made possible by new technologies and increasingly global circulation of economic and cultural capital.... Writings by Mo Yan, Su Tong, and Wang Anyi, three of the most prominent mainland literati, now often see first publication in Taiwan or Hong Kong.... Jin Yong and Li Bihua, two of the most popular writers based in Hong Kong, have become household names in China, Taiwan and Hong Kong, owing to cinematic adaptations of their works and to shrewd market

promotion.... All these Chinese writers are writing at a time when the master narrative is already fragmented and anachronized.[10]

From here, Wang's coauthor, Chi Pang-Yuan goes on to observe that "the grand epic narrative has dissolved into fragmentary impressions, fortuitous events, and pointless monologues, foregrounding a historical experience deprived of any authentic lived experience except linguistic configurations." She cites, as one example, the well-known Taiwanese writer Li Yu, "whose writing not only reflects social malaise and human aberrations; it is writing that can also become a remedy to soothe the wounds left by the atrocities of history."[11]

Without a doubt, China's government has been successful in convincing many millions of Chinese that its particular modernization program is a good thing and that it should be supported. It may also be succeeding, to a substantial degree, in convincing many millions of Chinese that further aggrandizement of China in the world at large is also a good thing. Indeed, it may well be convincing them that the risks associated with the implementation of a truly grand design—a design, for example, without precedent in the imperial history of the country but similar to one once propounded in the Maoist era, that is, becoming the world's hegemonial power—are well worth taking. But it has not convinced everyone.

There is, first of all, the legacy of what Ban Wang calls "the classic critique of modernity." It is still alive and well in China, especially since China has the benefit of examples of countries that came to modernity a century earlier.

Industrialization, technology, and urbanization, the prime movers of modern history, created a radically new environment that severed huge populations from traditional ways of life.... It was nothing less than an epochal transformation from a mode of social organization based on the traditional family and the village to a new socioeconomic structure embedded in urban existence, an anonymous market, and the rule-bound and abstract relations of a civil society.... Critics of modernity at the advent of the modern age characterized this new condition as alienating, abstracting, traumatic, and catastrophic. For them, the overriding image of technological progress was the metropolis; the urban environment was monstrous in its widespread impersonal power.[12]

The transformation of China now underway is a modernity of this kind, but even more so. It resembles the first coming of modernity in the late nineteenth and early twentieth centuries, and yet, in this way of looking at things, it is today even more intense, more rapid, and more disorienting because it is a part of so-called postmodern globalization. The main difference is that the first coming of modernization affected the Western world and propelled the West to a position of worldwide influence, such that it brought the Western version of modernity to the entire world. Modernity, in the countries of its birth, had many destructive and catastrophic consequences. The fear that some in China now express is that the postmodern globalization currently underway in what was once called the underdeveloped or, more politely nowadays, the developing world—a part of the globe less prepared for the shock of it—may bring catastrophes even worse than those that appeared in the West.

Thus, the skeptic in today's China will speak of the "psycho-cultural trauma of globalization," and "a disenchanting effect on communities once buttressed by tradition, collective memory, folklore, and kinship relations. . . . In the rush to embrace economic development, consumer goods, and a uniform mass culture, many societies risk losing their cultural heritage and history. . . . The lifeworlds constituted by relatively stable associations, by shared collective memory and commitments, by time-honored attachments and structure of feeling, are fading from the horizon. . . . The attempts to preserve the valuables of these lifeworlds are also fading. . . . The merger between the global metropolis and the village is all too treacherous and the prices for changing one's identity and inventing one's history every few minutes have not been calculated."[13]

Foreboding of this sort is not new. Chinese writers and philosophers in the late nineteenth and early twentieth centuries—whether welcoming of, or resigned to the necessity of, or grudgingly accepting of the inevitability of the modernization of a post-imperial Confucian China—worried about what could happen in the process. And in real life the actual events of China's story were far worse than any one of them imagined. Like the twentieth century, the twenty-first century in China begins with comparable dread in many of the same precincts. What should we make of it?

Even a brief encounter with Chinese literary and intellectual life is a reminder of how literary imagination—that is, what begins in a writer's imagination—can become an inspiration for subsequent political, including strategic, behavior. In fact, in China there has been a close connection between the two. After all, in the late Qing period the beau ideal of a proper Chinese man changed profoundly—from a Confucian *literatus* to a man of modern education and attainment. After the end of the imperial system, in the writings of the 1920s and 1930s, the beau ideal of a good and loyal subject of the old dynasty was replaced by the beau ideal of a good and civic-minded citizen of the new republic. With the establishment of the People's Republic, the literature of "socialist realism" announced that this mere "citizen" was now to become a "new socialist man." Even more significantly, as David Der-wei Wang emphasizes, the transformation in the portrayal of what it means to be a proper Chinese woman—from dutiful Confucian wife and mother, to modern career woman, to matriarch of but a one-child family—has been rapid and profound.[14] This alone has had, and will continue to have, enormous effects on Chinese life and society.

Twentieth-century science fantasy writing is also very suggestive, and David Der-wei Wang's discussion of the connections and parallels between those visions and today's creations is well worth pondering:

> Just as in the late Qing, utopia and dystopia remain Chinese science fantasy writers' favorite subgenres. By imagining a future landscape for Taiwan or China, these writers test their political anxieties or desires. . . .
>
> According to Yao Jia-wen (1942–) Taiwan will have declared independence from China and rejoined the stage of world politics, and helps the Chinese government solve ecological problems and even avert a political coup. . . . The mainland writer Liang Xiaosheng's (1952–) *Fucheng* (*Floating City*, 1992) deals with the disastrous consequences when a southeastern Chinese metropolis (Shanghai?) is mysteriously disconnected from the mainland; it drifts aimlessly. . . .
>
> In Bao Mi's 1991 novel *Huanghuo* (*Yellow Peril*), a stupendous novel of more than half a million words, China has split into parts, and politicians fighting a civil war employ nuclear weapons; . . . [M]ore than a billion Chinese emigrate to the rest of the world; wherever they go they cause political and economic crises. . . . Bao Mi's end-of-the century vision is a bleak one: the "new era" so anticipated by late-Qing writers may still arrive, but only after China has managed to ruin, not rule, the world. . . .
>
> Writing in an era of "post-history," contemporary Chinese writers have tried to make sense of history by invoking its fantastic other. . . . This fantastic inclination seems to take us full circle to a point almost a century before, when the forerunners of modern Chinese fiction imagined a new China by means of utopian constructs. . . . But unlike their predecessors, contemporary writers diversify the future of the new China by conjuring up various political and scientific possibilities.[15]

In this way the great ambition of Chinese strategists now vies for control of the Chinese imagination with the unsettling imagery of Chinese literary artists. As the strategists advance their political program, the novelists advance what is in effect a political program of their own by invoking China's memory of violence and destruction.

At the same time, the destruction wrought by Taipings and Maoists informs the outlook of others who have had no use for modernity in any of its variations. Such people, who have long dreaded the consequences of China's modernity whatever its guise, still repair to the Confucian ideal of *tatong*, the great harmony. Still other Chinese suggest another kind of Chinese approach, the Middle Way, an idea that the competitiveness, both internal and international, that history has shown necessary for China to move ahead and recover its proper standing, is not inconsistent with peace, and can therefore be sustained indefinitely without catastrophic breakdown either at home or in the world.

Yet the history of the last century's violence is the history of abrupt and dramatic change—from the Confucian Qing dynasty to the bourgeois Republic of China; from Chiang Kai-shek's Republic of China to Mao Zedong's People's Republic of China; and from Mao's China to Deng's China. It is only this last startling, and wholly unexpected, change that has been accomplished thus far without wholesale upheaval and without widespread violence and destruction. It is also the only one that is generally regarded as successful, at least for the moment, and it is, for any twentieth-century Chinese dispensation, comparatively long lived. An American must say this with some irony, for Deng's China is only thirty years old, not the span of even one generation. But in Modern China, that is a long time. One can only imagine how this unfolding experience is affecting China's strategic culture and how, or even whether, it is contributing anything to China's strategic tradition.

Both the judgment of Westerners and the competing judgments of Chinese seem shallow and even tongue-tied when placed against the verdict delivered by one of twentieth-century China's literary masters, Gao Xingjian (b. 1940). In 2000 Gao received the first Nobel Prize in Literature ever given to a Chinese. The government in Beijing kept conspicuously silent about this unprecedented international recognition of a still-living Chinese writer, but its silence is easily understood when contrasted with what Gao had to say. In giving the traditional lecture in Stockholm that follows presentation of the prize, he spoke on behalf of his lost comrades and against any renewed effort to enlist art in the service of any grand political design.

> Chinese literature in the twentieth century time and again was worn out and indeed almost suffocated because politics dictated literature: both the revolution in literature and revolutionary literature alike passed death sentences on literature and the individual. The attack on Chinese traditional culture in the name of the revolution resulted in public prohibition and in burning of books. Countless writers were shot, imprisoned, exiled or punished with hard labour in the course of the past one hundred years. This was more extreme than in any imperial dynastic period of China's history....
>
> During the years when Mao Zedong implemented total dictatorship even fleeing was not an option. The monasteries on far away mountains that provided refuge for scholars in feudal times were totally ravaged and to write even in secret was to risk one's life....
>
> This is an age without prophecies and promises and I think this is a good thing. The writer playing prophet and judge should also cease since the many prophecies of the past century have all turned out to be frauds, and there is no need to manufacture new superstitions about the future. It would be best also for the writer to revert to the role of witness and strive to present the truth.[16]

The Chinese text of Gao's lecture continues to circulate inside China and throughout the Chinese-writing world.

CHAPTER 9

THE STRANGE DEATH OF THE SOVIET EMPIRE

Any discussion of the future of national epics and national narratives in China should begin by examining the fate of the very story that was put forward not long ago as the greatest of China's modern national narratives—the coming of the People's Republic of China. And central to an understanding of that particular tale is the radical way in which it attached China's history and China's future to concepts that were not Chinese at all—Marxism, dialectical materialism, proletarian internationalism, and Stalinism. Beyond these abstractions, China's future was also attached to a recently established, actually existing, political regime—the Union of Soviet Socialist Republics—a regime that governed the lands of the former Romanov Empire. One might have imagined, as many Chinese had once done, that the denouement of the story of modern China would be a Sino-Japanese bloc, or a Pan-Asian bloc, or even some version of a Greater East Asian Co-Prosperity Sphere with China as its leader.

Instead, in a truly Great Leap to an unanticipated climax, modern China's story came to rest in none of these places. Instead, China left the Asia where it used to live, and migrated to a New World altogether. In 1950 Mao Zedong famously predicted that "the Soviet Union's today will be our tomorrow." Mao believed that the Soviet model would lead China toward its own economic development. In the early years of the People's Republic, Soviet material assistance and Soviet advisors were seen as integral to the success of China's revolution. The Soviet manual of economic and governmental organization was adopted in China, and Stalin's approach in the late 1940s to rebuilding his empire's war-damaged economy was closely studied and became decisively influential in developing New China's first central plans.

Overall, as Deborah Kaple, a careful student of the first years of Mao's China, summarizes it, this era is best characterized as the "Triumph of High Stalinism."[1] Later on, Mao Zedong came to prefer a more distinctly "Chinese" model of communism. This led him to undertake the hugely destructive and self-defeating political campaigns that began in the mid-1950s and lasted in one form or another until his death in 1976. In the polemical parlance of those days, these programs represented a Chinese critique of Soviet ideology, but from the Left. In Mao's view, after Stalin died the Soviet Union began to practice revisionism, not Marxism. With Mao's death and the subsequent adoption of Deng Xiaoping's reform program, China's discussion of the Soviet Union took yet another abrupt turn. Now, Chinese economists and sociologists were instructed not to document and denounce the Soviets' backsliding and revisionism but rather to look sympathetically at the history of liberalization and decentralization efforts within the Socialist camp, whether in Yugoslavia, Hungary, Poland, Romania, or, especially, the Soviet Union itself.

The results were disconcerting. In the late 1970s and early 1980s many insightful Chinese observers began to detect a reversal in the momentum of the Soviet-American contest and the first signs that the Soviet Union might enter a period of sustained decline. In a remarkable investigation into the situation as it appeared to both Soviets and Chinese at the time—published in 1987, four years before the doom of the Soviet Union was finally sealed—Gilbert Rozman laid out the content of these ominous discussions. The metaphor of a slow Pearl Harbor—a not-yet-recognized attack, like the one on the Qing dynasty in the early nineteenth century—certainly is applicable to the Soviet Union as the twentieth century was coming to a close. Its accomplishments were many, and its future seemed bright. But on January 30, 1982, *People's Daily* carried an article called "Signs of Crisis as Soviet Economy Enters a New Year" which quoted Western newspapers on Soviet failures to achieve planned economic growth rates. A week later *Xinhua* analyzed the Soviet global strategy for 1982. It asserted that the Soviet harvest shortfall of 1981, together with the protracted war in Afghanistan and the Polish crises, "has more or less shackled the feet of the Soviet giant in pressing ahead with expansion abroad."

Rozman further recapitulates this discussion, noting that a month later, in an article in a journal published by Shanghai University, the Chinese economist Zhang Yueming evaluated the prospects for the Soviet Union and the United States, "both still plotting to gain a monopoly position and world hegemony." In the 1960s the United States had been on the offensive; in the 1970s, and even on into the 1980s, it was the Soviets. But, Zhang said, a change in the balance was now visible. As Rozman summarized Zhang's argument, "In the mid-seventies Soviet economic development began to stagnate, and Moscow was no longer narrowing the gap with America. Entering the eighties, the Soviet economic situation further deteriorated, while it faced larger military competition from America.... The Soviet decline was underway.... Although the results of recent expansion had widened Moscow's sphere of power, its economic problems could not be overcome."[2] It is now known that much of the Soviet leadership had been reading the situation in the same way. It is also now known that Mikhail Gorbachev, who came to power in 1983, brought with him an agenda for large-scale reform in the Soviet Union not so very different in its spirit and in its sense of urgency from that of Deng Xiaoping's program.

The contents of these two programs were different, as were their outcomes. But even in the early 1980s, the terms of intellectual trade inside the Communist camp had been turned upside down. The Chinese Communist Party had been learning from the Soviet Union since the 1920s, but now it was the other way around. Many Soviet economists and sociologists, who had looked upon the Maoist version of communism as increasingly irrational and dangerous, studied Deng's program as a plausible way out of the USSR's crisis. As one of them quipped, "Communism had saved China, and it was now China's turn to save Communism."

By the late 1980s there was a palpable sense of crisis in both countries. Gorbachev arrived in Beijing for an official visit on May 15, 1989, with Eastern Europe already in turmoil and less than six more months before the end, when the Berlin Wall would collapse on November 9. Deng's China was less than three weeks away from the climactic events of June 4 in Beijing's

Tiananmen Square. Indeed, it seemed to many—not least to Deng Xiaoping himself—that it was the system *in China* that was in imminent danger of collapse.

Just as it was peculiar that China and Russia had become joined at the hip in a wholly unexpected way, equally unexpected has been China's reluctance to separate itself rapidly and wholly from its fraternal twin. It has been a slow process, with China still interested in asserting at least some formal continuity between the Soviet experience and its own. When China began its wholesale reforms of the late 1970s, it did so within the context of their relationship to other Communist countries. Chinese social scientists, economists, and Communist Party theoreticians labored mightily to fit Deng Xiaoping's program into the grand sweep of the world revolution's history. Thus, even if only by negative example, the death of the Soviet Union—and the discrediting of the ideology on which it had been constructed—remain important to China's understanding of its own situation. The fate of the Union of Soviet Socialist Republics and its ruling Communist Party is not easily quarantined, especially psychologically, from the future of the People's Republic of China and its ruling Communist Party.

At the time, the historic events of 1989 throughout the Communist world seemed closely connected, but in what ways? The final collapse of the USSR in 1991 came only two years into the post-Tiananmen era in China. Was this the end of the turmoil, or only its beginning? China and Russia once had a common Communist program, but as it turned out, after the historic events between 1989 and 1991, the People's Republic of China was left standing, but the Soviet Union was not. This was a traumatic event for Communists everywhere, and especially for the severely shaken Communists in China. Jiang Zemin, by designation of Deng Xiaoping, became general secretary of the Chinese Communist Party in late June 1989, then president of the country in 1993, and then, finally, preeminent leader after Deng's death in 1997. Jiang's rise to power had coincided with inauspicious omens. Jiang Zemin observed, "After more than seventy years of socialist construction in the Soviet Union, the great tragedy of the Soviet collapse occurred. Why? The reasons and the lessons need to be concluded profoundly and comprehensively. . . . The study of the reasons for the Soviet collapse is very important for China at this time. . . . It will help us build the foundation of socialism with Chinese characteristics and help us govern the country into the future and keep China safe, stable, and standing."[3]

China's "profound and comprehensive" examination of these issues has been carefully analyzed by Christopher Marsh, who has begun with, and then significantly expanded on, Gilbert Rozman's pioneering studies. In Marsh's summary:

> Following Jiang's call, research institutions that had previously studied the USSR as a means of generating insight into an adversary, such as the Institute for Soviet and East European Studies at the Chinese Academy of Sciences, switched their focus to examining the implications of the Soviet past for China's future. Other research centers were created, whose purpose is to analyze regime evolution and collapse, especially with reference to the former USSR. . . .
>
> Research into the Soviet collapse is not something the Party just left up to academics. The Communist Party formed working groups comprised of the country's leading specialists with the specific charge of studying the causes of the collapse and the lessons to be learned. These working groups have been the source of much of the research in this area, which has included government sponsored conferences and has resulted in numerous books on the Soviet collapse, many with special sections devoted to the lessons to be drawn from the Soviet experience.[4]

These efforts have produced a myriad of analyses, ranging across the ethnic conflicts in the USSR, to the competence of individual Soviet leaders, to ideological dogmatism, to excessive timidity in carrying out reforms, to choosing the wrong reforms, to moving too fast, to moving too slowly. To the extent that there is a consensus position, it is that the Soviet Communist Party could not make the transition from a revolutionary to a truly governing party; that Marxism-Leninism can no longer be the main source of legitimacy for the rule of the Communist Party in China, but that the party should rely instead on things more traditionally Chinese; that economic prosperity and honest leadership are required.

At the same time, some argued that there were other dangers to the Soviet regime, and in retrospect it is apparent how their analyses informed one part of future action by the Chinese government. "By their own admission," Marsh writes, "China's policymakers are pursuing their restrictive religious policy due to their understanding of the role that religion played in the collapse of Communism in Eastern Europe and the Soviet Union." As Marsh explains, one of the party's own journals saw the threat this way:

We need to learn from the lessons of the disintegration of the Soviet Union and precipitous changes in Eastern Europe.... As a result of the errors of the former socialist countries in their handling of the religious question, religion became an instrument in the hands of political dissidents for stirring up trouble when the domestic politics and the economy became mired in trouble and all kinds of social contradictions sharpened. That hastened the downfall of the Soviet and East European Communist parties.[5]

From these wide-ranging discussions of the Soviet experience, one can tease out many of the elements in contemporary China's domestic policies, both for better and worse—the commitment to high economic growth rates; the ongoing efforts to correct regional imbalances; the promotion of interest in Old China's cultural and literary achievements; the invocation of vaguely defined phrases such as Spiritual Civilization as adjuncts to the country's official materialist ideology; the unceasing police activities directed against dissenters of both a secular and religious bent.

But there is another part of the Soviet experience that is at least as relevant—the lessons of Soviet foreign policy. Many Chinese students of the Soviet collapse have seen in the USSR's international ambition the seeds of its ruin. In 1998, for example, Shen Jiru, an obviously well-connected researcher at the Chinese Academy of Sciences, published a book carrying an approving forward by the academy's vice president. His book, *China Doesn't Want to Be "Mr. No": Problems of International Strategy for Today's China*, was a four-hundred-page discussion of the future of China's international relations, based on the notion that the post-Mao reforms had so changed Chinese society as also to change the country's sense of itself, especially its sense of its place in the world and what it wanted from the world.

Shen's analysis began with a discussion of the causes of the Soviet collapse, and Soviet foreign policy figures prominently. The Soviet Union wanted to be a hegemonic world power, but with the result that "it created enemies, lost friends, and wasted national economic strength."[6] Soviet foreign policy was one of confrontation; Soviet military policy was reduced to attempting to match the United States weapons system for weapons system, thereby exhausting the Soviet economy.

Chinese readers knew the context of this analysis. The phrase "creating enemies and losing friends" had a special resonance, for it harked back to an essay written by Mao Zedong in 1926, which famously began: "Who are our enemies? Who are our friends? This is the revolution's most important question." Mao Zedong had picked the Soviet Union as China's friend, but the relationship turned out badly. As for the Soviet Union, its erstwhile friend and disciple, China, had somehow become a mortal enemy, in part because of avoidable errors in the conduct of the Soviet Union's foreign policy in general, and its China policy in particular.

In the 1970s China chose the United States as its new friend, and that turned out to be a shrewd decision. Capital and technology have poured into the country not only from the United States, but also from the European Union and Japan—both allies of the United States and both part of an American-dominated security and economic network. Relationships with other rich and powerful international networks, networks run by Chinese in Hong Kong, Taiwan, Singapore, and Southeast Asia, were reactivated, leading to the re-establishment of a China-dominated Asian economic system. In these respects, China's current project is well begun.

All of these things, whether openly stated or merely hinted at, argue for China's acceptance of the obligations of the international economic and political system and China's promotion of greater openness in its own society so as to become more competitive while remaining at peace. In Shen Jiru's view—and presumably in the view of his sponsors and mentors—this is a winning strategy over the long run; the problems posed to China today by American hegemony will solve themselves as American primacy slowly but surely recedes. Thus, for one example, China does not need military forces that even begin to approach the size and capability of those of the United States.

At one level, analyses of this sort are seemingly supportive of a liberal internationalist approach to world affairs. But one can also view it as "liberal internationalism with Chinese characteristics." After all, it projects calm self-confidence that China's patience and diligence will ultimately be rewarded; it implies that American foreign policy—in its global ambitions, in its impetuosity, in its desire for quick results, and in its costly worldwide military operations—will likely fall victim to the same self-destructive compulsions that destroyed the world position of the old Soviet Union. In this view China, on the other hand, can allow history and human nature to work on China's behalf, confident that the United States, like the Soviet Union, will succumb to its excesses, excesses that, in best dialectical fashion, are the products of its own virtues.

In this respect one can sense once again the dissonance that has been a prominent feature of the thinking of modern-minded Chinese intellectuals for more than a century: the West in general and the United States in particular are much to be admired and emulated, but only to a point.

In 1994 Beijing University inaugurated its China Center for Economic Research. The keynote speaker at the center's opening ceremony was Douglass North, an economic historian who, the year before, had received the Nobel Prize in Economics. North (b. 1920) was honored for his role in pioneering what he and likeminded thinkers called the new institutional economics. As the phrase suggests, North believes that the history of economic development—especially why it occurred at some times and in some places, but not at all times and in all places—can best be explained by reference to the complicated relationships among institutions, politics, belief systems, and cultural history in any particular country. In his Nobel lecture of December 9, 1993, North contrasted this approach to pristine economic theory:

> It is necessary to dismantle the rationality assumption underlying economic theory in order to approach constructively the nature of human learning. History demonstrates that ideas, ideologies, myths, dogmas, and prejudices matter; and an understanding of the way they evolve is necessary for further progress in developing a framework to understand societal change. The rationality assumption of neo-classical theory suggests that political entrepreneurs of stagnating economies can simply alter the rules and change the direction of failed economies. But it is not that rulers have been unaware of poor performance. Rather the difficulty of turning economies around is a function of the nature of political markets and, underlying that, the belief systems of the actors. The long decline of Spain, for example, from the glories of the Habsburg Empire of the sixteenth century to its sorry state under Franco in the twentieth century was characterized by endless self-appraisals and frequently bizarre proposed solutions. . . .
>
> We cannot account for the rise and decline of the Soviet Union and world communism with the tools of neoclassical analysis, but we can begin to do so with an institutional/cognitive approach to contemporary problems of development.[7]

North stresses the role of political communities in shaping economic performance. "Polities significantly shape economic performance because they define and enforce the economic rules. An essential part of development policy is the creation of polities that will create and enforce efficient property rights. However, we know very little about how to create such polities because the new political economy (the new institutional economics applied to politics) has been largely focused on the United States and developed polities. . . . While economic growth can occur in the short run with autocratic regimes, long-run economic growth entails the development of the rule of law."

In 2004 North was again invited to speak at the China Center for Economic Research to mark its tenth anniversary. His presence was confirmation that after another decade of debate in China, there were still some well-situated adherents to his belief that open-access political markets are as important as open-access commercial markets. Indeed, he and his Chinese supporters maintain that the main task before the country is in fact the application of the new institutional economics to the Chinese polity so as to build in China a regime that creates and enforces efficient property rights. Accordingly, after his return from Beijing, North recapitulated the uncertainty surrounding China's grand project as he had seen it unfold over the years:

> China has partially opened competitive access to its economic markets. But China is only halfway there. The society is still dominated by a political dictatorship and, as a result, personal exchange rather than impersonal rules dominate the economy. How will China evolve? It could continue to evolve open-access economic markets built on impersonal rules and gradually dissolve barriers to open political markets. . . . Or the political dictatorship could perceive the evolving open-access society as a threat to the existing vested interests, and halt the course of the past decades.[8]

The regime in power in China is thus called on to accelerate its own subversion today in the service of China's national greatness tomorrow—all in the name of yet another of the West's theories about the way to wealth and power.

CHAPTER 10

"THE CHINESE PEOPLE ARE A HEAP OF LOOSE SAND"

In the course of the past century the modern has presented itself to China in very appealing guises—only to leave disappointment behind. The promise of the first great age of liberal globalization at the turn of the twentieth century gave way to disillusionment, as European civilization collapsed in the wake of World War I. After that, the promise of a new revolutionary internationalism, when implemented in a new People's Republic, led not to a restoration of China's glories but to mind-boggling material and psychological damage, to international isolation, and almost to open war with a once-inspirational Soviet Union. Most recently, China has sought to explain its own good fortune in avoiding the fate of the Soviet Union, and how its alliance with the capitalist United States and its embrace of the American-dominated international system will somehow ensure the thriving of "socialism with Chinese characteristics."

Chinese today have a hard time making much sense of this story. Indeed, to many, the welter of details has foreclosed even the possibility of a coherent recounting of modern China; accordingly, they think it is inevitable that China's next great national undertaking will end up like the ones that have preceded it. At the least, there is great confusion about how the experiences that created Modern China should be represented. It is one thing to find such bewilderment among intellectuals and artists who pride themselves on being opponents of the regime in power. It is quite another thing to observe that the regime itself, led by a self-proclaimed all-knowing Chinese Communist Party, repeatedly shifts its ground. Whether the subjects are elevated ones like modern history, modern literature, or modern architecture, or mundane ones like tariffs, trade, and transportation, the party scrambles for ways of explaining how it thinks and why it acts in the ways that it does. Indeed, the regime in power is indefatigable in its search for a unifying theme or a consistent story to serve as a basis for a grand design and a national purpose.

In response to Jiang Zemin's call for a thoroughgoing inquiry into the causes of the Soviet demise, new institutes and research centers were created to study the evolution of regimes and their collapse. One such, the China Reform Forum, was set up at the Central Committee's Central Party School. The forum is also thought to be part of a network of think tanks connected to the State Council and to the prime minister's office. The forum, and its long-time head Zheng Bijian (b. 1932), are well known to research institutions in the West for organizing international conferences about China's economic and social policies. As for Zheng Bijian himself, his official biography tells us that he has also been involved in the development of the party's outlook on various things for many years. Indeed, he has lived through more than his fair share of party history.

He joined the Communist Party of China in 1952. He completed postgraduate studies in political economics at People's University of China in 1954. . . .

Zheng has conducted Party-oriented research for the State government, the Chinese Academy of Social Sciences, and the Party. He was deputy chief for the theory group of Mao Zedong Works Editing Committee at the CPC Central Committee in the late 1970s. He was later Deputy Director-General of the International Affairs Research Center at the State Council in the late 1970s. In 1988, he served a four-year stint as the vice-president of the Chinese Academy of Social Sciences. He concurrently worked as the Director of the Research Institute for Marxism, Leninism and Mao Zedong Thought at the Academy.

Following his Academy positions, Zheng became deputy head of the publicity department at the CPC Central Committee. He is Executive Vice-President of the Party school of the CPC Central Committee.

Zheng also has an unofficial biography as constructed by Western China watchers; he is believed to have served as a personal assistant to two more liberal general secretaries of the party—Hu Yaobang (1915–1989) and Zhao Ziyang (1919–2005)—who were both iconic and inspirational figures for the 1989 Tiananmen demonstrators. When Zheng Bijian began his service as vice president of the Central Committee's Party School, it was headed by the current president of the People's Republic, Hu Jintao. Among those who have survived the gauntlet of higher party politics these past five decades, Zheng Bijian is probably not unusual either in his intellectual adaptability or in his political agility.

In fact, he would not be the best exemplar of either, except for the fact that he has had his proverbial fifteen minutes of fame among China watchers; he is the inventor of the phrase Peaceful Rise as the definition of China's Grand Strategy. Zheng introduced the phrase in November 2003 and has frequently written and spoken about it. In fact, in June 2005 the Brookings Institution of Washington, D.C., published a small compendium of his speeches on the subject.

As much as the notion of a Peaceful Rise has been linked to globalization and liberal internationalism, the phrase has proved flexible enough to represent additional ways of relating China to today's world and to the history of the world. For one conspicuous example, Zheng Bijian himself, writing in April 2006, connects China's Peaceful Rise not to any Western-derived scheme but says, instead, that "the profound substance of China's peaceful development is the revival of Chinese civilization, a process in which Chinese civilization is rehabilitated through autonomous innovation; realizing the revival of Chinese civilization is the profound substance of China's peaceful development."[1]

A comment like this is not so much a culmination but, rather, another point on a three-decades-long continuum that connects China's most recent era of reform to things Chinese as well as to things Western. Almost as soon as Deng Xiaoping's program was launched, there was a conscious effort to link it to China's sixteenth-century commercial revolution. Indeed, as Harriet Zurndorfer elaborates, this was part and parcel of a trend throughout the Sinic world.

> In the 1980s, the governments of Taiwan, Singapore, and South Korea gave official approval to Confucian values as a collective guide to economic practices. . . . By the 1990s, the PRC authorities sanctioned historical

Confucianism as a major component of China's intellectual tradition and modern-day economic progress. It became common during that decade to find in the PRC's official newspaper, *People's Daily*, articles praising business leaders as *rushang* (Confucian entrepreneurs).

On the occasion of the PRC's forty-fifth anniversary, in October, 1994, an international conference was held in Beijing where various official and semi-official organizations from Singapore, Japan, South Korea, Taiwan, the United States, and Germany were invited. This meeting inaugurated a new organization, the International Society of Confucianism, with the former Singapore Prime Minister Lee Kuan Yew and Gu Mu, a former Chinese vice premier, elected honorary president, and vice-president, respectively.

Thus, it would seem that by the end of the twentieth century the PRC had aligned itself with traditional anticommunist ideologues in a purportedly non-political discourse that ultimately linked present-day economic initiative in a globalized capitalist world with a 2000-year-old cultural legacy.[2]

With impressive ease, the Communist Party of China transformed capitalism from a system forcibly imposed on China by militant Western imperialism into a system deeply rooted in China's millennia-old culture. But it is a mistake merely to be dismissive; analytically and politically, this one episode of conceptual legerdemain raises important questions about China's future understanding of itself as a nation, as a culture, and as a civilization. It may be a clue to how China may decide to project itself into the world and into the future history of the world.

In one respect, can it be surprising that China wishes to represent itself to the world as—China? If it is not China, what else could it be? Writing about "China's soft power offensive," Pernendra Jain and Gerry Groot report that in 2002 Beijing established what it calls the Confucius Institute, with a mission to promote the Chinese language, culture, and a range of other aspects of learning about China.

Several of these institutes have already been established around the world, in such places as Japan, Australia, Sweden and the United States, and Beijing aims eventually to open some 100 of them.

The choice of the name is instructive, since for years it was Communist Party dogma that Confucianism held back China's development. In recent years, however, Confucianism has undergone a kind of political resurrection in China, and in any case has no threatening connotations. A "Mao Zedong Institute" probably would not be welcomed in most countries.[3]

This seems straightforward enough on the face of it, a seeming indication that China may well be headed back to being just China, no more and no less. If so, Chinese everywhere will re-examine their decades-old debate—their still vigorous debate—about the meaning of China and things Chinese. And, as they have in the past, these speculations will figure prominently in how these words should be part of the country's ongoing strategic calculations.

To China's ever-changing understanding of itself in different contexts—whether as a geographical expression or as a cultural or even anthropological one—there should now be added a racial dimension. A discourse of race, to use Frank Dikotter's term, has been part of China's self-analysis, especially since the late nineteenth century when a presumed racial difference between the Chinese and their Manchu rulers began to matter in entirely new ways. This distinction, of course, was rooted in the very creation and enlargement of the Manchu Empire, and cultural and ethnic sensibilities influenced the governance of the empire for centuries. Indeed, they were inseparable from the Manchus' larger strategic sensibility.

A discourse of race was also introduced into the analysis of international relations. At the turn of the twentieth century, many Chinese—and Westerners also—saw world politics as a white-yellow race war to the death. Racial solidarity figured on both sides, as the white man's burden and civilizing mission encountered pan-Asianism. As China's political system devolved, first into a republic and then into a People's Republic, "race" became "nation" became "class."[4]

Thus, the twentieth century's invocation of the Yellow Peril, the Aryan race, and the Yamato race remains a conscious part of contemporary China's experience. It is a memory invoked ironically, and sometimes bitterly, by Chinese themselves, as in the 1991 novel *Huanghuo* (*Yellow Peril*), a fantasy in which a Chinese writer imagines a China that has become a threat to the world. Meanwhile, in the larger world, both a clash of races and a clash of classes have, for the moment, given way to a clash of civilizations as the catch phrase for defining major political fault lines. Should a rising power bet its future on any such slogan?

This is not the only available shorthand. Chinese have connected their sense of themselves to things that were not Chinese at all—to liberalism, socialism, Christianity—but, most of all, to the modern, and to all the ways that term has been interpreted for the past 150 years. A perennial frustration of China's most important political figures of modern times was with what they took to be the backwardness of their country and its people. Sun Yat-sen—father of the republic, whose political program was suffused with what today would be called anti-Manchu racism—was for all his Chinese racial sensibility a quintessentially un-Chinese man, a maritime Chinese, an outsider reared in Hawaii, a physician-practitioner of Western medicine, and a baptized Christian. It was he who, in 1924, famously described the Chinese as "a heap of loose sand," maddeningly incapable of creating a modern state.

In this, Sun was reiterating the judgment of the renowned Liang Qichao, who, during his exile from China in the first years of the twentieth century, had similar frustrations. Liang visited North America in 1903. As K. Scott Wong describes it,

> Liang came to the United States ideologically rooted in Confucian ideals of political reform and social hierarchy, but also influenced by Social Darwinist notions of race and power that privileged Anglo-Saxon supremacy. Dismayed by the turn of events in China and inspired by the example of growing Japanese power, Liang believed that the nature of the "Chinese character" had to be transformed in order for political and social reform even to be possible. That transformation, however, would call for national self-examination, generated by and resulting in a restructuring of the Chinese worldview.
>
> "Chinese can be clansmen, but not citizens," Liang wrote. "They cling to the family and clan systems to the exclusion of other things."[5]

In the century since Liang Qichao, visiting his countrymen in an already functioning modern state, despaired of their ever being able to create a modern state of their own, the effort to relate what is quintessentially Chinese to what is quintessentially modern has only intensified. Today's self-consciously academic phrase for this quest is "the construction of China's national identity," but the activity itself is not especially exotic. Americans, for example, have been at it for quite a long time, sometimes relying on a foreign observer like Alexis de Tocqueville (1805–1859) or on a native-born historian like Daniel Boorstin (1914–2004) to explain themselves to themselves. Americans continually work at defining themselves as a nation, as a country, as a people, and as a culture. More specifically, and related to the formation of what we have been calling Grand Strategy, Americans have pursued national strategies based in large part on their assessment of the ways in which other peoples are like them, the ways in which they are different, and, therefore, the ways in which America's own views about politics and economics are transferable to other people and transplantable into other places.

These are fundamental issues in the history of China also. For three great dynasties—two of which, Mongol and Manchu, were not Chinese at all—the definition of what was inside and what was outside, of what was civilized and what was barbarian, figured decisively in the formation of imperial strategies. In the waning days of Manchu rule, both the dynasty and its internal enemies struggled for control of the very definition of the words *China* and *Chinese*. Modern China lived through two episodes of violent revolution—the Taiping uprising of the nineteenth century and the Maoist insurgency of the twentieth. Both revealed great intellectual flexibility and adaptability among China's people; indeed, the leaders of these movements assumed that belief systems from the other side of the world as taught by two Jews, Jesus Christ and Karl Marx, would somehow become the basis of a durable Chinese political and social order. There were debates about the applicability of the West's modern to China's own modernization in every realm of life. Though the largest ambitions of Hong Xiuquan and Mao Zedong were not fulfilled, Christianity and communism still exert powerful influence; high modernity did not prevail either, but it occupies a prominent place in China's culture.

The post-Mao reforms are yet another chapter in the story of China's effort to relate developments in a world to which China is daily more connected, on the one hand, to changes in what Liang Qichao called "the Chinese character" on the other. One pole in this discussion is represented by the work of Chinese intellectuals like Sun Longji and Jin Guantao, who are associated with the idea of the "ultrastability" of China as a cultural system. As summarized by Tim Oakes,

> Sun and Jin found in cybernetics and systems theory alternatives to the
> orthodox historical materialism of Chinese Marxism and argued that China,
> as a cultural system, displayed an "internal resilience" and "a capacity for
> adjustment" so that revolutionary upheavals and disruptions were absorbed
> into an "ultrastable" system. . . . As Jin Guantao writes, "China has not yet
> freed itself from the control of history. Its only mode of existence is to relive
> the past. There is no accepted mechanism within the culture for the Chinese

to confront the present without falling back on the inspiration and strength of tradition."[6]

Oakes draws on this idea of an essential Chineseness, but to make another kind of argument. He uses the term *cultural regionalism* to distinguish among the increasingly disparate definitions of *Chineseness* as between coastal and interior areas, and he maintains that the province in turn is becoming the focal point of this regionalism; many provinces in China are promoting ideas about provincial culture and provincial identity. In Oakes's observation, these efforts are similar. "They seek to convey a message about the 'spirit' of Chineseness as distinct from the West, but a spirit that is equally distant from China's own revolutionary Marxist heritage."

The provincial elites who do this may very well believe it, but it is also their strategy for connecting themselves to people and things Chinese all over the world, not only to those in China. "It is here," Oakes thinks, "that we encounter the link between the broader civilizational discourse of 'Asian values' and the flexible accumulation of global capitalism."[7]

Some argue that the successes of Chinese businesses anywhere are related to time-honored Confucian values everywhere; some academics regard such explanations for the success of Chinese capitalists as myths, while others believe in them. As we have also seen, the Chinese governments in Greater China endorse the connection, even as they often see in Confucianism an obstacle to modernization. But the non-Chinese governments, especially those in Southeast Asia that are the sovereign hosts of powerful Chinese business networks, are leery of claims of an irrevocable connection between their Chinese citizens and some other mother country or mother culture.

On the face of it the efforts to offer a culturalist explanation for the successes of China and the Chinese during the late twentieth century appear to be in the interest of the nation-state that is the People's Republic of China. And, moreover, it is incontrovertible that Beijing's patriotic appeal to Chinese around the world to invest in China's post-1978 reform project has been a successful strategic initiative, in every sense of that term. But at the same time, the preferred method of reform, post-1978, has placed Beijing's preferred definition of Chineseness under great stress.

By now, most people in the world who pay close attention to China are familiar with a phrase coined by Deng Xiaoping to encapsulate the aim of his reform program—"socialism with Chinese characteristics." Since then, the beguiling notion of Chinese characteristics has been linked in China's policy pronouncements to many products of the Western world—democracy with Chinese characteristics especially. But what do Chinese understand the qualifying phrase to mean? "The Chinese drive for modernisation," writes Elena Barabantseva, "has brought about the reinterpretation and reformulation of the origins, composition, and ideals of the Chinese nation." She continues:

> In the Republic and under Mao, it was believed that the Chinese people since ancient times were centered in North China . . . [but] it is currently believed that China originated not in the isolated northern-plain culture, but in the interplay between several centers. Within the framework of this conviction, the southern provinces have become the vanguard and the personification of the ideals of Chinese modernisation. . . .
>
> The qualities and values cherished by communities on the outskirts of "civilizational China," and condemned for decades, have come to the fore and shape the cultural image of China. . . . Dynamism, flexibility, commercialism, and openness have been promoted from the regional to the national level.[8]

A Chinese patriot, in the literal rendering of the Chinese characters that make up the term, is someone who loves his country. But what is it that he is supposed to love? To what is he supposed to be loyal? Over the decades of the modern era, as China's situation went from bad to worse, Chinese patriotism had a constantly changing agenda. As Michael Hunt has written,

> the continued decline of the state and the widespread popular apathy over China's future convinced Chinese patriots that only a China thoroughly made over could be made to function effectively in international affairs, perhaps even to survive at all. The idea of a revolution that would "make the people new" by effecting fundamental social and economic changes gradually gained adherents. . . . But the result was to push patriots into positions that seemed paradoxical. To save China meant destroying important parts of it. . . . The state would have to be torn down. . . . Destruction of the old political order and social system was the painful but unavoidable path to unity and order and ultimate renewal.[9]

It was always assumed that building a state powerful enough to save China would, in and of itself, produce solidarity and cohesion that would, in turn, make the state even more powerful and effective. Today no one disputes that, by the customary measures, the People's Republic of China is the most powerful and efficacious Chinese state of the past two centuries. And yet, in several different contexts and from several different perspectives, the process of creating an efflorescence of Chinese power is also corroding the very unity and order that were its original inspiration. It is this trend that has brought China to what may prove to be a dividing line, a crossover point—perhaps even a point of no return—between the modern sensibility and a postmodern one. The regime in power in Beijing may continue to insist that there is an unbreakable union among nation, state, people, party, and culture, but the more it persists in its reform program, the more it brings on a kind of destruction—hopefully creative destruction from *its* point of view—but far from inevitably that.

Indeed, the regime in power proclaims "one country, two systems," yet many observers now imagine "one country, many systems." The People's Republic of China, which represents itself as the one and only China, has become but one of several Chinas within Greater China. At the same time, the China mega-economy is creating intranational regions that seek their own independent relations with the outer world. The great cities on the China coast could well come to join a league of their own with other great cities, similarly situated, but within other national jurisdictions. The energy and creativity in contemporary Chinese cultural creation, more often than not, works against the People's Republic of China's ongoing national project. In these and other ways, the very notions of Chineseness, and of the Chinese nationalism it is supposed to produce, are becoming elusive, not merely to outside observers but to the Chinese themselves.

The great legacy of the Qing dynasty to the new Republic of China was the terminological sleight of hand that transformed a multinational empire into a national state. That republic now claimed vast territories and whole peoples whose relationship to China and Chineseness had long been problematical, and whose place in Chinese consciousness and in China's strategic and political scheme of things had changed many times over the preceding centuries; sometimes they were seen as useless wastelands, other times as vital assets. These shifting judgments reflected the state's sense of its own internal governance requirements, its assessment of regional and international power balances, and its judgments about the relationship between the domestic and the foreign. All these became central to the strategic calculations of the new People's Republic, and they still are.

People interested in contemporary China's changing perspectives on the country's modern history anticipate the publication in 2012 of the official history of the Qing dynasty that will mark the one-hundredth anniversary of the Manchu abdication. And, as the date approaches, the questions propounded a century ago—about the shape and size of the country, its governance, its identity, its culture, its expectations for the future, its relations to the world—are still very much in play today. The terminology may seem abstract and somehow disconnected from actual facts, but it is well embedded in the facts on the ground. If Chinese people inside the People's Republic of China—that is, people who think of themselves as Chinese in some sense—have opposing views of what the term means and are therefore conflicted to one degree about their own relationship to the People's Republic as a state, what about people who are in no sense Chinese? Such ethnic minorities, to use the sociological term, are only about 7 percent of the population of the People's Republic—some 90 million of 1.3 billon. But the five so-called autonomous regions in which one or another constitutes a majority of the population comprise about half of the state's territory—about 1.8 million square miles of some 3.7. To look at a map of the People's Republic is to see that China proper is nestled within a crescent formed by the autonomous regions. It is thus obvious that the autonomous regions are inside the People's Republic of China because they are strategically located—which is why, of course, they were incorporated into the Qing Empire in the first place and, later, into the Republic of China.

In that there have been almost a hundred years of republicanization in the non-Chinese parts of the venerable Manchu Empire, how successful has this undertaking been? Tibet and East Turkistan—or sometimes Chinese Turkistan, but *always* Xinjiang ("New Territories") in Beijing's designation—are the most conspicuous for their discontents, and there is substantial evidence that neither the Nationalist nor the Communist version of Chinese republican rule is regarded as satisfactory in these areas. In the early 1950s Tibet's de facto autonomy was ended by its forcible incorporation into the People's Republic. Yet the very brutality of Tibet's reconquest created strategic vulnerabilities for the new overlords. Indeed, the United States, for almost a decade, was able to draw upon Tibetan discontent and supported a guerrilla war by Tibetans against the Chinese army. The Dalai Lama, who then went into exile in 1959, became a man of international renown; more to the point, he is today Beijing's best-known interlocutor in discussions about Tibet's future governance. Tibet remains a problem that China has still to solve, one made no less worrisome by the widely bruited rise of India.

Meanwhile, the Muslim population of Xinjiang—thirteen million in toto, of whom about eight million are Turkic Uighurs and the rest an assortment of other Central Asian ethnicities—has acquired a strategic salience out of all proportion to its numbers. The Qing dynasty pondered the role of this immense piece of territory—about six hundred thousand square miles, or three times the size of France—as the dynasty had to balance the threats of barbarian incursions, Russian expansion, and Western aggrandizement.[10]

Today Beijing's concern with Xinjiang is the product of the Islamic revival, the clash of civilizations, the energy crisis, and the war on terrorism. With the outer world, China shares five literal borders with Islam—Afghanistan, Kazakhstan, Kyrgyzstan, Pakistan, and Tajikistan—and Chineseness in its many varieties shares metaphorical borders with various manifestations of Islamness. China relies for trade and investment on a Chinese diaspora in Islamic Southeast Asia. It also relies increasingly on oil from countries like Iran and Saudi Arabia, which are influenced by China's treatment of its Islamic minority and which could have considerable influence on that Islamic minority if they ever chose to exercise it. As China competes for influence in Central Asia, it is comparably mindful of the kinship among the Central Asian peoples. That the Xinjiang Autonomous Region is not today an independent Islamic Republic of East Turkistan is one of history's accidents. All this gives to Muslim inhabitants of China's northwest substantial leverage in their ongoing wrestling match with Beijing about their future in China's grand scheme of things.

Indeed, in modern times especially, Xinjiang's relationship to China has been influenced by the ebb and flow of politics elsewhere. The Manchu dynasty ended in 1912, the Romanov in 1917. The other empires based in Western Europe either disappeared or were debilitated after World War I. Xinjiang was too far from Wilson's influence to gain its independence, but even though the new Chinese Republic acquired legal title to the place, the struggles among the warlords, and the Nationalists and the Communists, and the Chinese and the Japanese, were tantamount by default to Xinjiang's independence from China. During the same period, however, Xinjiang's Central Asian neighbors suffered the return of Russian influence in the form of the Soviet Union and its Stalinist mode of governance. Thus, East Turkistan had good reason to cherish its separateness from its Sovietized neighbors in the adjacent "Stans." In fact, between 1944 and 1949 there was even a formally proclaimed East Turkistan Republic. It was soon brutally crushed by the new People's Republic of China, even as Beijing was enthusiastically offering support to decolonization movements elsewhere. In this convoluted way the reassertion of a Beijing-based authority as envisioned by Manchu and Chinese strategists in the nineteenth century was finally brought about.

In the early 1950s the regimes in both Stalin's Soviet Union and Mao's People's Republic were sufficiently synchronized in their brutality so that a Turkic person on one side of the line had no particular reason to envy his brother on the other. But with the death of Stalin in 1953, the inhabitants of East Turkistan began to see some moderation of conditions to the West, in contrast to their own experiences of Maoist madness during the Great Leap Forward and then the Cultural Revolution. In the late 1970s and 1980s the advantage moved again to the East, for the post-Mao reforms could be contrasted favorably to the last-gasp effort to shore up the Soviet Union. However, with the Soviet collapse in 1991, the Muslim peoples of Xinjiang could only envy their brethren who had not only gained independence but, in an astonishing feat of bureaucratic legerdemain, had even become a part of Europe—as members of the Organization for Security and Cooperation and with their country desks in the Bureau of European Affairs of the U.S. Department of State.

Thus, the geopolitical map of China's boundary with Islam has shifted over time, and a geocultural map has been as hard for China to draw as a topographical one. The rise of Islam is itself closely coincidental to the flourishing of China's great Tang dynasty (618–907), a dynasty renowned through the ages for its many splendors. There are Chinese accounts of Arab traders in Canton offering a dazzling array of goods. There are records of intrepid Chinese pilgrims like Xuanzang, the AD seventh-century monk who traveled the Silk Road westward. There are Chinese versions of the travels of Hungarian-British archaeologist Aurel Stein (1862–1943) and the Swedish explorer Sven Hedin (1865–1952), famed travelers in Central Asia once well known to European schoolboys as well as to their Chinese contemporaries. There have also been many political travelers across the centuries, many of them advocates of expanding Chinese influence—whether imperial, Confucian, republican, or Communist—into historically Islamic domains. Recently some contemporary Chinese literary travelers have been recovering an older Chinese sense of the journey to the West (that is, to Inner Asia) as a route to personal self-discovery and introspective escapism.

China also produced its own version of a *chinoiserie* mania in the form of a venerable interest in natural and manmade artifacts from far-off Islamic lands. A generation ago the aspiring student of Tang-era China learned how the country created part of its sense of wealth, worldliness, and conspicuous consumption by reading Edward Schafer's canonical catalogue of wonders, *The Golden Peaches of Samarkand* (1963). In earlier centuries, of course, the cultivated Chinese mandarin had come to the topic through books based on this sensibility, pre-political in a way, yet celebratory of the great Islamic emirates that provided the Chinese empire and those who ran it with useful and beautiful things from all over the world.

The contemplation of such vaguely defined and exotic realms far away was, for a very long time, just a pleasure and not a problem for Chinese scholar-officials. But it became a problem when first the Manchu Empire and then its republican successors concluded that many millions of Muslims of Central Asian origin belonged inside China. An empire's subjects may have become a new republic's citizens, but Xinjiang and its people were in China then and simply had to stay there now. The political relationship, born of mere strategic calculation, even has also been given an aura of geological permanence. Indeed, majestic mountain ranges like the Pamirs and the Tianshan almost surround the territory, but Xinjiang's defining topographical feature is at its center—the great Taklamakan Desert. The writer Christopher Tyler, who visited there to retrace the route of Sven Hedin, found it "a true wilderness," "intimidating, beautiful, dangerous, a place that preys on the mind and enslaves the senses."[11] These are phrases that capture the forbidding spirit of an inland ocean of silicon that can record fifty degrees below zero (centigrade) in the winter and experience blinding sandstorms in the summer. A traveler in Xinjiang today will be told by local Chinese that "Taklamakan" means "you go in, but you don't come out." This aptly expresses what they think about Xinjiang's entry into China more than two hundred years ago.

Here, then, is a fine example of an encounter between the imperial and the modern. Xinjiang is still part of someone else's imperium, that of the People's Republic of China, and yet it is also up-to-date in its very modern name. Xinjiang may be a "self-governing autonomous region of the People's Republic of China," but Beijing is not at all modern minded in the matter of diversity; it proclaims a total sameness of Xinjiang and China. In the same way Xinjiang is also thoroughly up-to-date in the Islamic internationalist character of the political challenge it presents to Beijing—an Islamist problem instantly recognizable in its form, in its vocabulary, and in its worldwide connections. But it is modern only in its immediacy. The *modern* liberation struggle had as its objective the creation of a democratic republic, but an *Islamic* liberation struggle has as its objective another kind of regime entirely. This is a novel problem for China, and a droll Chinese general, sensitive to this particular manifestation of the struggle between the old and the new, might describe it as "People's War with Islamic Characteristics."

Like the Tibetan Buddhists, the Xinjiang Muslims seem incorrigible, but there has been no worldwide upsurge in Buddhist fundamentalism to inspire a resumption of violence in Tibet. In Xinjiang, on the other hand, there has been ongoing violence, and Beijing reports to us about it from time to time. Executions are announced, and successes against local separatist and terrorist cells are publicized. The "splittists" will occasionally assassinate pro-Beijing collaborators, murder local officials, and set off bombs, not only in Xinjiang, but even in China proper. Sometimes there are reports of communal rioting. People outside the country who support their Xinjiang kinsmen describe Chinese repression even beyond that which Beijing publicizes. Beijing admits to "hundreds" of arrests, while others say "thousands"; Beijing admits to "dozens" of executions, while others say "hundreds." We also know that Beijing has deployed to the territory ever-larger numbers of regular army forces as well as so-called People's Armed Police. Further to transform Xinjiang into China, Beijing sponsors migrations of Han Chinese into the area and promotes large-scale investments, which are also intended to help narrow a growing and politically dangerous income gap between the country's hinterland and its far more prosperous coastal areas.

The longer-term success of this enterprise will depend on Beijing's capacity to disentangle Xinjiang from a premodern Islamic consciousness, even as the requirements of its own modernization strategy push China into ever-closer relationships with the contemporary Islamic world. To be sure, these efforts have a history. Long before it worried about Islamic extremism, China was hard at work building back doors through the geographical Islamic world to the world beyond. For one example, the fabled Karakoram Highway was chiseled out of forbidding mountains and was designed ultimately to connect China's far west to the Pakistani port of Karachi and to the new Chinese-financed port of Gwadar. There is also the need for oil; China is now a major importer and, therefore, a competitor for access to energy in the Persian Gulf area, the Caspian region, the Indonesian archipelago, and the waters adjacent.

Obviously, these and other projects are advanced by the co-optation and isolation of extremist Islam, not only by China, but also by others. In the end, though, we can imagine how these experiences of Islam at home and abroad have created a kind of cognitive dissonance in the Chinese political mind. Everywhere it encounters Islam it appears at best opaque, more often as irrational and dangerous to China and the Chinese. Yet the imperial memory lingers, a major component of an as-yet unalterable commitment by Beijing to keep millions of un-Chinese-minded people under Chinese control.

Han-Turkic relations in Xinjiang offer the most conspicuous example at the moment of the inherent difficulty Beijing faces in producing a Chinese national consciousness on the territory of what was once a multiethnic empire. But the problem is deeper, more persistent, and, indeed, structural. In the first place, "Han nationality as invented national unity"—to borrow Dru Gladney's phrase—is itself of recent vintage, a product of twentieth-century anthropology and linguistics. Today's Chinese state, which, for one example, controls the content of the entrance examinations for access to higher education (just as mastery of the Confucian curriculum was required by the old imperial examination system to institutionalize a common cultural outlook), also has available to it the centralizing tools of a modern state—railroads, highways, broadcasting, national banks, stock exchanges, currency printing presses. The army is supposed to be another such centralizing institution supportive of the creation of a truly national outlook. Yet, as Gladney points out, "In June 1989, when China's future hung in the balance, there was significant concern about which armies would support Deng's crackdown, especially those based in Sichuan, Hunan, Canton, or Beijing, all with their own local concerns."[12]

Even if, as a result of conscious attention, greater national unity within the armed forces has been achieved since then, other policies essential to economic growth have been having precisely the opposite effect. The economic activity that has propelled China into the first rank of states over the past generation has set in motion many powerful centrifugal forces. To these must now be added the problem of Chinese identity as such, for as Gladney notes, "China's very economic vitality has the potential to fuel ethnic and linguistic divisions," and strategically significant religious ones also. For a regime in Beijing that still seeks greater understanding of the Soviet collapse, such widely circulated phrases as national disunity, national disintegration, and the Soviet Union as China's prologue are very unsettling.

To observe China's rise in the world is thus to be in the grip of two powerful, yet conflicting, concepts—yet another fine example of cognitive dissonance—for our speculation about the future must somehow combine radically different visions. How will contemporary strategy embody that ancient Chinese sense of the interaction between *yin* and *yang*, between unity and disintegration, between honor and humiliation, between victory and defeat, between hegemony and subjugation, between survival and extinction?

From ancient times, Chinese philosophy existed to help its students find the Middle Way. Even before being tutored in the classics of statecraft and strategy, the aspiring man of affairs was presumed somehow to have absorbed the sensibility of Chinese cosmology and its notion of perpetual change. Indeed, the most ancient of the classics, the *Yijing* (the *Book of Changes*), is an impenetrable text that has defied explication for centuries. But to some commentators, the book's indecipherable sentences are itself its message: the ebb and flow of unfathomable impermanence and inexpressible unpredictability—these are the ways of the universe and, therefore, of human affairs also. Ordinary, more easily understood teachings, such as Confucianism or Daoism, exist to cultivate the self-control that any person—the statesman most of all—must have in order to steer through it all.

CHAPTER 11

RISING CHINA'S GRAND DESIGN

The present invariably imposes itself on its understanding of the past, and these perceptions of the past then come to interact in the present when making grand plans for the future. Still, an examination of past eras of Chinese greatness shows far more adaptation to changed circumstances—often dangerous circumstances—than it demonstrates an implementation of some pre-existing vision. Indeed, whatever can be said about the fixed principles and enduring philosophical assumptions of Chinese strategy, its implementation was frequently the product of bitter, and even violent, argument within the political system, argument that was, in turn, the result of a very complicated relationship between the system of governance and the content of high culture. Circumstances in the world around China could change abruptly, thereby setting in motion wholly unanticipated developments inside China. Even with the passage of centuries, the inner workings of those relationships in the distant past are still fodder for spirited debates in the present.

Today, the recollection of past national greatness occurs within a context that can fairly be described as a modern milieu, even as its idiom changes and may yet be on its way to something new. But that has not happened—

yet—and thus modernity as such remains a very rich concept. The modern is certainly bound up with the advance of science, the progress of technology, and the wealth that combination produces; we connect the modern to the productive and to the efficient. But the modern is also a way of thinking about things, or an outlook, or a sensibility. The term "modern" is also a way of describing some cultural products, for modern art and modern literature are recognizable from what preceded them. Thus, there is more than one way for a person to be modern minded, and the person who embraces the modern as a way of living in one realm of life can utterly reject the "modern" as a way of living in another.

Chinese observers were, and still are, deeply fascinated by the consequences of modernity in the Western world. And precisely because China's own encounter with modernity, in all its aspects, has thus far proved both highly productive and immensely destructive, Chinese today are both highly energized and immensely unsettled by it. All of this is on display in central Beijing; it is as if the contending forces of the past two centuries have converged on one small piece of urban real estate. The Forbidden City of the Qing emperors abuts the northern edge of Tiananmen Square. Its complex of palaces and offices is a quintessential expression of the finest in traditional Chinese architecture—symmetrical, balanced, and reflective of ancient Chinese principles of cosmological harmony. But the Forbidden City was more than a work of art; it was also the nerve center of one of the great empires in the history of the world, designed to intimidate and to inspire awe.

Across the street, immediately adjacent to the Forbidden City, is another two-hundred-acre imperial compound of the eighteenth century, the Zhongnanhai (literally, "the South and Central Seas," sometimes called the Water Palace). Since 1949 the Qing-era buildings enclosed within its walls have served as offices and residences for the highest-ranking officials of both the Chinese Communist Party and the national government; both Mao Zedong and Zhou Enlai lived there, as the highest-ranking officials today still do. Like its next-door neighbor before it, the Zhongnanhai serves as the nerve center of a truly enormous polity—New China. The compound today is as forbidden and as forbidding as it was in High Qing times, and it is an impressive example of the expropriation of a great past by an ambitious present.

But the modern, in more than one guise, is close by. A short walk from Zhongnanhai will take a Chinese citizen to the Great Hall of the People, at the western edge of Tiananmen Square. In all its Stalinoid ugliness, this huge building was completed in 1959 to mark the tenth anniversary of New China's founding. At the southern edge of the square, the citizen will also find the Mao Zedong mausoleum, which contains the embalmed remains of the Great Helmsman. The structure is topped by a large portrait of the chairman, who gazes out over the square as if benignly blessing what is transpiring beneath him. Between the Great Hall and the Mao Mausoleum sits the new National Theater, another milestone in Beijing's urban history. This so-called Big Egg is a titanium-clad structure designed by contemporary French architect Paul Andreu. It is another version of modernity, as incongruous and, yes, as ugly and as off-putting in its own way as the proletarian *grotesquerie* right next to it—and also as spectral as Mao Zedong's resting place. And, just steps away, another representative of modernity is on display. In 1992 McDonald's opened the first of its now hundreds of outlets in China, just off the southeast corner of Tiananmen Square. Thus, in 2006, when China's President Hu Jintao declared as his main goal the creation of "a harmonious society," he assumed the leadership of China's mediation between the great Qianlong emperor and those iconic figures of the modern age—Joseph Stalin, Mao Zedong, Walter Gropius, and Ronald McDonald.

Contemporary Chinese political leaders are familiar with various approaches to the governance of vast territories in Asia, each one impressive in its scale and its success. In the past the achievement of the peace inside these realms, and the continuation of that peace, depended on the ability of the political leadership to recognize the implications of changes on a regional and a world scale. But they may not be so much interested in understanding the past in its own terms as they are in learning how contemporary concepts could inform their sense of the past; in other words, they seek to translate the successes of the past into the political language of the present day. The present government in China is constantly seeking to legitimize its post-1978 policies by finding relevant antecedents in past heroic epochs.

Yet these great ages are very different from each other, and they embody decidedly different strategic concepts and modes of political organization. Indeed, during the time of the *Pax Mongolica*, China functioned successfully as part of someone else's empire, a genuinely global scheme of things. In that China's culture was just one of several great cultures represented in the Mongol Empire, a high imperial policy of disinterest and acceptance made perfect sense. China, in particular, was encouraged to reflect on its connections to world history and world civilization rather than dwell on Chinese characteristics. Seen in this way, the theory and practice of *Pax Mongolica* is readily translatable into the familiar twenty-first-century political jargon of multiculturalism and provides a certain practical component to it. No matter the intention of the creators of the concept, it can be interpreted as a potential contributor to China's rise in the world; to use a term from ancient China's lexicon of strategy, it has *purchase*.

Another historical echo of the *Pax Mongolica* is that China today is once again part of someone else's global system. Theorists now argue whether the post-Soviet world order dominated by the United States is at bottom an empire of some sort, but today's global system, however one praises it or insults it, operates by rules that were established by people who were not Chinese. The system, in its formal aspects, derives from post–World War II arrangements for the United Nations, the World Trade Organization (then known as the General Agreement on Tariffs and Trade), the International Monetary Fund, and a host of other institutions; some—like the International Postal Union and International Telecommunications Union—even descended from the long-defunct League of Nations. The original Republic of China may have been present at the creation of these organizations and have been a founding member of almost all of them, but it had very little to do with their real establishment. Later, the new People's Republic of China dissociated itself from them altogether, opting instead to join another international system also of someone else's making—the Socialist camp, designed and dominated by the Soviet Union. The Soviet Union was a more dominating hegemon inside the Socialist camp than the United States was within the Free World, but China's rejoining of the American-designed global system was China's acknowledgment that it had to acquiesce in arrangements not of its own making.

That was thirty years ago; circumstances have changed since then, and so has the balance of influence within the system. How is this balance going to evolve? As a matter of strategic self-interest, how hard should China push the pace of that evolution, and to what result? Should it seek somehow to supplant over time the United States as the system's dominant figure so that China's long-term strategic objective becomes one of inheriting the existing global regime more or less intact? Or is China's strategic self-interest better served by the establishment of an altogether new, or at least substantially altered, global regime?

China has already lived through a series of world systems, each one expressing the vision of the hegemon of the age—whether the Mongols, the Manchus, or the West—and each of these systems has been supplanted in its turn. China may think that this time, through its continuing accretion of wealth and power, it will finally gain an opportunity to get out in front of history and to be present at the creation of a new international system in a way it has not been for centuries. If so, how might such a system come into being? How might it work?

Comparable questions descend from the historically different situation of Ming times, the *Pax Sinica*. Then, there was a more cohesive and unitary China—a China with a more highly developed sense of itself and of its difference from others—but a China also drawn very deeply into a worldwide revolution in technology, commerce, and economics. That presaged a comparable transformation of world politics. In particular, in the importance of worldwide maritime commerce to the China of that era, the Chinese government of today has found an irresistible analogue to its own policy preferences. As China's contemporary scholars, thus empowered, investigated this era more carefully, they have discovered not only new statistics about the terms of trade but also how the effects of participation in a world economy stimulated Chinese thinking about economics and politics. Chinese, then, discovered that they could be powerfully affected by new economic forces now loose in the world, but they were not at all satisfied by how well they understood them. The workings of what is now called the global market were mysterious, and the inability of the Chinese to decipher them to their satisfaction created a sense of vulnerability. Thus, there were those, then, who embraced the new way and those who rejected it.

Meanwhile, there is yet another argument from history—one that descends from the history of the Qing dynasty and its *Pax Manjurica*—that haunts ongoing debates inside the Zhongnanhai. For the Chinese leaders who live there, the task is to assess the vulnerabilities presented to their country by the globalization of today and then to devise a way to hedge against them. Here, mediation between the imperial and the modern is well established, for modern history is instructive about how rising powers cope with the vulnerability and uncertainty that accompany the growth in wealth and power that derive from involvement in the international economic system.

For one pertinent example, a generation ago James B. Crowley wrote a canonical book describing modern Japan's strategy for squaring this particular circle.[1] Japan sought not so much to overturn the entire global system as to reorganize the system of political economy in East Asia and South-east Asia that had been set up by Westerners. In China particularly, this meant replacing the system of treaty ports, leaseholds, perpetual Chinese indebtedness, and spheres of influence—which, having supplanted the *Pax Manjurica* with a new Western-dominated regime, had turned China into a faux sovereign state in any case.

Japan set out to supersede both of these old orders with a new scheme, a plan for integrating a Japan-dominated China into an Asian regional economy also dominated by Japan. This arrangement, which the Japanese called the Greater East Asia Co-Prosperity Sphere, would function as an essentially self-contained unit to the benefit of all, yet would give to Japan both prosperity and self-sufficiency at the same time. This was a very ambitious undertaking, and violence would prove essential to its implementation. Meanwhile Japan, as the dominant political, economic, and military impetus to this vast reorganization, contemplated a variety of political arrangements within its sphere of control. Thus, Korea was to be an outright Japanese colony; northeastern China was to be a monarchy with its own emperor—and a Manchu emperor at that; China, now reduced to its old pre-Qing-dynasty dimensions, would have a new national government, one that harked back to the spirit of the early twentieth century, when many Chinese patriots, such as Sun Yat-sen and Chiang Kai-shek, believed that the salvation of their own country lay in Sino-Japanese collaboration against the West. The West's colonies in Southeast Asia would become independent republics, based on a revival of an earlier twentieth-century pro-Japanese pan-Asian sentiment. This was an ambitious plan, a genuinely grand design, but in its scale and pretentiousness it was no more ambitious or pretentious than the great reorganizations of Asia successfully carried out by Manchus and, later, by Westerners. In fact, it was less ambitious and pretentious than the total political and economic reorganization of Asia that the People's Republic of China would later attempt between 1950 and 1970.

"What need have we for the world?" This renowned though probably apocryphal query is said to have been posed by the emperor Qianlong in 1793 as he pondered his formal response to proposals from Britain for expanded trade. But even in the late eighteenth century, ideas about the Manchu Empire's self-sufficiency were not well founded; the Qing state was very much involved with the world, but it was not wholly dependent on the world. Around 1800 the Manchu Empire's economy may have accounted for about 30 percent of the world's gross domestic product, and it was to that economy that the rest of the world sought expanded entrée, not the other way around. The Manchu court had both defenders and deniers of the value of international trade. The benefits and risks of the great prosperity in High Ming times were intensely discussed from many perspectives, including a moral one: the traditional Confucian view was that great wealth was the precursor to great ruin and that splendor and decadence went hand in hand.

For all of this, the Qing dynasty had been in its own way a Greater East Asia Co-Prosperity Sphere nonpareil. It thus presents an imperial memory with intriguing modern possibilities, for it might figure into contemporary China's analysis of the deep structure of the world. The China megaeconomy of today is creating a regional economy that is already huge and growing rapidly. Its parts include the very large East Asian economies of Japan, South Korea, Taiwan, Singapore, and Hong Kong, and the not-so-large economies of mainland Southeast Asia, Indonesia, and austral Asia. The even less-developed economies of Central Asia and Russia's Far East are also being drawn into it. This regional integration may proceed by fits and starts, but the process seems inexorable. At some point in this century, it will certainly account for 30 percent of the world's domestic product; indeed, the Greater China component alone will be able to do that.

However, it seems improbable that this economic arrangement, though clearly destined to grow in scale, will enhance the region's self-sufficiency, for it will remain a trading and manufacturing enterprise above all, inextricably connected to the larger world economy beyond. Its ever-growing requirements for energy and commodities have already extended its reach into Latin America and Africa, but it is a reach that exceeds its grasp. The fear in the rest of the world is that China will feel required—and will become rich enough to become emboldened—to try to bring its expanding market under an expanding security umbrella of its own making. It may well be thinking about how to do this, but as of today, this seems a daunting, close-to-impossible task.

Moreover, this China-dominated regional entity, though more closely integrated economically, remains an area of great political diversity. In addition to China, the founding members of this second coming of the Greater East Asia Co-Prosperity Sphere include the constitutional monarchies of Japan, Thailand, Cambodia, Malaysia, and Brunei; the parliamentary regimes of South Korea and Taiwan; the reformist Communist regime in Vietnam and its antediluvian cousin in North Korea; members in good standing of the British Commonwealth of Nations, Australia and New

Zealand; the world's largest functioning constitutional Islamic Republic, Indonesia; and even a place ruled by an old-fashioned military junta, Burma. Steering this entity in a single direction is already a challenging task for the government in Beijing, and it can only become more so.

Moreover, economic integration within China has, paradoxically, created powerful centrifugal forces inside the country that are very challenging and that by themselves raise serious questions about the durability of China's new internal dispensation. And it is more than a merely political or administrative problem, for at the base of it all are the bedrock arguments about the competing variants of modern life and which among them is best for China. These arguments define the tension between strategists whose work is construction and culturalists whose work is deconstruction. In one form or another and at one level of intensity or another, all of China's Asian neighbors have had comparable distress with their lives in the modern world.

In the twentieth century, none of these problems could be confined to the national or the regional; instead, they spilled out into the larger world, becoming part of the great violence that swept through it. The twenty-first century is the product of the astonishing worldwide transformation that resulted. Its problems will be resolved, if they are ever resolved at all, on a worldwide basis, and the failure to resolve those problems will be played out on the same worldwide scale.

China's own consideration of strategy, politics, economics, and culture, as it has turned out, is not readily divisible into separate components. In 1953 Joseph Levenson began his exploration of what he called the mind of modern China by wondering: "How can a Chinese be reconciled to the observable dissipation of his cultural inheritance? How can a China in full process of westernization feel itself equivalent to the West?"[2] Levenson's questions, beguiling in their simplicity yet maddening in their power to pull us in a myriad of directions, are now the starting point for this book, more than fifty years after Levenson posed them.

However one might have imagined the mind of Modern China more than five decades ago, it is surely something else today, and it will be something different a decade from now. And because the mind of Modern China is now inseparable from the mind of the Modern West, it cannot be studied in isolation from thought in the rest of the world. In this respect

China and the West will proceed in tandem, whether along a parallel course whose lines will never get closer, along an asymptotic course whose lines may come tantalizingly close but will never quite touch, or along paths that will eventually intersect.

Events of the past century have been suggestive of all three possibilities. Many Westerners and Chinese who actually lived through these experiences believed that somehow the great issues would soon be resolved. Thomas Metzger, who has written extensively and described in considerable detail the relationships between Western and Chinese ways of thinking about the world, cites studies that have demonstrated that modern and modernizing societies are becoming increasingly similar in their institutions and political and cultural patterns. But he also cites those who, with equal acuity, have observed "that culture and religion lead to great differences in how the good society is conceptualized. They have an equal effect on how the actual given world is perceived, for they are the saga of suffering and glory with which every 'community of memory' defines its goals. . . . It is thus clear that Chinese today are still free to influence these trends, tilting their civilization one way or the other. Policy-makers will do some of that steering, but so will public opinion and the intellectual trends competing to influence it."[3]

Whatever China becomes in the next decades, the country's story will not unfold in isolation, for it cannot exist alone and cannot float above the rest of the battle, as if embodying some uniquely immutable set of principles. Instead China, too, will be an ever-changing product of the meeting of memory and modernity, a part of the world's saga of suffering and glory from which every great nation must now create its future.

EPILOGUE

In the prologue that introduced this book, I recalled that my first lesson about Modern China came from George Orwell. It has turned out that in the decades since that introduction, this was not a bad place to begin. Cerebral analysis and its talk of dialectic and metaphysics can all too easily overlook the Modern Fate of those who have actually lived the story, but who lived it not dialectically or metaphysically, but tragically. And even amid the more benign version of modernity that settled into China after the death of Mao Zedong in 1976, life is lived neither sociologically nor economically only.

Deng Xiaoping's (1904–1997) program has now lasted longer than Mao's, and it continues to move forward. Indeed, in almost all of the manifestations of the modern, the pace of China's grand project has accelerated. Mao had hoped that the countryside and all that it represented would surround and finally destroy everything that the city was and what it represented— and not only in China, but throughout the world. But the city has more than fought the countryside to a draw; it is now counterattacking and will win. China will soon leave behind its past as a predominantly peasant society, and most of its people will live in urban settlements. Soon there will be no countryside at all. Of course, the countryside will be more than a just memory for a long time. Postmodern China will have within it hundreds of millions of new urbanites who carry the countryside's habits of mind with them. The world as a whole may not yet be configured in the way Late Qing–era writers of science fiction imagined it, but China's newest cities—indeed, all the newest cities around the world—resemble the projections of prescient fantasists and pioneering filmmakers. The World City is now more than mere metaphor. It is a thing called megalopolis, and it does not acknowledge national boundaries in its unstoppable sprawl.

Urbanologists and economists study these developments as physical phenomena; they worry about sources of water and power, the construction of transport, the removal of trash, and the treatment of sewage. They rightly focus on natural resources, and whether the world will have enough of them to sustain the new World City's way of life. But we do not think much about the world's store of cultural, psychological, and spiritual resources—how rapidly the new World City will consume them, and how, or even whether, they can be replenished. In these respects some places in Modern China are already frightening—filled with social and personal pathologies of every description—and Postmodern China is fated to create many more of them.

Deng's Xiaoping's blueprint, which set all this in motion, had consisted of four modernizations—agriculture, industry, technology, and defense. Though the absence of a fifth—democratization—has long been noted, political change, whatever one decides to call it, is also now a fact of life. In today's China political words may still have a Lewis Carroll affect; like Humpty Dumpty, the regime will use them to mean what it wants them to mean. But if there is still any Marxism left in the Communist Party of China, the doctrine makes it plain that that there is a political specter that must eternally haunt China. Marxists believe that the political "superstructure" of a society must change as its economic and productive "substructure" changes. Today China's leaders term their country a developing socialist market economy with Chinese characteristics. However one construes that tortured phrase, it describes a tiger with ever-changing stripes.

Those of us who came in on this story during the mid-twentieth century—at the time of the first episode of madness in Mao's China—were relieved by what we thought was good news as the twentieth century ended. The great changes in China since 1976 seemed to vindicate Western ideas about the way the world worked. Every day, China was coming ever more to resemble what we thought a modern Asian society ought to be—Japan, South Korea, Taiwan. China's transformation was not yet complete, but it seemed unlikely that China would create a new, unique variant of modern society that would stand against the irresistible forces of the age. Much reassurance was offered, but it did not overcome the concern and then the anxiety and, now in many quarters, the plain dread about what today's Rising China portends for the United States and the rest of the world.

In this we are not alone, for twenty-first-century Rising China must now live with the curse of hopes fulfilled. China is rich and powerful, but it is the product of the same modern history that, having created the riches and the power, may also have planted inside the country the seeds of its possible undoing. Should a twenty-first-century prophet announce, then, that that there is now a specter haunting Modern China, and that it is the specter of, say, postmodernism? The next new era in China will need to have a name, however elusive. Postmodernism, it is its very imprecision, makes it a useful catch-all adjective, like *Confucian*, *modern*, or *rising*. Still, it will not supersede more enduring terms. Whatever else may happen, there will always be a Left and there will always be a Right, though not at all in the confining way that Mao Zedong understood the words. In fact, the actual content of the programs of both the Left and the Right has changed across the centuries and will continue to do so; it is only that, in some version, the two will continue to oppose each other. Two other conjunctions will also endure. There will always be an Old and there will always be a New; there will always be a Then and there will always be a Now; how people live and think in the Now will always be influenced by how they think people once lived and thought in the Then.

Nor are Westerners alone in seeing in China a long-sought result that may prove problematical. Rising China has been with us, and with the Chinese, for a generation. Rising China is now becoming part of the stuff of memory; today most Chinese were not born, or were not conscious, when it started. Should we now begin to imagine how modern memories will fare in a postmodern milieu?

The basic geographical structure of Rising China, resting on the great multinational empire it inherited from the work of eighteenth-century Manchus, runs contrary to the twenty-first century's ideas about identity and autonomy for ethnic groups and their cultures. This newer movement is being helped along by technological innovations that make easier the formation of affinity groups and ongoing communication within them. Rising China's basic mode of governance—"democratic centralism," an increasingly creaky arrangement based on a now universally repudiated Leninist political theory—runs contrary to a worldwide trend, if not toward classic representative democracy then at least toward greater decentralization. Rising China may very well contemplate a traditional national strategy of traditional expansionism supported by equally traditional nationalism and patriotism. But this, too, is now coming up against the emerging postmodern high culture, whose mission for cultural studies is the deconstruction of culture as a mainstay of the political order in China and throughout the world. This emerging high culture is wholly unlike the high culture of previous rising nations in great ages of imperialism; it seeks not to buttress great national projects but to undermine them.

This is a noticeably powerful trend in today's China, where intellectuals and creative artists of every stripe recall Mao's brutal efforts to put politics in command of culture and believe that it is their bedrock obligation to resist even the half-hearted attempts to do so by China's government of today. Beyond this, there is a more mundane threat to the inherited political order. It is appearing in the political counterpart of economic globalization—regionalism, multilateralism, transnationalism—which works to restrict the freedom of action of major nations and to subordinate them to international organizations, whether governmental or nongovernmental.

In this book the stories of the Yuan, Ming, and early Qing eras were instructive for the expansive global settings they described, and how China benefited thereby from opportunities for increased wealth and power. The story of Modern China began in the Late Qing era, when the world had become an existential threat; many Chinese feared that Confucian China would dissolve into it, never to be heard from again. When Rising China appeared after the death of Mao Zedong in 1976, the world was something else yet again, but still very dangerous. But after 1991, following the collapse of the Soviet Union and the benign worldwide ascendancy of the United States, the world seemed to revert to a place China had not seen for centuries—a safe place, hospitable to China's aggrandizement.

The substructure of the world is, therefore, no immutable thing, and each era also produces a climate of opinion or a spirit of the age. Ideas swirl around, and the people who have charge of a nation's affairs absorb those ideas and connect them to their own personal ambitions and their ambitions for their country. They use them to make some sense of what has happened before. Therefore, it matters very much *when* in History a country and its leaders get drawn into this process. Wealth and power always matter, but the times also matter, because the times supply the vocabulary and the concepts that inform deliberations about what should be done with that wealth and power.

We Americans know about this from our own history. In 2002 retired ambassador Warren Zimmerman published a book called *First Great Triumph: How Five Americans Made Their Country a World Power*. Of course, these five—Theodore Roosevelt, Alfred T. Mahan, Henry Cabot Lodge Sr., John Hay, and Elihu Root—did not do this literally by themselves. All of them had absorbed the regnant ideas of the day about how a newly powerful country such as the United States could secure—indeed, had no choice but to secure—its place in the world. In that era words like *navalism* and *imperialism* were prominent in the deliberation of every important chancery. That vocabulary—to borrow from twentieth-century academic jargon—was the hegemonic discourse of the day. In 1945 and 1955, when comparable discussions took place after World War II and during the Cold War, leaders acquired a new shorthand—containment, deterrence, balance of terror. These terms derived from, and were used to describe, real circumstances, circumstances very much different from those of 1895.

The circumstances of 2009 are again different, and new catchwords are competing to describe them. China is affected by this discussion, just as it was in the twentieth century when it got caught up in an age of Communist revolution or, as in the nineteenth century, when Christianity inspired an enormous armed insurrection called the Taiping Rebellion. Neither of these ideas was invented in China, but both of them entered into the country and were modified—sinified—with results quite different from what the originators of those ideas could have imagined. Accordingly we need to think about how the postmodern hegemonic discourse of the present day, a discourse again not invented in China, is being assimilated and how Rising China is making use of it. We cannot know how this will proceed, only that it will once again confirm the law of unintended consequences. China's sense of itself and its place in the world is thus always a work in progress. Just as Chinese thinkers and political leaders in the late nineteenth century had sought a formula to revive China in the world as it was then, China's thinkers and political leaders in the early twenty-first century must assimilate yet another century of experience, and yet another new vocabulary in which to evaluate it.

Above the life of ordinary political and economic affairs, a larger intellectual and cultural life, connected both to things Chinese and things international and filled with always-inventive connections between the old and the new, advances relentlessly. Chinese culture has never been a stagnant thing and is certainly not one today. As in earlier eras, when the Yuan and the Ming and the Qing were all ascending, Chinese cultural production is energetic and creative. Today it is even more so, for it is the product not only of Chinese in China but of Chinese all over the world. Though now beyond the control of any government in Beijing, this part of China today generates pressures all its own on the workings of Chinese society at home, akin to when Chinese outside the country intervened decisively in politics during the Late Qing dynasty or when they provided the enormous amount of capital that was the seed money for the economic reforms of the 1980s. Rising China is not now, and will not be, the creation of only a handful of isolated politburo members in Beijing, but the result instead of the now always-changing give and take of real life throughout the Chinese world.

Throughout, this book has held to the idea—without putting it quite this starkly—that China and the People's Republic of China are not the same thing. The two never got along very well with each other. On behalf of the People's Republic, Mao Zedong waged a brutal campaign against

China and sought to destroy it, but China fought the PRC to a standstill and then went on to defeat it outright. The meeting of the Confucian and the modern set the stage for this epic struggle, and its outcome created today's Rising China. Of all the memories that will live on into the mind of Post-modern China, this decisive battle—and how and why it was fought—will be the most important.

NOTES

Chapter 1. A Memory of Empire: The New Past of Old China

1. Q. Edward Wang, "Encountering the World," 40.
2. Krebs, "New Historical Thinking," 21, 22.
3. Schwartz, "Jews and China," 333.

Chapter 2. The Yuan Dynasty and the *Pax Mongolica*

1. Allsen, *Culture and Conquest*, 83, 85, 87.
2. Richard van Glahn, foreword to Struve, *Qing Formation*, xiii, xiv.
3. Mote, "Chinese Society," 626.
4. Rosabi, "Reign of Khubilai Khan," 416.
5. Ibid., 431.
6. Ibid., 436.
7. Hok-Lam Chan, "Chinese Official Historiography at the Yuan Court: The Composition of the Liao, Chin [Jin] and Sung [Song] Histories," in *China and the Mongols*, 56.
8. Ibid., 99.
9. Polo, *Travels of Marco Polo*, 208.

Chapter 3. The Ming Dynasty and the *Pax Sinica*

1. An English edition of vol. 1, translated by Li Zhengde, Liang Miaoru, and Li Siping, was published in 2000 as *Chinese Capitalism, 1522–1840*.
2. Yang Zhaoyun, "Maritime China in the 'Long Sixteenth Century' (1450–1640): A Revision of the World Systems Approach," undated paper, *China History Forum*, 3.
3. Marme, *Suzhou*, 2, 3.
4. Gang Deng, *Maritime Sector*.
5. Ibid., 94–95.
6. Ibid., 95.
7. De Bary, *Self and Society*.
8. Ibid., 188.
9. Ibid., 196.
10. Gang Deng, *Maritime Sector*, 113.
11. De Bary, *Self and Society*, 225.
12. Rosen, "Strategic Tradition."
13. Xinhua, September 18, 2003.
14. Xinhua, May 17, 2005; May 25, 2005.
15. Government of Hong Kong, press release, June 28, 2005.

16. Zhang and Zhang, *Great Voyages of Zheng He*.

17. An excellent summary of the historiography of the Zheng He voyages, which this passage follows closely and has drawn on *in extenso*, is provided by the China Heritage Project of the Australian National University in its newsletter no. 2, June 2005, devoted entirely to the sexcentenary of the Zheng He voyages.

18. Von Glahn, "Myth and Reality," 437.

19. R. Bin Wong, "Role of the Chinese State."

20. Ibid., 12, 13.

21. Ibid., 14, 15.

22. Ibid., 20.

23. Hsiao Hung-te, "Fleet and Wall, " 2.

24. Ibid., 8.

25. Ibid., 24, 28.

26. Wade, " Zheng He Voyages," 12.

27. Ibid., 7, 8, 9.

28. Ibid., 11, 12, 13, 14, 15, 16.

29. Ibid., 18.

30. Ibid., 1.

31. Wade, "Ming *Shi-lu*," 27.

32. Ibid., 28.

33. The discussion of this important though lesser-known figure follows the introduction in Landeg White, trans., Luis Vaz de Camoes, *The Lusiads* (New York: Oxford's World Classics, 2001), ix–xxv.

34. Xu Dongfeng, "Traveler as Host."

Chapter 4. The Qing Dynasty and the *Pax Manjurica*

1. Elman, *Cultural History of Civil Examinations*, 54–55.

2. Crossley, *Orphan Warriors*, 216.

3. He Bingdi (Ping-ti Ho). "Significance of the Ch'ing Period," 189–95.

4. Ibid., 191.

5. Ibid., 194.

6. Ibid., 191, 192, 193.

7. This discussion is based on the more detailed description in Horner, "China and the Historians."

8. Chen, "Final Chapter Unfinished."

9. *Xinhua*, September 8, 2002; August 25, 2003.

10. Pokong, "Toward the Republic," 73.

11. Di Cosmo, "European Technology and Manchu Power," 2.

12. Ibid., 17.

13. Yang, "Water Worlds."

14. Von Glahn, *Fountain of Fortune*, 215, 216.

15. Perdue, *China Marches West*, 10.

16. Ibid., 565.

17. Ibid., 443.

18. Rawski, "Qing Empire," 19, 20.

19. Waldron, *Great Wall of China.*

20. Millward, *Beyond the Pass.*

21. Ibid., 245.

22. Perdue, "Culture, History, and Imperial Chinese Strategy," 261.

23. Ibid., 265, 266, 275.

24. Ibid., 279.

25. Gao Zhao, "Reinventing China," 3–30.

26. Quoted in Richard J. Smith, "Mapping China's World," 14.

27. *People's Daily*, September 12, 2002.

28. See, for example, Foret, *Mapping Chengde.*

29. Wohlstetter, "Slow Pearl Harbors," 23, 24.

30. Wills, "Great Qing," 10.

31. Swanson, *Eighth Voyage of the Dragon*, 127–29.

32. Leonard, *Wei Yuan and China's Rediscovery*, 2, 3.

33. Elman, *Cultural History*, 625.

34. Goldman, "Restarting Chinese History," 52.

35. Ibid.

36. Herrman-Pillith, "Importance of Studying Late Qing."

37. Zelin, *Merchants of Zigong.*

38. Bernhardt and Huang, *Civil Law in Qing*, 4, 6, 9.

39. Karl and Zarrow, *Rethinking the 1898 Reform Period*, 2, 3, 6.

40. Cited in Reid, *Manchu Abdication*, 298.

41. Elman, *On Their Own Terms*, 355.

42. Ibid., 356.

43. Ibid., 387.

44. Ibid., 355.

45. Ibid., 394–95.

46. Yuan Weishi, "Modernization and History Textbooks" (translated from the Chinese), *Bingdian* [*Freezing Point*], January 11, 2006.

Chapter 5. The Proletarian Dynasty of Chairman Mao

1. Kirby, "Internationalization of China," 183.

2. Wittfogel, *Oriental Despotism.*

3. Boorman and Boorman, "Strategy and National Psychology," 152.

4. Johnston, "Cultural Realism and Strategy," 256.

5. Kawabata, *Master of Go*, 57.

6. Plaks, *Four Masterworks*, 392, 393.

7. West, "Quest for the Ur-Text."

8. Buck, Nobel Lecture, *Nobel Lectures, Literature, 1901–1967* (1969).

9. Edward C. O'Dowd, "Last Maoist War."

10. Lin Paio, *People's Liberation Army Daily*, September 1, 1965.

11. Ibid.

Chapter 6. The History of the World as China's Own

1. Nathan, *Chinese Democracy*, 19.

2. David Der-wei Wang, *Fin-de-Siecle Splendor*, 302–4.

3. Ibid., 306.

4. Ibid., 307, 308, 309.

5. Ibid., 310.

6. Sheridan quoted in Tang, *Global Space*, 170.

7. Ibid., 179.

8. Liang, *Excerpts from Impressions of Travels in Europe*, 23:1, quoted in Tang, *Global Space*, 181.

9. Ibid., 181, 182.

10. Liang Shuming quoted in Alitto, *Last Confucian*, 125, 105, 106.

Chapter 7. China's Continent and the World City

1. McNeill, *Rise of the West*, 1963 ed., 807.

2. Ibid., 811.

3. McNeill, *Rise of the West*, 1992 ed., xvii.

4. McNeill, *Pursuit of Truth*, 127.

5. McNeill, *Rise of the West*, xx, xxi, xxii.

6. Ibid., xxix.

7. Wallerstein, *World-Systems Analysis*, 24, 59, 77.

8. McNeill, foreword to Christian, *Maps of Time*, xv, xvi.

9. Christian, *Maps of Time*, 245.

10. McNeill, foreword to *Maps of Time*, xvii.

11. Dirlik, "Confounding Metaphors," 132.

12. Ni Fangliu, "Shanghai's New Secondary School Textbook Raises a Dispute," *Phoenix Weekly*, May 31, 2006, 2–7. Professor Zhou also discusses the project in Joseph Kahn, "Where's Mao? Chinese Revise History Books," *New York Times*, September 1, 2006, 1.

13. Blue, "China and Western Social Thought," 60.

14. Ibid., 70, 73.

15. Huters, *Bringing the World Home*, 175.

16. Zhou Qun and Lin Yanhua, "Shanghai Modernity."

17. *China News*, Nanning, November 11, 2005.

18. Philips, "Drastic Urbanization."

19. Dong, *Republican Beijing*, 100, 101.

20. Wu, *Remaking Beijing*, 7, 8, 240, 241.

21. Qin, *Culturing Modernity*, 2, 3.

22. Bergere, *Sun Yat-sen*, , 3.

23. Ibid., 281.

24. Kirby, "Engineering China," 37.

25. Ibid., 139, 140.

26. Skinner, "Regional Urbanization,", 211.

27. Skinner, "Cities and the Hierarchy," 307.

28. Ibid., 338.

29. Chu, " Hong Kong–Zhujiang Delta," 78.

30. Ibid.

31. Smart, " Hong Kong/Pearl River Delta," 104.

32. Cartier, *Globalizing South China*, 235.

33. Ibid., 235.

34. Oakes and Schein, *Translocal China*, 19.

35. Several related aspects of "translocalism" are discussed in Oakes and Schein, *Translocal China*, 19.

36. Martin Wolf, "National Wealth on City Life's Coattails," *Financial Times*, May 2, 2006.

37. Jacobs, *Cities and the Wealth of Nations*, 218.

38. Ibid., 209.

39. Laquian, *Beyond Metropolis*, 139, 140.

40. Ibid., 140.

41. Ibid., 421.

42. Lewis and Wigen, "Maritime Response," 81.

43. Ibid.

44. Cartier, "Cosmopolitics," 104.

45. Blank, "Pacific."

46. Sumida, "Reimagining the History," 180.

47. French, "Shanghai's Boom.".

48. Geoff Dyer, "How China Looks to the Future to Forget the Past," *Financial Times*, June 13, 2006.

49. Deyan Sudjic, "Engineering Conflict," *New York Times Magazine*, May 21, 2006, 23, 25.

50. Antoaneta Bezlova, "Friction Builds over Beijing's Olympic Revamp," *Asia Times*, March 18, 2003, 2.

51. Elsea, "Chang Yung Ho's New Chinese Architecture," 1, 2.

52. Ibid.

53. Arthur Labow, "The China Syndrome," *New York Times Magazine*, May 21, 2006, 70.

54. Pepe Escobar, "The Accumulation of the Wretched," *Asia Times*, May 20, 2006.

Chapter 8. A Peaceful Rise and Memories of Violence

1. David Der-wei Wang, *Monster That Is History*, 2.
2. Ibid.; emphasis in the original.
3. Smith, "Talking Toads and Chinless Ghosts," 423, 405.
4. David Der-wei Wang, *Monster That Is History*, 7.
5. Wang Ban, *Sublime Figure of History*, 5.
6. Ibid., 238.
7. Benjamin, "Theses on the Philosophy of History,"257–258.
8. Ban Wang, *Sublime Figure of History*, 229.
9. Li, "Resistance to Modernity," 143.
10. David Der-wei Wang, introduction to Chi and Wang, *Chinese Literature*, xxxiii, xxxv.
11. Ibid., xxxvii.
12. Ban Wang, *Illuminations from the Past*, 183.
13. Ibid., 182.
14. David Der-wei Wang, *Fin-de-Siecle Splendor*, 163–66.
15. Ibid., 335, 336, 337, 341.
16. Gao, Nobel lecture, December 7, 2000.

Chapter 9. The Strange Death of the Soviet Empire

1. Kaple, *Dream of a Red Factory*, 108–15.
2. Rozman, *Chinese Debate about Soviet Socialism*, 101, 103, 107.
3. Marsh, *Unparalleled Reforms*, 107.
4. Ibid., 108, 109.
5. Ibid., 115.
6. Shen is cited by Zhao Suisheng in "China's Pragmatic Nationalism," 139.
7. "Economic Performance through Time," Lecture in Accepting the Svenges Riksbank Prize in Economic Sciences in Memory of Alfred Nobel, Stockholm, December 9, 1993.
8. Douglass North, "The Chinese Menu for Development," *Wall Street Journal*, April 7, 2005, A-14.

Chapter 10. "The Chinese People Are a Heap of Loose Sand"

1. "China's Peaceful Development and China's Civilized Renaissance," *People's Daily*, April 10, 2006.
2. Zundorfer, "Confusing Confucianism with Capitalism," 2–3.
3. Pernendra Jain and Gerry Groot, "Beijing's Soft Power Offensive," *Asia Times*, May 17, 2006.
4. Dikotter, *Discourse of Race*, is the definitive discussion of this subject.
5. K. Scott Wong, "Transformation of Culture," 213.
Ibid.
6. Oakes, "China's Provincial Identities," 667, 682.

7. Ibid., 673.

8. Barabantseva, "Chinese Nation-Negotiation," 13, 14.

9. Hunt, "Chinese National Identity," 69.

10. Horner, " Other Orientalism," is the basis for this discussion.

11. Christopher Tyler, *Financial Times*, May 18, 1996, 11.

12. Gladney, "China's National Insecurity."

Chapter 11. Rising China's Grand Design

1. Crowley, *Japan's Quest for Autonomy.*

2. Levenson, *Liang Chi'ch'ao*, 5.

3. Metzger, *Cloud across the Pacific*, 291.

BIBLIOGRAPHY

Alitto, Guy S. *The Last Confucian: Liang Shu-ming and the Chinese Dilemma of Modernity*. Berkeley: University of California Press, 1986.

Allsen, Thomas T. *Culture and Conquest in Mongol Eurasia*. Cambridge: Cambridge University Press, 2001.

Barabantseva, Elena. "Chinese Nation-Negotiation in the Period of Modernisation." University of Sheffield. *School of East Asian Studies Working Papers* 2, no. 5 (2004): 13, 14.

Benjamin, Walter. "Theses on the Philosophy of History," no. 9 (1940). In *Illuminations: Essays and Reflections*, by *Walter Benjamin*, edited by Hannah Arendt, 257–58. New York: Schocken Books, 1969.

Bergere, Marie-Claire. *Sun Yat-sen*. Translated by Janet Lloyd. Stanford: Stanford University Press, 1998.

Bernhardt, Kathryn, and Philip C. Huang, eds. *Civil Law in Qing and Republican China*. Stanford: Stanford University Press, 1994.

Blank, Paul W. "The Pacific: A Mediterranean in the Making?" *Geographical Review* 89, no. 2 (April 1999): 265–77.

Blue, Gregory. "China and Western Social Thought in the Modern Period." In *China and Historical Capitalism: Genealogies of Sinological Knowledge*, edited by Timothy Brook and Gregory Blue, 57–109. London: Cambridge University Press, 2002.

Blue, Gregory, and Timothy Brook, eds. *China and Historical Capitalism: Genealogies of Sinological Knowledge*. London: Cambridge University Press, 2002.

Boorman, Howard L., and Scott A. Boorman. "Strategy and National Psychology in China." *Annals of the American Academy of Political and Social Science*, March 1967, 152.

Buck, Pearl S. Nobel Lecture, December 12, 1938. *The Nobel Lectures: Literature, 1901–1967*. Vol. 1. Amsterdam: Elsevier, 1969.

Cartier, Carolyn. "Cosmopolitics and the Maritime World City." *Geographical Review* 89, no. 2 (April 1999): 278-89.

———. *Globalizing South China*. Oxford: Blackwell, 2002.

Chan, Hok-Lam. *China and the Mongols: History and Legend under the Yuan and the Ming*. Aldershot, U.K.: Ashgate, 1999.

Chen Hsi-yuan. "Final Chapter Unfinished: The *Qingshi gao* and the Making of the Official Memory of the Last Chinese Dynasty." Paper prepared for a conference on modern Chinese historiography, Leiden University, the Netherlands, September 15, 2000.

Chi Pang-Yuan, and David Der-wei Wang, eds. *Chinese Literature in the Second*

Half of a Modern Century: A Critical Survey. Bloomington: Indiana University Press, 2000.

China Heritage Project of the Australian National University. Newsletter no. 2. June 2005.

Christian, David. *Maps of Time*. Berkeley: University of California Press, 2005.

Chu, David K. Y. "The Hong Kong-Zhujiang Delta and the World City System." In *Emerging World Cities in Pacific Asia*, edited by Lo Fu-chen and Yueng Yue-man. Tokyo: United Nations University Press, 1997.

Conlan, Thomas D. *In Little Need of Divine Intervention: Takezaki Suenaga's Scrolls of the Mongol Invasions of Japan*. Ithaca, N.Y.: Cornell University Press, 2001.

Crossley, Pamela Kyle. *Orphan Warriors: Three Manchu Generations and the End of the Qing World*. Princeton, N.J.: Princeton University Press, 1990.

———. *A Translucent Mirror: History and Identity in Qing Imperial Ideology*. Berkeley: University of California Press, 1999.

Crowley, James B. *Japan's Quest for Autonomy: National Security and Foreign Policy: 1930–1938*. Princeton, N.J.: Princeton University Press, 1966.

de Bary, William Theodore. *Self and Society in Ming Thought*. New York: Columbia University Press, 1970.

di Cosmo, Nicola. "European Technology and Manchu Power: Reflections on the 'Military Revolution' in Seventeenth-Century China." Paper prepared for the International Congress of Historical Sciences, Oslo, 2000, p. 2. Published as "Did Guns Matter? Firearms and the Qing Formation," in *The Qing Formation in World Historical Time*, edited by Lynn A Struve. Cambridge, Mass.: Harvard University Press, 2004.

Dikotter, Frank. *The Discourse of Race in Modern China*. Stanford: Stanford University Press, 1994.

Dirlik, Arif. "Confounding Metaphors, Inventions of the World: What Is World History For?" In *Writing World History, 1800–2000*, edited by Benedikt Stuchtey and Eckhardt Fuchs. New York: Oxford University Press, 2003.

Dittmer, Lowell, and Samuel S. Kim, eds. *China's Quest for National Identity*. Ithaca, N.Y.: Cornell University Press, 1993.

Dong, Madeleine Yueh. *Republican Beijing: The City and Its Histories*. Berkeley: University of California Press, 2003.

Dreyer, Edward L. *Zheng He: China and the Oceans in the Early Ming Dynasty, 1405–1433*. New York: Pearson, 2007.

Dunnell, Ruth W., James A. Millward, Mark C. Elliott, and Philippe Foret, eds. *New Qing Imperial History*. London: Routledge Curzon Press, 2004.

Edmonds, Richard Louis, and Fredric E. Wakeman Jr., eds. *Reappraising Republican China*. Oxford: Oxford University Press, 2000.

Elman, Benjamin A. *A Cultural History of Civil Examinations in Late Imperial China*. Berkeley: University of California Press, 2000.

————. *On Their Own Terms: Science in China, 1550–1900*. Cambridge, Mass.: Harvard University Press, 2005.

Elsea, Daniel. "Chang Yung Ho's New Chinese Architecture," *Metropolis Magazine*, March 15, 2005.

Finamore, Daniel, ed. *Maritime History as World History*. Gainesville: University Press of Florida, 2004.

Foret, Philippe. *Mapping Chengde*. Honolulu: University of Hawaii Press, 2000.

Franke, Herbert, and Denis Twitchett, eds. *The Cambridge History of China*. Vol. 6. Cambridge: Cambridge University Press, 1994.

French, Howard W. "Shanghai's Boom: A Building Frenzy," *New York Times*, April 13, 2006.

Fuchs, Eckhardt, and Benedikt Stuchtey, eds. *Writing World History, 1800–2000*. New York: Oxford University Press USA, 2003.

Gang Deng. *Maritime Sector, Institutions, and Sea Power of Premodern China*. Westport, Conn.: Greenwood Press, 1999.

Gang Zhao. "Reinventing China: Imperial Qing Ideology and the Rise of Modern Chinese National Identity in the Early Twentieth Century." *Modern China* 32, no. 1 (January 2006): 3–30.

Gao Xingjian. Nobel Lecture, December 7, 2000. *The Nobel Lectures: Literature, 1996–2000*. Vol. 5. Amsterdam: Elsevier, 2002.

Gao Zhao, "Reinventing China: Imperial Qing Ideology and the Rise of Modern Chinese National Identity in the Early Twentieth Century." *Modern China* 32, no. 1 (January 2006): 3–30.

Gladney, Dru C. "China's National Insecurity: Old Challenges at the Dawn of the New Millennium." Paper presented at a symposium sponsored by the National Defense University, Washington, D.C., March 8, 2000.

Goldman, Merle. "Restarting Chinese History." *American Historical Review* 105, no. 1 (February 2000): 153–64.

Goldstein, Jonathan, ed., *The Jews of China: Historical and Comparative Perspectives*. Armonk, N.Y.: M. E. Sharpe, 1999.

Government of Hong Kong. Press release. June 28, 2005.

He Bingdi (Ping-ti Ho). "The Significance of the Ch'ing Period in Chinese History." *Journal of Asian Studies* 26, no. 2 (February 1967): 189–95.

Herrman-Pillith, Carsten. "On the Importance of Studying Late Qing Economic and Social History for the Analysis of Contemporary China, or: Protecting Sinology against Social Science." Duisberg Institut fur Ostasienwissenschaften, *Working Papers on East Asian Studies no. 3*, July 2002.

Horner, Charles. "China and the Historians." *National Interest* (Spring 2001).

————. "The Other Orientalism: China's Islamist Problem." *National Interest* (Spring 2002).

Hsiao Hung-te. "Fleet and Wall, 1405–1435: The Zheng He Expeditions and Ming

Empire Policy." Paper presented at the 15th biennial conference of the Asian Studies Association of Australia, Canberra, July 2, 2004.

Huters, Theodore. *Bringing the World Home: Appropriating the West in Late Qing and Early Republican China.* Honolulu: University of Hawaii Press, 2005.

Jacobs, Jane. *Cities and the Wealth of Nations.* New York: Vintage Books USA, 1984.

Johnston, Alistair Iain. *Cultural Realism: Strategic Culture and Grand Strategy in Chinese History.* Princeton, N.J.: Princeton University Press, 1995.

————. "Cultural Realism and Strategy in Maoist China." In *The Culture of National Security: Norms and Identity in World Politics,* ed. Peter J. Katzenstein. New York: Columbia University Press, 1996.

Kaple, Deborah A. *Dream of a Red Factory: The Legacy of High Stalinism in China.* New York: Oxford University Press USA, 1994.

Karl, Rebecca E., and Peter Zarrow, eds. *Rethinking the 1898 Reform Period: Political and Cultural Change in Late Qing China.* Cambridge, Mass.: Harvard University Press, 2002.

Katzenstein, Peter J., ed. *The Culture of National Security: Norms and Identity in World Politics.* New York: Columbia University Press, 1996.

Kawabata, Yasunari. *The Master of Go.* Translated by Edward G. Seidensticker. New York: Alfred A. Knopf, 1972.

Kirby, William C. "Engineering China: Birth of the Developmental State." In *Becoming Chinese: Passages to Modernity and Beyond,* edited by Wen-hsin Yeh. Berkeley: University of California Press, 2000.

————. "The Internationalization of China: Foreign Relations at Home and Abroad in the Republican Era." In *Reappraising Republican China,* edited by Richard Louis Edmonds and Frederic Wakeman Jr. Oxford: Oxford University Press, 2000.

Krebs, Edward S. "New Historical Thinking in China's Reform Era." *Chinese Studies in History* 38, no. 3 (Spring/Summer 2005): 21, 22.

Laquian, Aprodicio A. *Beyond Metropolis: The Planning and Governance of Asia's Mega-Urban Regions.* Baltimore: Johns Hopkins University Press, 2005.

Leonard, Jane Kate. *Wei Yuan and China's Rediscovery of the Maritime World.* Cambridge, Mass.: Harvard University Press, 1984.

————. *Wei Yuan and China's Rediscovery of the Maritime World.* Cambridge, Mass.: Harvard University Press, 1984.

Levathes, Louise. *When China Ruled the Seas: The Treasure Fleet of the Dragon Throne, 1405–1433.* New York: Oxford University Press, 1994.

Levenson, Joseph R. *Confucian China and Its Modern Fate: A Trilogy.* Berkeley: University of California Press: 1958, 1964, 1965.

————. *Liang Chi'ch'ao and the Mind of Modern China.* Berkeley: University of California Press, 1967.

————, ed. *Modern China: An Interpretive Anthology.* London: Macmillan, 1971.

Lewis, Martin W., and Kären Wigen. "A Maritime Response to the Crisis in Area Studies." *Geographical Review* 89, no. 2 (April 30, 1999): 161–68.

Li Tuo. "Resistance to Modernity: Reflections on Mainland Chinese Literary Criticism." Translated by Marshall McArthur and Han Chen. In *Chinese Literature in the Second Half of a Modern Century: A Critical Survey*, edited by Pang-yuan Chi and David Der-wei Wang, Bloomington: Indiana University Press, 2000.

Lin Biao. "Long Live the Victory of People's War!" *People's Liberation Army Daily* (Beijing), September 1, 1965.

Logan, John R., ed. *The New Chinese City: Globalization and Market Reform*. Oxford: Blackwell, 2002.

Luo Fu-chen and Yueng Yue-man, eds., *Emerging World Cities in Pacific Asia*. Tokyo: United Nations University Press, 1997.

Marme, Michael. *Suzhou: Where the Goods of All the World Converge*. Stanford: Stanford University Press, 2005.

Marsh, Christopher. *Unparalleled Reforms: China's Rise, Russia's Fall, and the Interdependence of Transition*. Lanham, Md.: Lexington Books, 2005.

McNeill, William H. Foreword to *Maps of Time*, by David Christian. Berkeley: University of California Press, 2005.

———. *The Pursuit of Truth: A Historian's Memoir*. Lexington: University Press of Kentucky, 2005.

———. *Retrospective Essay*. Chicago: University of Chicago Press, 1992.

———. *The Rise of the West: A History of the Human Community*. New York: New American Library, 1963.

———. *The Rise of the West: A History of the Human Community*. Reprint, with a new introduction. Chicago: University of Chicago Press, 1992.

Meisner, Maurice, and Rhoads Murphy, eds. *The Mozartian Historian: Essays on the Works of Joseph R. Levenson*. Berkeley: University of California Press, 1976.

Metzger, Thomas A. *A Cloud across the Pacific: Essays on the Clash between Chinese and Western Political Theories Today*. Hong Kong: Chinese University Press, 2006.

Millward, James A. *Beyond the Pass: Economy, Ethnicity, and Empire in Qing Central Asia, 1759–1864*. Stanford: Stanford University Press, 1998.

Mote, Frederick W. "Chinese Society under Mongol Rule, 1215–1268." In *The Cambridge History of China*, vol. 6. Cambridge: Cambridge University Press, 1994.

Nathan, Andrew. *Chinese Democracy*. Berkeley: University of California Press, 1985.

Newman, Robert P. *The Cold War Romance of Lillian Hellman and John Melby*. Chapel Hill: University of North Carolina Press, 1989.

Oakes, Tim. "China's Provincial Identities: Reviving Regionalism and Reinventing 'Chineseness.'" *Journal of Asian Studies* 59, no. 3 (Autumn 2000): 667–92.

Oakes, Tim, and Louis Schein, eds. *Translocal China: Linkages, Identities, and the Re-imagining of Space.* London: Routledge Falmer, 2006.

O'Dowd, Edward C. "The Last Maoist War: Chinese Cadres and Conscripts in the Third Indochina War, 1978–1991." PhD diss., Princeton University, 2004.

Pang-yuan Chi Wang and David Der-wei Wang, eds. *Chinese Literature in the Second Half of a Modern Century: A Critical Survey.* Bloomington: Indiana University Press, 2000.

Perdue, Peter C. *China Marches West: The Qing Conquest of Central Eurasia.* Cambridge: Belknap Press, 2005.

———. "Culture, History, and Imperial Chinese Strategy: Legacies of the Qing Conquests." In *Warfare in Chinese History*, edited by Hans van de Ven. Boston: Brill Leiden, 2000).

Plaks, Andrew H. *The Four Masterworks of the Ming Novel.* Princeton, N.J.: Princeton University Press, 1987.

Pokong, Chen. "Toward the Republic: A Not-So Distant Mirror." *China Rights Forum* 4 (2003): 72–74.

Polo, Marco. *The Travels of Marco Polo.* Ed. Henri Cordier, trans. Henry Yule. 1903 ed. New York: Dover Books, 1993.

Qin Shao. *Culturing Modernity: The Nantong Model, 1890–1930.* Stanford: Stanford University Press, 2003.

Rawski, Evelyn. "The Qing Empire during the Qianlong Reign." In *New Qing Imperial History*, edited by James A. Millward, Ruth W. Dunnell, Mark C. Elliott, and Philippe Foret. London: RoutledgeCurzon Press, 2004.

Reid, John Gilbert. *The Manchu Abdication and the Great Powers: An Episode in Pre-War Diplomacy.* Berkeley: University of California Press, 1935.

Rosabi, Morris. "The Reign of Khubilai Khan." In *The Cambridge History of China*, vol. 6. Cambridge: Cambridge University Press, 1994.

Rosen, Stephen Peter. "Strategic Traditions for the Asia-Pacific Region." *Naval War College Review* (Winter 2001).

Rozman, Gilbert. *The Chinese Debate about Soviet Socialism, 1978–1985.* Princeton, N.J.: Princeton University Press, 1987.

Schwartz, Benjamin. "Jews and China: Past and Present Encounters." In *The Jews of China: Historical and Comparative Perspectives*, edited by Jonathan Goldstein. Armonk, N.Y.: M. E. Sharpe, 1999.

Skinner, G. William. "Cities and the Hierarchy of Local Systems," In *The City in Late Imperial China*, edited by G. William Skinner. Stanford: Stanford University Press, 1977.

———. "Regional Urbanization in Nineteenth Century China." In *The City in Late Imperial China*, edited by G. William Skinner. Stanford: Stanford University Press, 1977.

Smart, Alan. "The Hong Kong/Pearl River Delta Urban Region: An Emerging Transnational Mode of Regulation or Just Muddling Through?" In *The New*

Chinese City: Globalization and Market Reform, edited by John R. Logan. Oxford: Blackwell, 2002.

Smith, Richard J. "Mapping China's World: Cultural Cartography in Late Imperial Times." Fairbank Center for Chinese Studies, Harvard University, October 28, 1996.

Smith, S. A. "Talking Toads and Chinless Ghosts: The Politics of 'Superstitious' Rumors in the People's Republic of China, 1961–1965." *American Historical Review* 111, no. 2 (April 2006): 405–27.

Struve, Lynn A. *The Qing Formation in World Historical Time*. Cambridge, Mass.: Harvard University Press, 2004.

Sumida, Jon Tetsuro. "Reimagining the History of Twentieth-Century Navies." In *Maritime History as World History*, edited by Daniel Finamore. Gainesville: University Press of Florida, 2004.

Swanson, Bruce. *Eighth Voyage of the Dragon: A History of China's Quest for Seapower*. Annapolis, Md.: Naval Institute Press, 1982.

Tang, Xiaobing. *Global Space and the Nationalist Discourse of Modernity: The Historical Thinking of Liang Qichao*. Stanford: Stanford University Press, 1996.

Van de Ven, Hans, ed. *Warfare in Chinese History*. Boston: Brill Leiden, 2000.

von Glahn, Richard. *Fountain of Fortune: Money and Monetary Power in China, 1000–1700*. Berkeley: University of California Press, 1996.

———. "Myth and Reality of China's Seventeenth-Century Monetary Crisis." *Journal of Economic History* 56, no. 2 (June 1996): 429–54.

Wade, Geoffrey. "The Ming *Shi-lu* as a Source for the Study of Southeast Asian History." Singapore: Asia Research Institute, National University of Singapore, 2005.

———. "The Zheng He Voyages: A Reassessment." *ARI Working Paper* 31. Singapore: Asia Research Institute, National University of Singapore, October 2004.

Waldron, Arthur. *The Great Wall of China: From History to Myth*. Cambridge: Cambridge University Press, 1990.

Wallerstein, Immanuel. *World-Systems Analysis: An Introduction*. Durham, N.C.: Duke University Press, 2005.

Wang Ban. *The Sublime Figure of History: Aesthetics and Politics in Twentieth Century China*. Stanford: Stanford University Press, 1997.

———. *Illuminations from the Past: Trauma, Memory, and History in Modern China*. Stanford: Stanford University Press, 2004.

Wang, David Der-wei. *Fin-de-Siecle Splendor: Repressed Modernities of Late Qing Fiction, 1849–1911*. Stanford: Stanford University Press, 1997.

———. *The Monster That Is History: History, Violence, and Fictional Writing in Twentieth-Century China*. Berkeley: University of California Press, 2004.

Wang, Q. Edward. "Encountering the World: China and Its Other(s) in Historical Narratives, 1949–1989," *Journal of World History* 14, no. 3 (September 2003): 327–58.

West, Andrew C. "The Quest for the Ur-Text: The Textual Archaeology of the Three Kingdoms." PhD diss., Princeton University, 1993.

Wills, John E., Jr. "Great Qing and Its Southern Neighbors, 1760–1820: Secular Trends and Recovery from Crisis." Paper presented at a conference titled "Interactions: Regional Studies, Global Processes, and Historical Analysis," Washington, D.C., March 3, 2001.

Wittfogel, Karl A. *Oriental Despotism: A Comparative Study of Total Power*. New Haven, Conn.: Yale University Press, 1957.

Wohlstetter, Roberta. "Slow Pearl Harbors and the Pleasures of Self-Deception." *Washington Quarterly*, Winter 1979.

Wong, K. Scott. "The Transformation of Culture: Three Chinese Views of America." *American Quarterly* 48, no. 2 (1996): 201–32.

Wong, R. Bin. "The Role of the Chinese State in Long-Distance Commence." Paper presented at a conference of the Global Economic History Network, London School of Economics, May 2004.

Wu Hung. *Remaking Beijing: Tiananmen Square and the Creation of a Political Space*. Chicago: University of Chicago Press, 2005.

Xu Dongfeng. "The Traveler as Host: Cultural Imperialism in *the Three-Treasure Eunuch's Travels to the Western Ocean*." Paper presented at a convention of the Association for Asian Studies, Boston, 1999.

Yang Shaoyun. "Water Worlds: Piracy and Littoral Societies as 'Non-State Spaces' in Late Imperial China." *China History Forum*, November 10, 2005.

Yeh Wen-hsin, ed. *Becoming Chinese: Passages to Modernity and Beyond*. Berkeley: University of California Press, 2000.

———. *Landscape, Culture, and Power in Chinese Society*. China Research Monograph 49. Berkeley: Institute for East Asian Studies, University of California, Berkeley, 1998.

Zelin, Madeleine. *The Merchants of Zigong: Industrial Entrepreneurship in Early Modern China*. New York: Columbia University Press, 2005.

Zhao Suisheng. "China's Pragmatic Nationalism: Is it Manageable?" *Washington Quarterly* 29, no. 1 (Winter 2005-6): 131–44.

Zhou Qun and Lin Yanhua. "Shanghai Modernity: Commerce and Culture in a Republican City." In *Reappraising Republican China*, edited by Richard Louis Edmonds and Frederic Wakeman Jr. New York: Oxford University Press, 2000.

Zurndorfer, Harriet T. "Confusing Confucianism with Capitalism: Culture as Impediment and/or Stimulus to Chinese Economic Development." Paper presented at the third conference of the Global History Economic Network, Konstanz, Germany, June 5, 2004.

INDEX